A HISTORY OF THE
WORLD IN 100 TALES

A History of the World in 100 Tales

Sharon Jacksties

ILLUSTRATED BY JEM DICK

First published 2024

The History Press
97 St George's Place, Cheltenham,
Gloucestershire, GL50 3QB
www.thehistorypress.co.uk

British Library Cataloguing in Publication Data.
A catalogue record for this book is available from the British Library.

ISBN 978 1 80399 174 0

Typesetting and origination by The History Press.
Printed and bound in Great Britain by TJ Books Limited, Padstow, Cornwall.

Trees for LYfe

WITH THANKS TO

Tim Bates, Ina Bulzan, Sally Pomme Clayton, Jem Dick, Debbie Felber, Alida Gersie, Lesley Hughes, Csilla Laszadi, Karolina Mackiewicz, Dr Roger Middleton, Elaine Mendoza, Stephen Moss, June Peters, David Trevis, Dr Daniel Weinbren and all the countless storytellers who have inspired me over the decades.

DEDICATION

For Alida, who once took me on a journey to the moon with Eland, there and back again. For all those who know that when a story ceases to be told, somewhere in the great firmament, a star stops shining.

CONTENTS

Foreword by Alida Gersie   11

Introduction   13

A Story for Starting: The Diamond of Truth   19

Chapter 1 – Africa   21

How Sun Reached the Sky – *South Africa*   23

How the Dead Caused Rain – *Madagascar*   24

Why the Sun Ate the Stars   25

From a Buffalo to a Lion – *Mali*   26

The Epic of Isis and Osiris – *Egypt*   29

The Music of the Night – *Nigeria*   31

Ananse and the Three Calabashes – *Ghana*   33

The Hare and the Baobab Tree – *Senegal?*   36

Spider Brings Fire – *Kenya*   39

The Blacksmith and the Clever Madman – *Uganda*   41

Do You Believe in Witches? – *Democratic Republic of the Congo/*
Central African Republic   42

The Stolen Baby – *Morocco*   45

The Trickster Tortoise – *Cameroon*   48

The Hungry Ghoul – *Libya*   50

The Blind Hunter – *Zambia*   53

Why Crocodile and Fox Never Meet – *Somalia*   56

Who has Earned their Weight in Gold? – *Togo*   57

An Unequal Contest – *Sudan*   59

Lion, King of the Beasts – *Central African Republic*   60

The Man Who Came Back – *Eswatini* (*Swaziland*)   61

Chapter 2 – The Americas and Caribbean   65
Quetzalcoatl, the Beloved and Defiled – *Mexico*   67
The Men with Fog in their Eyes – *Mayan, Guatemala*   69
Sedna – *Inuit, Canada*   70
Coyote Brings the Seasons – *Zuni, North America*   71
First Man Meets First Woman – *Amazon Rainforest*   73
The Girl Who Danced with the Sun – *Mayan, Honduras*   75
Skeleton Woman – *Inuit, Canada*   77
The Story Stone – *North America*   80
The Potato Farmer and the Star Maiden – *Peru*   82
Beautiful Brother – *North America*   85
How the Birds Got their Colours – *Guyana*   87
Trapped in the Ice – *Quebec/Newfoundland, Canada*   90
Johnny Appleseed – *Massachusetts, North America*   91
Momo – *North America? Internet*   95
No Mouth Woman – *Jamaica*   99
Jorge Plays for the Giants – *Brazil*   101
Unholy Meat – *Otomi tribe, Mexico*   103
Monkey See, Monkey Do – *Sint Maarten/Saint Martin, Caribbean*   104
The Devil's Dulcimer – *Appalachia, North America*   107
The Old Couple and the Volcano – *Chile*   110
The Old Woman and the Soup – *White River Sioux, North America*   112

Chapter 3 – Asia   115
How the World was Made – *China*   117
The First Sacrifice – *Iran (Zoroastrian, Ancient Persia)*   118
From the Dark Comes Light – *Japan*   119
Gilgamesh, Demi-God, Tyrant, Hero, Mortal – *Iraq
    (Ancient Mesopotamia/Sumeria)*   121
The Tale of Draupadi in *The Mahabharata* – *India*   128
Koblandy, Warrior, Suitor, Protector of His People – *Kazakhstan*   136
A Hero Humbled – *Iran (Ancient Persia)*   138
Why the Roma Keep Moving – *Roma (Gypsy)*   141
The Parsee's Arrival in India – *Zoroastrian/Indian*   143
The Tears of a Giant – *Philippines*   144
Watermelon – *Armenia*   145
The Shadow of Shame – *Korea*   149
The Magic Pomegranate Seed – *Yemen*   152
The Champion Poets – *Vietnam*   156

Mohammed and Another Mountain – *Kurdistan*   157
Hodja and the Sparrow – *Turkey*   158
The Powerful Prawn – *Myanmar*   159
The Good Wish – *Pakistan*   161
Don't Complain About the Rain – *Sumatra*   163

Chapter 4 – Europe   **165**
Sun and Moon Give Birth to Earth – *Lithuania*   167
Hare Here on Earth – *Roma (Gypsy)*   168
Sun Boat, Sun Chariot – *Scandinavia and Denmark*   169
Divine Retribution or Natural Forces? – *Crete*   170
Dido and Aeneas – *Ancient Rome*   172
Gudrun's Dreams – *Iceland*   175
Who is Blameless? – *France*   177
The Ill-Fated Princess – *Germany*   180
The Jewel Prince – *Hasidic Tradition, Ukraine*   184
Twelve Swan Brothers – *Sweden*   186
The Snake and the King's Dream – *Russia*   193
The Faery Flag of Dunvegan – *Isle of Skye, Scotland*   196
The Woman Who Had Two – *England*   199
Rich Mother, Poor Mother – *Greece*   202
Stone Soup – *Traveller Community, Scotland*   209
The Shoemaker and the Water Nymph – *Poland*   211
Half a Chicken – *Spain*   213
The Stone Spirit – *Romania*   215
The First Mirror – *Ireland*   217

Chapter 5 – Oceania   **219**
Making the World in a Shell – *Nauru, Micronesia*   221
Rainbow Serpent Finds Companions – *Australia*   222
Matariki – The Little Eyes (The Pleiades) – *Aotearoa (New Zealand)*   224
Rainbow Serpent – *Murinbata Tribe, Northern Territory, Australia*   225
Disobeying Nakaa, Lord of Plenty – *Kiribati*
    (formerly the Gilbert Islands), Micronesia   227
Divine Pig, Monster and Benefactor – *Papua New Guinea, Melanesia*   228
The Heroine's Journey – *Hawaii, Polynesia*   232
Maui Trickster, Hero, Helper – *Polynesia*   235
The Epic of Seia, the Beautiful – *Samoa, Polynesia*   240
Fiery Passion – *Hawaii, Polynesia*   242

Daughter of the Ocean – *Aotearoa (New Zealand)*   244
The Dancer and the Whirlwinds – *Australia*   246
Snake Daughter – *Solomon Islands, Melanesia*   248
Whale Rider – *Aotearoa (New Zealand)*   250
The Ghost in the Image – *Banks Islands, Melanesia*   252
Rich Brother, Poor Brother – *Papua New Guinea, Melanesia*   253
Why Tasmania is an Island – *Tasmania*   255
Stealing the Sky Maiden – *Northern Vanuatu, Melanesia*   257
Eel Lover Spurned – *Tahiti, French Polynesia*   258
Eel Lover Welcomed – *Maui, Polynesia*   259
Why Termites Became Stars – *Australia*   260

To Make an Ending: Three of the Same?   261
Bibliography   262

FOREWORD

I love the first word in the title of this book. The modest, indefinite article 'a'. Through its delicate, easily missed presence, that simple 'a' denies the umbrella term 'history' its potential irrefutable status. This 'History in 100 Tales' is, in the optimum sense of that term, a common history, as in a history familiar to many people. The 100 tales are myths, epics, legends and folk tales. Wonderfully retold. Some tales have for the first time made the transition from an oral to a printed tale. Others have oral, written or visual roots. But all share one key feature: they have been told around a table, in a sacred or ceremonial place, on a stage, by a fire, or in a car on the road. In these pages they clamber for attention and inspire a longing to get to know them more intimately. Then to tell them so that they can continue their stimulating journey in our cultural universe.

The literary critic Maria Tatar notes that folklore, including the study of tales, is a discipline without boundaries. It requires, she says, the palaeontologist's love of the archaic, the historian's appetite for fact, the psychologist's curiosity about causes, and the anthropologist's passion for understanding cultural differences. I add the philosopher's commitment to clarity and meaning, as well as the artist's gift of newness. The tales you are about to read sparkle with these six nouns: love, appetite, curiosity, passion, commitment and newness. They do so individually and collectively.

As I travelled through the book, I was reminded that not only the tales themselves, but also the names of a country or continent are tied to context, place and time in all their corners. People listening to one of the tales may think that their country actually belongs to another continent than to the one suggested here, or know their land or peoples by a different name. To illustrate: Irish citizens call Ireland 'Eire'. While in China many people refer to Europe as The Far West. Subject to where we are on the globe your East may be my West and my down-under your up-there. The evocation of thoughts such as these is yet another of the book's intriguing gifts.

The 100 stories entail a wide array of marvellous and harsh facts and fictions. For example, the acquisition of great wealth by a king or queen frequently involves tough labour by disenfranchised adults, children or a maltreated beast. Then, as now, 'fair trade' and 'kindness for all' remain an important aspiration. That said, taken together, the tales inspire hope and a desire to realise more equal, peaceful times. In every story, people's dreams, visions, knowledge and culture are deeply intertwined.

The historian and broadcaster Zeinab Badawi says in her recent book, *An African History of Africa*, that she likes to tell history through personalities because history is best understood if it is seared into the imagination. Several stories in this collection will undoubtedly do this, and thereby generate an ongoing dialogue with the past. Especially because the story's historical, factual background and its relationship to actual people, events or places was and will remain a matter of both controversy and significance.

Thanks to these exciting characteristics, the tales in this book will undoubtedly elicit multiple uses – at home, in workshops, in schools or university and on stage. It is a big-hearted gift to the story of life.

Alida Gersie Phd

SOURCES

Tatar, M., *The Hard Facts of the Grimms' Fairy Tales*, Princeton: Princeton University Press, p. xix, 1987.

Gersie, A., King, N., *Storymaking in Education and Therapy*, London: Jessica Kingsley Publishers, 1990.

Day, M., 'Africa's Secret History', *The Independent*, April 27, 2024.

INTRODUCTION

As a traditional oral storyteller for thirty-five years, with an eclectic repertoire of tales from all over the world, I sometimes refer to the inside of my head as 'the soup of stories'. Sustaining, delicious, with multiple ingredients, recipes that are followed conscientiously or that are tweaked and added to – who does not like a good soup? The soup is mostly served as live performances in all kinds of spaces, whether formally in designated public performance venues or informally in community settings such as youth clubs and care homes.

However, sometimes these servings find their way into book-shaped receptacles, emerging as anthologies of folk tales or myths. Just as with a performance consisting of a sequence of selected tales, a written journey through these chosen stories is one in which each member of the collection sheds light on its fellows, as well as being worth reading in its own right. In my occasional efforts to tame those internal soupy tidal surges into recipes, I have written several anthologies for The History Press, the more recent having a wider remit than their predecessors.

By its title alone, *A History of the World in 100 Tales* implies perceptions of human time across a vast span – while referring to all possible physical places on the planet. These invoke a huge mouthful of traditional narratives to savour and swallow. 'How on Earth are you going to do that?', many horrified, wondrous and all-stages-in-between colleagues and friends have asked. How indeed? Several possible structures were considered within the recently developed trope of describing 100 examples of something significant through the perspective of a timeline. Perhaps my earliest inspiration was Neil MacGregor's *A History of the World in 100 Objects*, whose radio broadcasts I listened to several times, and whose book I distributed to as many of my friends as I could afford to favour. Is it too obvious to say that given the countless thousands of traditional stories in the world, it is almost impossible to choose those that are most representative of time and place?

However, without that almost incantatory formula of 100, I would be swimming or sinking in the soup of stories for the rest of my lifespan. When it comes to the choosing, I am reminded of that Korean story in which the lazy listener has confined all the stories he has heard into a sack rather than tell them. The stories rebel until he sees reason and lets them out by sharing them. I beg forgiveness of all those stories I have heard and not been able to share here in written form for reasons of time and space, forces to which mortals are subject, but which stories easily transcend.

So how to approach this ambitious title? Conversations with historians, anthropologists, cultural attachés and storytellers revealed pitfalls and provided suggestions. My first obstacle was that I am not a historian, although being an outsider perhaps helps me to see how very subjective interpretations of the past are, and how these change, according to scientific discoveries and to the social attitudes that interpret them. However, historians are themselves not necessarily didactic about perspectives. During a conversation with social historian Dr Daniel Weinbren, we discussed his assertion that, 'history is about a relationship between the past and the present that is always shifting'.

Perhaps more controversially, he went on to say that this interpretation through time is one of the ways we 'make ourselves feel more "composed", comfortable or integrated'.

While thinking about individual and collective biases towards interpreting scientific facts and physical archaeological finds, I came across an article in which even the expression 'through time', or the term 'timeline', are not necessarily relevant or applicable in some cultures. In an interview for *Emergence* magazine with Tyson Yunkaporta entitled 'Deep Time Diligence', he attempts to explain his culture's approach to time by describing aspects of his language, Wik-Mungkan, which is one of the few intact indigenous languages spoken in Australia today:

> So there's no abstract nouns at all in Wik-Mungkan, which is the language I speak, so it's really tricky. But the thing about time is that there's not a discrete word for just 'time', you know? Time is always the same as place … If you are asking like, you know, what time something's gonna happen, you use the word for place and you say, 'What place?' So, it's not confusing when you're speaking the language, but it's confusing when you try to explain it to other people – because they haven't got any frame of reference for you, you haven't got any frame of reference for them, and it's all just a muddle.

So here I am with a title in which the very terms, whether relating to time or place, are so open to question. Working within my cultural linear perception of time and my perspective of the world geography as represented by five continents, I have been playing with another construct, more closely related to my practice as a storyteller. This consists of different kinds of stories, running in my mind along a timeline with the earliest being creation myths that describe how the world was made, all the way through to urban legends of which internet legends are the latest example. This model, with its various story forms of creation myths, pantheonic myths, epics, legends, wonder tales, folk tales and urban legends may be useful for categorising what are known as 'Indo-European' traditional narratives, but which do not necessarily apply to other continents. I can go to somewhere near where I live and within a 2-mile radius see the places whose story history comprises examples of creation myth, epic, wonder tale, folk tale and urban legend. Where these genres of story can be found, I have replicated this continuum, believing it to be a timeline of story development relevant to some places and cultures.

However, I could stand elsewhere in the world and the same would not be true. Cultures have developed differently and so have their respective stories, this variety being reflected also in what they represent and how they are understood in their places of origin. One man's myth, therefore, could be another man's reality. I have benefitted from the advice to consider the difference between people's connections to real and imagined events. I can be sure in my own mind about the distinction between them, but I can't guarantee that everyone would agree with me. Being raised in a place where the Abrahamic faiths are the most common, I have noticed that the stories written in sacred texts can be a source of conflict between those who believe that they are factual, those who think their truths are symbolic, and those who think that they are entirely fictitious – that is one of the reasons why I have not included any examples here.

How then can I justify using stories that have religious importance to other cultures? There are certainly hundreds if not thousands of years' worth of precedents in the rewriting and retelling of different versions of Hindu religious stories, and many Hindus believe that Hinduism celebrates a plurality of perspectives. I feel less uncertain, therefore, about my doing so here, and being blessed with Hindu Indian adoptive family, feel that I can be immersed in their traditional literature without a uniquely European perspective. I may never know if I am offending people from very different cultures by misrepresenting their traditional oral literature in this book, either in the way I present it, or by the act of including it in this context. If I do offend, I hope that I may be forgiven.

These thoughts are leading to the consideration of a salient topic of our times, and one that is particularly pertinent to this place, England, from where I am writing. The topic is cultural appropriation, which has been one of huge importance among oral traditional storytellers and among whom opinions vary. They vary also among indigenous storytellers from other places, some not wanting their stories told by representatives of a colonial power and some believing that the world needs their stories and that these should be shared. I know storytellers who can be vehement on the subject, proposing that traditional stories, originating from and/or representing their respective cultures, should not be told by others; they are something to be protected. Another, from the same part of the world, has asked me to retell the stories he has shared with me because they have a message for the whole world. I have also been told only to tell stories from my own culture by a person who mistakenly assumed that our backgrounds were culturally similar. However, as one who is entitled to five passports spanning three continents, I wouldn't know where to start! I write this to reveal a bias that inclined me to write this book.

I have never noticed or been told that people from different countries have objected to my telling a story that comes from their culture of origin, but acknowledge it is a possibility. My own experience is to the contrary, when people have expressed their appreciation at my knowing something about their part of the world represented by a story from that place. Many years ago, when living in London, I worked in settings providing services for refugees who, finding themselves facing discrimination, were pleased that their cultures were being honoured by my telling stories from their homelands. The most poignant example of this kind of approbation was when I was invited to tell stories to a group of African women. I chose a story that is accompanied by a song in the Sotho language, taught to me by a European storyteller, who hadn't visited Lesotho. As soon as I started, one of the women began to cry. When I asked the reason for her tears, she replied that it was because she was so happy to hear her own language again after so many years. I asked her to sing the song with me so that I could correct my pronunciation and we did so holding hands. The story is reproduced here, entitled 'Hare's Lucky Day', and, because of my place of birth and some of the culture that has shaped me, it also carries for me a metaphor for the rapine aspects of colonialism.

Colonialism is fuelled by racism, but some are eloquent about the danger of equating all cultural appropriation with racism. Whilst formerly known for controversial opinions in relation to other matters, the African-American poet and critic Amiri Baraka has said:

> If the Beatles tell me that they learned everything they know from the blues singer Blind Willie Johnson, I want to know why Blind Willie is still running an elevator in Jackson, Mississippi. It's that kind of inequality that is abusive, not the actual appropriation of culture because that's normal.

As Kenan Malik reflects in *The Guardian*, 'Conflating racism and cultural appropriation does little to challenge racism but much to rob culture of subtlety and depth.'

Closer to home, the traveller people of Scotland and Ireland have a rich store of traditional stories, perhaps better preserved because they are a people who have fiercely maintained their identity, surviving persecution for centuries. One such was consulted by a friend and colleague about how he would feel if she were to retell a story for which he was her source. This was his reply:

> The tales are okay to share, traditionally we do so within a tradition that grounds itself in three ways.
>
> 1. If a tale comes to you, you have the responsibility to carry it forwards, even just once – as for a tale to die on anyone's lips, is a terrible thing.
> 2. No matter the situation, they are told as truthful, for they carry a truth within them.
> 3. Honour when you can by letting people know where it came from. The tales are free to grow, in the ways they wish to grow, while always being honoured as the heart of the teller holds it – and please do not worry about speaking it rather than reading it. We don't 'settle' our stories and they can come through us in all the ways they want to. Thanks again for your message and I hope the tales travel far in you. x

I am grateful to Alida Gersie for mentioning the inconsistencies in the ways in which tribes, peoples, cultures, nations and countries have been named as sources. Whilst trying to implement changes to address this valid observation, I found that some stories were impossible to trace back along their original routes to the original source, so I have decided to omit some of my favourite stories from this collection, as not even the storytellers who were my original oral source, knew from which continent they originated.

There is also the phenomenon of the same stories being prevalent all over the world; it is the garments in which the storyteller clothes them to appear in public that differ. Some of my sources are from old books, written in English and products of Britain's colonial history. Since then times and names have changed, with many countries regaining their independence. These stories, however, are no respecters of the borders that colonialism imposed, and the history and information around these developments is extensive and varied. As a result, in consultation with the publisher, I would welcome any relevant information or updates that can be supplied by readers, for inclusion in any future reprints.

I remember the first time I ever told a traditional story in a storytelling club. It is rewritten here as 'The Magic Pomegranate Seed' from Yemen. Rumour has it that the club's host, who was to become a huge influence on my becoming a storyteller, travelled next day to Scotland to meet a renowned storyteller from the travelling community. Excited at having heard this story the night before and eager to repeat it, he told it to his companion, who snorted derisively, 'Pomegranate seed from Yemen, nonsense! [or some less printable expression involving the human anatomy, as I too knew this individual]. It's a Scottish traveller story about a pear seed ...!' I heard this rumour many years later but it highlighted an unconscious reason for my love of traditional stories – the ways in which they encapsulate so many of the concerns and values that are shared across cultures, speaking of our common humanity.

> Story, as it turns out, was crucial to our evolution – more so than opposable thumbs. Opposable thumbs let us hang on; story told us what to hang on to.
>
> *Lisa Cron, Wired for Story*

In what is for me an ambitious venture, I am comforted by Rosalyn Poignant's words, 'There are as many valid versions of a myth as there are storytellers to recount it, and very often the interest lies in the difference.'

A STORY FOR STARTING: THE DIAMOND OF TRUTH

When Time was no longer new, Lord Brahma, who could create anything, found his brother, Lord Vishnu, weeping on Earth's tallest mountain. In his hands was a gleaming lump that Lord Brahma instantly recognised as coming from the largest diamond he had ever made. Its innumerable facets mirrored all that was happening in the world below, which is why it was called 'the Diamond of Truth'. Somehow it had fallen from heaven and broken on the summit of Earth's highest mountain. Pieces from that mighty shattering had rolled down slopes and been carried away by the rivers that ran in all directions.

'Dear brother Vishnu, are you weeping because my diamond has been broken and your purpose is to maintain all that exists? Do not weep, for I, creator, can easily make you another diamond!'

'No, dear brother Brahma, I am weeping because people have found many pieces of the Diamond of Truth.'

'Are you weeping then, for those pieces that have not yet been found?'

'No brother, I weep for the people because each one of them believes that they have the whole diamond, and is holding the whole truth.'

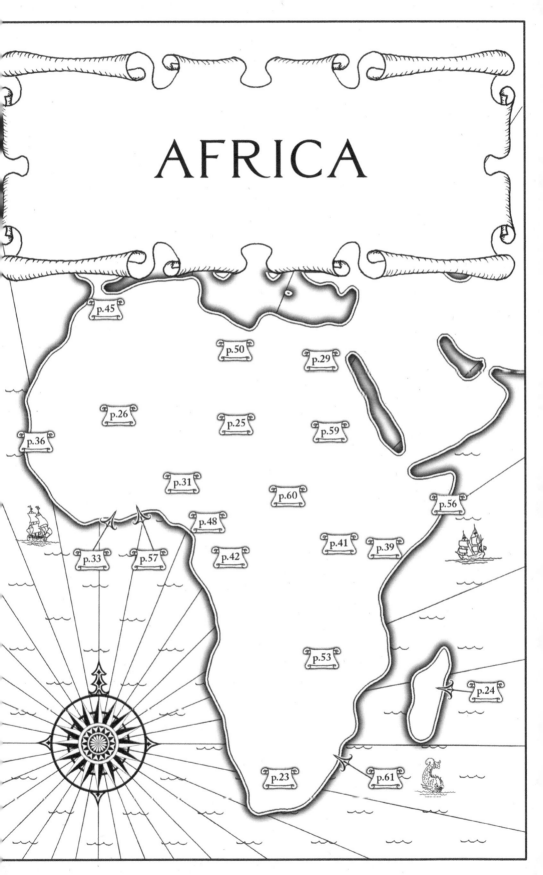

AFRICA

p.45

p.50

p.29

p.26

p.36

p.25

p.59

p.31

p.60

p.56

p.48

p.33

p.57

p.42

p.41

p.39

p.53

p.24

p.23

p.61

'We are vessels of speech, we are the repositories which harbour secrets many centuries old. The art of eloquence has no secrets for us; without us the names of kings would vanish into oblivion, we are the memory of mankind.'

Djeli Mamadou Kouyate, as quoted in Sundiata: An Epic of Old Mali, *Djibril Tamsir Niane.*

HOW SUN REACHED THE SKY

|XAM (SAN) PEOPLE, SOUTH AFRICA

This is among the oldest of the world's surviving stories, written by colonialists in the mid-nineteenth century from an oral storytelling in a language that is now extinct.

Old Man Sun stayed by himself in his own shelter, mostly sleeping. Light seeped out of his armpit, but it shone for him alone. If he lifted his arm, a shaft of sunlight cut through the darkness and when he lowered it all would become gloomy again. Any heat was also for him alone. That is why the women couldn't dry the ant eggs properly for people to eat and they went hungry, especially the children.

At last, their grandmother told them to creep up on Old Man Sun without waking him. They were to take him by surprise and hurl him up into the sky. That way his light would be shared with the people, the people who did not know what it was not to share, the people who lived in such a way that nobody went without. The children had seen how their fathers hunted. They knew how to wait patiently without being noticed. They knew how to creep up silently and when it was the right moment to spring.

All together they had the strength to throw Old Man Sun so high that he reached the sky. As he hurtled upwards, he rolled over and over and as he did so, Sun lost his man shape and became round. When he was as high as he could go, the children told him the story of his journey. They had listened to their grandfathers telling stories, and they knew how to tell Sun his own story. They told him of how he would shed heat on his journey as well as light, how he would chase away the darkness when he had rested, how he would catch up with Moon on his way across the sky and slice pieces off him with his knife. Sun knew what to do because the children had listened to their grandparents. What had happened was for their children, for our children, for everybody's children.

HOW THE DEAD CAUSED RAIN

The creator, Ndriananahary, and the world were one. When he had separated the sky from the earth, he wanted to see what possibilities there were below, so he sent his son down to Earth to see what kind of life forms should be placed there.

God's son found Earth so hot and dry that to survive the baking temperatures he buried himself in the ground. Deeper and deeper he dug to find somewhere cooler. When he did not return to his father in the sky, God became worried and sent his servants, the humans, to find him. How the people suffered as they spread across the inhospitable world, looking for God's son. Nobody was able to find him. Despairing at the failure of their efforts, some of them went back to heaven from time to time, to ask what they should do next about his missing son.

However, none of these emissaries ever returned to Earth and those who left to go back into the sky died as they left Earth behind. They became the first of the dead. They must have told God about the suffering of his servants, because he created rain as a token of his gratitude for their efforts. With the gift of rain, life on Earth became much more tolerable. As none of the messengers ever returned, people didn't know whether to continue the search or not, but as they haven't been told otherwise, they continue to search for God's son. The dead still take messages to reassure Him that the search continues, and the dead never return to the living.

WHY THE SUN ATE THE STARS

Long ago, Sun and Moon were married. They had many children, which are the Stars. There they were at their camp, sharing a meal. They do not eat what we eat; Sun and Moon eat fire, and it is that which gives them their brilliance. They had an unexpected visitor, a chief of great beauty and wealth who brought them many gifts. During the visit Moon had eyes only for their guest, she felt so attracted to him. Before he left, he gave Moon a sign that only she saw, and, that night, she slipped away and joined him at a distance from her camp.

When Sun discovered her absence, he was furious and demanded of the Stars whether any of them had helped their mother escape. The Stars were terrified of him and spread out across the sky to run away. Sun was so angry that he devoured those he could catch, and those who witnessed that are still frightened and disappear when his light approaches. Nobody speaks of, or remembers, the Stars their father swallowed. Sun spent his time chasing Moon and Moon often hid from him, changing her hiding place whenever she could. If Sun ever caught up with her, he would take bites out of her too, so she got smaller and smaller and would have to hide away until those wounds had healed and her body had grown back.

Most of all, Moon loves her children and spends as much time as she can with them as long as Sun is not chasing her out of the sky. This has been happening for so long that the Stars also have their own children. Moon would go to their weddings wearing the most exquisite veil, the same one she wore to her own. When they all need to leave the sky because of Sun's appearance, just one of her children remains, always the same Star, which can be seen in the morning and the evening. That Star is there as a lookout, to warn his mother of his father's approach.

Some people say that this cycle will end when Sun catches Moon and buries her in a ditch on Earth, where he will keep her prisoner. Then he will swallow up all of his children too. Others say that eventually the cycle will end of itself and only then will order on Earth be restored.

FROM A BUFFALO TO A LION

MALI

In the forests of Africa, the buffalo is the most powerful and dangerous of animals. On the savannah it is the lion. This is a fragment of an epic that describes the beginnings of one of Mali's greatest rulers, Sundiata Keita, who established an empire in the year 1235 (Gregorian calendar) or 632 (Islamic calendar).

A great king is one who is beloved by his people. Such a one was seated outside the palace in the shade of a silk cottonwood tree, when a stranger approached. From his garb, covered in cowrie shells, all could see that this was a great hunter. Had not the king himself descended from royalty who were also master hunters? As was the custom, the stranger presented the king with a portion of the doe he had just killed, saying that she had guided him to his palace. At this sign of respect, the king's griot, keeper of traditions, reciter of royal lineages, teller of stories, invited the hunter to sit with them. As the griot could also discern that he had skills of another nature, he was also asked whether he would care to practise his special powers of soothsaying.

The hunter emptied his pouch of cowrie shells and on casting them made the following prediction: this was a turning point of the kingdom's destiny, which could become the greatest that the whole of Africa had ever known, that is, if the king followed the prophecy. First, he would have to sacrifice a red bull, the sign for this destinic journey to begin. Afterwards, two other hunters would arrive with the ugliest woman ever seen at any royal court. Despite her hideousness, the king must marry her as she would bear him a son who would raise his people and his nation up, so that griots would be singing of its greatness for centuries to come.

Soon after the sacrifice, all passed as had been prophesied. The two hunters arrived with a young woman, so grotesque that she concealed her face. But nothing could hide her solid shapeless body, the massive limbs, the huge hump on the back of her neck. As she abased herself in the dust as a mark of respect before the king, it seemed she was more at ease on all four limbs than on two. Stranger even than this woman was the story the hunters had to tell.

Far away, in the land of Do, a magical buffalo was on the rampage. She had killed or wounded more than 200 people and destroyed crops and villages, and no hunter's weapon could pierce her hide. Nevertheless, these two had determined to kill the beast. On their way to her most recent area of destruction, they came upon a hideous old woman crying for help. After they had fed the starving crone until she was satisfied, she told them that many had passed her by, but as they were the only ones who had stopped, so she would reward them. She explained that she was the spirit of that buffalo, a destructive form that she had assumed in order to revenge herself against her brother, King of Do, who had stolen her inheritance. This 'Buffalo Princess' then told them how to kill the beast when all others had failed. Pointing three times with her staff to help aim their fatal arrow, they were also to break the egg she gave them when the wounded beast pursued them. This would become a swamp into which the enraged buffalo would be trapped, allowing them to kill her. But, after their success, there was one condition that they had to fulfil.

As a reward, the King of Do would offer them their pick of the loveliest maidens, but they must refuse them all and ask for the ugliest – the one who was so hideous that she sat apart from the others, easy to distinguish because of the hump on her back. This one would be the spirit, or double, of the Buffalo Princess, reborn into that maiden's body. Whoever succeeded in having marital relations with her would be the father of a son of destiny, a lion among kings, who would bring Mali to a greatness impossible to imagine. After hearing these marvels and remembering the first hunter's prophesy, the king married Sogolon, ugliest of all, the double of the Buffalo Princess.

The king's first wife was jealous of this newcomer, but how easy it was to insult and ridicule this hideous interloper! Sogolon had to endure this treatment from the queen and from the rest of the court, who emulated her example. When her first son was born, the bullying intensified, as he too was monstrous-looking and backward with it. He never smiled, his head was too large for his body, and at the age of 7 he still wasn't walking. Sogolon's mistreatment came to a head when she asked the first wife for some baobab leaves to cook with. Traditionally these were brought to the women by their sons, who would climb the trees with agility. Seizing another opportunity to add insult to injury, the queen told Sogolon to send her son to pick some.

For the first time, Sogolon lost her temper with her child and struck him. Upon his asking her what was the matter, all her grievance came pouring out. The boy told her to instruct the royal smith to make him an iron staff. When she reached the smithy, it was already waiting, fashioned by a master smith who, like many who practised this semi-divine craft, was also a soothsayer. He knew that he too had a part to play in this prophesy and had forged it in readiness for this moment of reckoning. It took six to carry it to the prince, where they dropped it with a great clamour. How the onlookers marvelled when they heard the proclamation:

> The waters of the Niger can efface the stain from the body, but they cannot wipe out an insult. Arise, young lion, roar, and may the bush know that from henceforth it has a master.

The child who had never walked, heaved himself upright by means of the metal staff and took his first step. It was a giant step that took him to a young baobab tree. Using the staff, he uprooted it and brought the entire tree to his mother, who sang out a song of praise.

The prophecy made to the king more than eight years ago now showed signs of being a promise. Not long after, the king died, nominating this son of a Buffalo Princess as his heir. Still young, and with a maligned mother, he was easily usurped and he and his mother went into exile when the king's first wife placed her own son on the throne. Too long to relate here are the stories of how that throne was regained by its rightful heir. By the time he had been escorted back from exile, the people were long disillusioned with those who had seized power. A warm welcome awaited him and his mother, and this ostracised and ridiculed child soon became a lion among men, a lion among kings, whose roar still echoes down the ages.

THE EPIC OF ISIS AND OSIRIS

There is no guarantee of brotherly love between siblings. Between the gods and goddesses, pride, anger and revenge are as common as among people, but with greater power to harm. Set, trickster god of chaos, war and destruction, droughts, storms and earthquakes, was not beloved of humans due to his violent nature. How he envied his brother Osiris, who was revered rather than feared, worshipped because of all the gifts he had given to humanity, and the knowledge he had shared. How the god Set would have preferred the title of this story to be 'The Epic of Set and Osiris', or, as a compromise, 'The Epic of Set and his Nephew Horus', because … but, dear reader, you can see how he is taking over this story just as he sought to take control of both Upper and Lower Egypt.

Among the gods and goddesses, siblings could marry each other and Osiris and Isis were both brother and sister as well as husband and wife. Their brother Set was married to their sister Nephthys, but theirs was a less happy union. At that time the deities were also pharaohs who mingled with and ruled the Egyptian people. Having shared all he could with them, Osiris left Egypt to spread his teachings in distant lands. His loyal and ingenious consort Isis ruled in his stead, keeping a watchful eye on Set, who she didn't trust. This did not stop Set from plotting to seize power, but he knew that he would have to do so by cunning and not by force. Slowly, secretly, he corrupted enough supporters to play their part when his trap was ready, and he was prepared to play a long waiting game.

After an absence of many years, Osiris returned to Egypt and a great celebration was prepared. How they feasted, how they sang praise songs, what quantities of beer they drank, with perhaps the exception of Set and Nephthys, who wanted to keep a clear head for their secret and separate plans.

At last, when the guests had retired, Nephthys anointed herself in her sister's perfume and crept into Osiris' chamber. There he lay between sleeping and waking, not too drunk to be able to make love, but not sober enough to be fully aware of what was happening. Neither of them knew that Set too was already there, hiding in the dark for the moment that he had been waiting for. Nephthys was there because she had decided to seduce Osiris so that she could conceive a child. She knew that Set was infertile and could never make her pregnant. Some said that it was Osiris himself who had caused his infertility to prevent any offspring who might resemble their father. Did Osiris know that this was not his wife when they made love? Set certainly knew, and yet another reason to hate his brother was born, just as he would hate the child who was conceived and would be Set's nephew but not his son. Nephthys did not know that Set had witnessed her infidelity and hoped that, somehow, she could pass her son off as his.

When she had slipped away, Osiris fell into a deep sleep, which was what Set had been waiting for. So gently that anyone who did not know better could have taken it for tenderness, Set began to measure Osiris – length, width, depth and then, possessed of his brother's exact dimensions, he too melted away. The next day he gave precise instructions for an exquisite chest to be built, matching his brother perfectly in size. The object was beautifully and extravagantly decorated and everybody marvelled at it when it appeared at the next feast. How Set was praised when he announced the evening's entertainment: everybody was to lie in it to see how well it fitted, and it would be given to the one who fitted it most closely. Of course, everyone was eager to try, and, of course, it only fitted the one who had been measured for it. Osiris was the last to try it. The lid was slammed shut and the chest surrounded by Set's henchmen, weapons drawn.

Isis hurled herself at the coffer that had now become a coffin, but, before she could reach it, it had been borne away by the conspirators and cast into the Nile. Then began her tireless journey to find her beloved Osiris and to restore him to life. Too long a story to relate here how she was at last successful in her quest to find him – and how his corpse had then been dismembered and scattered by Set. Too long a story to tell how Isis, with her persistence, found her beloved's remains all over Egypt and had the courage and cunning to trick the first of the gods, Ra, into giving her the secret of creating life.

With Osiris now living in the world beyond this one, she nevertheless managed to conceive his son, but he too was not safe from Set's vengeance. If Set had not rejected his wife, Nephthys may not have joined her sister in her quest to hide and protect Isis and Osiris's son, so that Horus could grow up in safety. But the sisters made a formidable pair and after many trials and dangers, the young Horus confronted his wicked uncle. Isis helped her son to use Set's methods of trickery against him, when force alone would not prevail. His successes in outwitting as well as fighting Set at last convinced the gods and goddesses that Horus was a rightful challenger, and he was permitted to depose his uncle to become ruler of all Egypt.

THE MUSIC OF THE NIGHT

The people lived in a clearing in the forest. In the daytime they went among the trees with their bows and arrows to hunt the wild animals, but in the night-time they surrounded their village with fences made of thorns, because that was when the animals came out of the forest to hunt them.

On this morning, one of the villagers did not go off with the hunting party because he had found a stick. If you live in a forest, sticks are to be found everywhere, but this was clearly a special stick because it was completely hollow and completely straight. He wanted to examine it at his leisure. After handling, sniffing and tasting it, he noticed that it made a curious sound he hadn't heard before. There were some round marks along its bark, where twigs had broken off, and, taking his knife, he whittled through these until there were holes along its length. Now a range of sounds could be heard if he placed his fingers over some of the holes. He had invented the first flute, but he didn't know what to play because music hadn't been discovered yet.

So the man listened. He heard the wind among the leaves and played wind music with the flute. He heard running water in the stream, so he played water music with the flute. He heard the song of the birds, so he played bird music with the flute. High up in a tree, the King of the Birds heard him and called out to his subjects, 'Hey, all you birds! Listen there is a man down there who can speak bird language!'

At that, he and all the birds of the forest flew down into the clearing and sat on the ground in front of the man to hear him play bird language. There they still were when the hunting party came back from the forest. They set arrows to their bowstrings and shot all the birds dead.

For the next few days there was plenty of meat to eat and feathers with which to adorn themselves. When everything had been eaten, the villagers went to the man and told him to blow down his magic stick to make the birds come again. Somehow he knew that he did not want to do this and he refused. The villagers then got very angry with him and threatened him with punishment if he didn't do what they wanted. Although he felt frightened, the man knew that this would be a wrong thing to do and still he said 'no'.

After a long meeting, the villagers decided that his punishment would be to leave him outside the fence of thorns at night, so the wild animals would eat him. And that is what happened. At first, he was frightened as he had never been outside the village at night, but as nothing happened, he grew bored until he remembered his flute. But when he put it to his lips, he didn't know what to play because the sounds of the night were so different from the sounds of the day. So he listened. Then he began to play the music of the night.

Gradually lights began to appear out of the darkness – red, yellow, orange, green. Still playing, he noticed that as the lights approached, they were moving in pairs. He played on, and could now see that the lights were the gleaming eyes of the wild animals. Silently lion and leopard and jackal, and even the snake that slithers, had come to listen to their music, the music of the night. When the dawn came, they slipped back into the forest and the man went to sleep in the early sunlight.

The villagers drew back the fence of thorns and hurried outside to look for his bones. How surprised they were to see him sleeping peacefully. How they marvelled when they saw the tracks of lion and leopard and jackal and even the snake that slithers, all around him in the dust. Feeling their gaze upon him, he awoke. When he stood up, he knew that he would not return to those who had tried to harm him. He also knew that with his flute he would be safe wherever he went through the forest, and so he started his journey. This took him to other villages where he taught those who welcomed him how to make their own flutes. That is how music spread through the world.

ANANSE AND THE THREE CALABASHES

GHANA

Ananse is a trickster character who sometimes manages to achieve the impossible and at other times gets put in his place when he overreaches himself.

Ananse is a spider, Ananse is a man
Ananse is West African and Caribbean
Ananse he leave Ghana on banana boat
When the people see him they all give a shout:
'Ananse! magic spider man, Ananse! he do what he can.'

Traditional children's song

Nyame, sky god, rolled back the clouds to see what people, those creatures of which the gods were most proud, were up to. Dismay gave way to anger as he saw all the bad behaviour below. Deceit, theft, fighting, murder and worse were all happening wherever he looked. He thought to wipe out the human race with a deluge, but decided instead to give them another chance. What these so-called intelligent beings needed to do was to start using the brains they had been given. He would encourage them to do this by setting a test for them for which the winner would be well rewarded. A thunderous voice echoed over the Earth so that none could avoid hearing it, and people learned that whoever would be the first to accomplish Nyame's task would receive both fame and fortune.

Next day Nyame rolled back the clouds again, anticipating a long queue of contenders. His anger returned when he saw nobody waiting; people were too stupid even to try. He was about to disappear into thunder when he heard a tiny voice calling out that he was ready to do the task. But who was it? Nyame could barely make out Ananse, Spider Man, who had come to take on the challenge. Perhaps because Nyame was still so angry, the task was especially difficult: it was to get an entire tribe to cross the great river with just one grain of corn in only three days. Nyame did not believe that this little Spider Man could do it, but Ananse insisted he could. A shaft of sunlight appeared, Ananse lifted one of his many hands and the sky god blew down a single grain of corn, golden in the sun's rays, golden in his grasp.

Ananse went singing and dancing through the bush until he came to a village where the children were waiting to greet the stranger. They were told that he was God's messenger and to take him to their chief immediately. How honoured the chief felt to have a visit from God's messenger. He ordered a great celebration. The feasting and dancing went on until late and when it was time to sleep, Ananse showed the chief God's grain of corn, explaining that it too had to go to sleep, but because it was so special, it should not be put to bed with all the other grains of corn – and did the chief have any chickens? The chief was rather put out that anybody should think he had no chickens – and led Ananse to the hen house himself. There he watched as Ananse tucked the straw lovingly around God's grain of corn for the night, then everyone went to sleep.

In the morning Ananse went to collect the grain, but couldn't find it. He remonstrated with the chief about God's favourite grain of corn being lost. The chief began to sweat, he didn't want to offend Nyame, he didn't want to be punished. He wondered if one of his chickens had eaten it and suggested that Ananse take all the chickens in exchange. Ananse pretended to be rather put out at this, and proudly said that he was no thief and would only take the guilty chicken. The chief looked at the dozens of hens in despair. How would he know which of them it was? At last, Ananse pointed out the fattest one and the chief tried to catch her. If you have ever tried to catch a particular chicken in a full hen house, you can imagine what his robes looked like by the time he finished. So it was that Ananse left that village with a chicken under one of his many arms instead of a grain of corn.

News travels fast through the bush, and by the time he reached the next village he was already expected. Much passed as it had done before, and when it was time to sleep, Ananse explained that because God's favourite chicken was so special, she couldn't sleep with ordinary chickens, so did he have any cows? The chief was rather offended as he was famous for his great herd and eagerly showed Ananse his corral. There the hen was tucked into the dust for the night. In the morning only some crushed feathers remained, and the chief was distraught at the thought of his cattle trampling God's favourite chicken to death. All the cows were offered to Ananse in recompense, who, in turn, was offended at being taken for a thief. They agreed that he would only take the guilty cow, so he left with the fattest.

Journeying onward, he met a funeral procession. All the mourners were exceptionally thin and all were weeping at the death of a child.

Ananse explained that he was on his way to meet Nyame and that he could take the corpse straight to the sky god so that the child would reach heaven sooner. At first the parents were shocked at this suggestion – give up the body of their dear child to a stranger even if he was God's messenger? Then Ananse said that he could see that they had experienced a period of famine and had walked far. He promised to give them the cow for the funeral feast in exchange. Wouldn't God prefer one person to die of hunger than many? Thus persuaded, the parents handed over the body of their son, wrapped in a cloth.

The feast was ready and waiting for Ananse at the next village. There he explained to the chief that he was carrying God's favourite son, who was already asleep. Because the body was covered, the chief did not see that he was dead. Ananse asked whether the chief had any children as, being special, this child should be put to rest with the most important children of the village. Proud of his many wives, and his many, many children, the chief immediately showed him to his children's large sleeping hut. There the corpse was gently laid down and the celebrations began.

At last, when all had gone to their beds, the corpse, which by now had been dead for some time, began to smell. The rotten odour awoke some of the chief's children, who began to complain and search for its source, which was soon identified as coming from the stranger. By now all the children were awake and saying that if the newcomer was too young to attend to his own hygiene, he should still be sleeping with his mother. They tried to rouse him to send him outside but, of course, the child didn't stir. Angry at being ignored, they shook him roughly and when he still didn't respond, somebody struck him. Once the first blow has been struck, others easily follow. In the morning all the children ran out of the sleeping hut except for one.

When Ananse and the chief went to collect God's favourite son, they couldn't rouse him. Gently the chief pulled back the cloth and was appalled to see the bruised and broken body. Weeping, he asked Ananse to intercede for him and his children with Nyame.

After some thought Ananse announced that the only remedy would be for the chief, his family, and the rest of the tribe to come with him across the great river to his appointed meeting with the sky god, and ask for forgiveness in person. The order was given and the whole tribe took to their canoes. When they ran out of boats, people travelled on hastily felled tree trunks, using branches as paddles. So it was that on the appointed day, Nyame rolled back the clouds to see an entire tribe crossing the great river with Ananse in the leading canoe. Nyame was delighted that there was at least one creature on Earth that could use his intelligence. He immediately restored life to the dead child, who was soon reunited with his parents.

The sky god fashioned a rope out of clouds for Ananse to ascend and claim his reward. When he reached the heavens, he was invited to pull out two calabashes from beneath Nyame's throne. The first was very light; it contained Ananse's fame. The second, full of gold, was so heavy that Ananse could barely drag it out. As he was struggling with it, he noticed a third calabash, and, pushing his luck as usual, he asked Nyame if he could have that one too. Still delighted with this little Spider Man, Nyame roared with laughter and told him he could take it, but to make sure he didn't unplug it until he reached the ground.

Maybe it is still hard to descend a cloud rope with three calabashes even if you have eight hands, or maybe Nyame's gales of delighted laughter made a gust that knocked him off balance, but Ananse dropped the third calabash. As it turned over and over in its fall, the plug came out and its contents were scattered all over the world. It contained the most precious treasure of all and that was stories! They were swept to every corner of every country, which is why, from that day to this day, stories are found everywhere on God's Earth. Ananse took his gold home, but didn't share it with his wife. And as for his fame, well don't we still tell his stories today?

THE HARE AND THE BAOBAB TREE

SENEGAL?

I only know this story from the oral tradition, so am not certain about its origin. However, I came across a written version inspired by hearing an oral Senegalese folk tale that has many similarities in the details. The hare is an animal also attributed with great cleverness or wisdom throughout southern Africa, which also abounds in baobab trees. These are revered for their medicinal properties, their sustaining fruits and the great reservoirs of water they contain. They are an anchor for ecosystems, sustaining many life forms in challenging habitats.

From the first light of dawn, Hare knew that this was her lucky day. She could feel it in her twitching whiskers, at the tips of her strong paws and in every hair of her alert ears. Wasting no time, she set off across the great savannah in her great zigzagging leaps to find her luck. Soon she knew where to find it: there, on the horizon, rose the huge silhouette of Baobab Tree. As soon as she saw that, the good luck feeling seemed to swell inside her as though she would burst.

When she reached Baobab, she gently hopped into the dappled shade that its spindly branches and sparse leaves barely managed to create.

'Oh! Baobab Tree, how sweet and cool your shade is,' said Hare politely.

To her amazement, Baobab laughed, and said in a huge rumbling voice, 'Do you like my shade, Little Hare? Why don't you come a little closer?'

So Hare hopped a little closer and lay back, looking up at those sparse leaves.

'Oh! Baobab Tree, how sweet is the music that the wind makes among your leaves.'

'Do you like the sound of the breeze in my leaves, Little Hare, why don't you come a little closer?'

Hare hopped up to the tree as close as she could and laid her long, strong paws on the trunk.

'Oh Baobab Tree, how strong your great trunk feels.'

'Do you like the strength of my trunk, Little Hare? In that case, how would you like to see my heart?'

Hare was more than surprised to hear this, and also surprised to hear her own weak voice saying that she would like to see Baobab's heart very much. Then came a terrible tearing sound and the ground juddered around the tree as a crack appeared all down its trunk from the branches down into its roots. The crack widened until it became a cavern from which a dark tunnel led right under the earth. Yes, Hare was frightened, but she could feel her good luck bubbling and fizzing away inside her and bursting through every hair of her body. With a leap and a lollop she was inside that beckoning darkness and following the tunnel to wherever it led.

Another cavern opened out before her, lit mysteriously from the light of countless jewels and heaps of gold and silver coins. Necklaces, crowns and rings were piled high, and jewellery was hanging from the cracks in the bark. Baobab's heart was a cave full of treasure. Then came that thunderous voice again, 'Well, Little Hare, how do you like my heart?'

'Oh! Baobab Tree, I like it very much, it is so beautiful,' squeaked Hare.

'If you like my heart, Little Hare, please take a present. Help yourself to anything you would like.'

Hare was so astonished to be offered anything at all after the gift of being shown Baobab Tree's heart that she was quite bewildered. She had no idea what to take, until she noticed just one gold watch wedged in a fissure. She decided to take that as her present and then pass it on as a gift to her husband. Along the tunnel she bounded and across the cave, out into the bright hot sun, and back home across the wide savannah, as Baobab Tree closed its trunk with a terrible grinding sound.

Mr Hare had been getting anxious, but now came a wonderful story to still his questions and then came Hare's present, passed on now as a gift to himself. He was certain that he was the only animal in the whole of Africa to be wearing a gold watch. How he longed to show it off! His turn now to cross the savannah: how he puffed out his chest and strutted, his paw held out so that the watch flashed golden, twinky-winky in the sunlight. The first animal to see it was Hyena, who raced up and demanded to know where Mr Hare had found it. Mr Hare told Hyena everything that Mrs Hare had told him. Hyena wasted no time and rushed to Baobab Tree in a cloud of dust.

Hyena didn't pause to admire the shade or the music of the wind in the leaves. He laid his claws on the trunk and scratched deep gouges, saying, 'Baobab Tree, show me your heart!'

A sound like a whip as the crack appeared down its length and then the creaking and juddering as the great trunk split and opened. Hyena tore across the cave and down the dark tunnel until he reached the heart. There he too was surrounded by treasure of every kind. But he didn't wait to be invited, he wasted no time in grabbing anything he could carry. Necklaces were slung over his head, crowns were looped around his ears, rings jammed onto every claw. But then there were the heaps of gold coins and he hadn't brought anything to carry them in. Hyena drooled in frustration but then realised that if he swallowed them, using his stomach as a bag, he could vomit them up later. He was so busy swallowing the gold that he didn't feel the ground shaking or hear that mighty trunk creaking as it closed, trapping him inside.

From that day to this day, Hyena always smells of death. From that day to this day, Hyena vomits up his food. From that day to this day, Baobab Tree never reveals his heart.

SPIDER BRINGS FIRE

KENYA

People have not always had fire. They ate raw food, shivered when it was cold and went to bed early because there was no light. Worst of all, they could not sit in a circle and tell stories by firelight. However, fire did exist in a deep chasm on the other side of the world; it was just a question of fetching it. How much better everyone's life would be if somebody would just do it.

The king's adviser suggested that he offer a reward for whoever would bring fire from the other side of the world. But the king was too mean to give a reward, so he refused. The next day, the advisor suggested that the king announce that whoever brought fire from the other side of the world could eat with him at his own table. But the king was too proud to share his table with just anybody, so he refused again. The advisor was not going to give up. The next day he suggested that whoever brought fire from the other side of the world could eat at any table in the land. The king thought that anyone who succeeded might want to sample food here, there and everywhere, and as he wouldn't necessarily have to share his food or his company, he agreed.

Were people too lazy or too timid? The only one to attempt the task was Spider. Off she went on her eight feet – or was it four feet and four hands? – but even with so many feet, it was still a long way. At last, she reached a place where the ground felt warm, and the air was thick with smoke, something that she had never smelt before. Nothing grew, there were no trees or bushes or plants of any kind, and because there were no plants, there were no animals. Spider had never felt so alone. Then she could go no further because across her path lay a great chasm, with a red heaving mass at the bottom. She had found fire at last, but how would she retrieve it?

There was only one way. Letting out a long thread of spider silk, she stuck it to a nearby rock, then she let it out slowly and surely, descending on it towards the molten furnace. When she was close enough, she seized a burning lump and retreated on her thread as fast as she could. To prevent her eight hands – or was it four – from blistering, she juggled the lump of fire as quickly as she could so it didn't have time to burn her. Then she was back on the Earth's surface again, and all she knew was that she was so tired, she couldn't move another step. Curling her eight limbs around herself, she fell into a deep sleep.

Far away, on the other side of the world, was another creature with a very acute sense of smell. He knew that he was smelling something he had never smelt before and decided to follow his nose, as he usually did. What a strange scent it was, with considerable potential, thought Fly. Eventually, after flying for a long time through ever thickening air, he could see its source. There, glowing through the smoke, he could see something that looked like a winking red eye. Flying lower, he could discern Spider fast asleep next to it. What a treasure to show the king. Fly seized the lump of fire and flew back with it to the king's court.

When Spider woke up, she was so distressed to see that the fire was missing. Realising that someone must have stolen it, she determined to tell the king and ask for justice. Anger hastened her steps, making her return journey all the faster. When she reached the royal court, what a sight met her eight eyes! Wherever she looked she saw fires cooking food. There were fire pits with meat cooking wrapped in clay. There were maize cobs wrapped in leaves roasting over embers. There were great cooking pots of soup bubbling on metal stands. On every shelf and in every niche, lamps were burning. She rushed towards the king's table and then she stopped. There was Fly shovelling food into his mouth sitting opposite the king! Now she knew who was the culprit.

'Your Majesty, Fly has stolen my fire. I demand justice!'

But the king didn't care. He was enjoying delicious cooked food, luxurious warmth and light long into the night, so why make a fuss? Spider's protest was ignored. From that day to this day, Spider is still angry with Fly and tries to trap him in her web. From that day to this day, Fly is still claiming his reward and eats at every table in the land. One of the reasons we don't like Fly is because he is so dirty, vomiting up his food and rubbing it on his hands. That's because they are still sore from stealing fire, but Fly doesn't mind, because he knows that there is plenty more food where that came from.

THE BLACKSMITH AND
THE CLEVER MADMAN

There was once a king whose word was law, and everybody feared him. One day he had an idea of how to show everyone just how powerful he was, so he summoned a master blacksmith, Walukaga, the most skilful in the land. To reach the palace, Walukaga needed to pass through the forest and there he encountered an old friend of his, who, due to living too long among foolish people, had lost his reason and was living like a wild man in the jungle. The madman was grateful for the food his old friend shared with him, and told Walukaga that he knew he was travelling to comply with a royal summons. He then prophesised that his friend would be faced with an impossible task.

Soon after, having prostrated himself before the king, the blacksmith was commanded to build a life-sized man out of metal, who could move, think, feel and act just like a real man. Walukaga knew that he could make a metal statue, but that everything else was beyond the powers of any mortal. Even though blacksmiths were among the most respected people in the land, Walukaga knew that he would be punished if he did not succeed, and if he ran away, his family would be punished instead. Already the servants were loading huge bundles of iron onto donkey carts to be taken to his forge. In despair, he followed them.

As they rattled on ahead, Walukaga's steps grew slower at the burden the king had placed upon him. Now that the jungle path was quiet once more, his friend the madman reappeared and listened to the blacksmith's troubles. Then he started to laugh,

'My friend, you are a blacksmith, so you know to fight fire with water. But now you are not beating metal, you are dealing with the iron will of a man. Now you must fight fire with fire. He has asked you to do something impossible, so you too must ask for something impossible!'

Walukaga listened to what he must do and gratitude and relief whipped his heels all the way back to the palace. There he told the king that he was eager to start the task but ordinary materials would not suffice for such a wonderous creation. To make the iron man he would need special fuel for his fire. This would have to be charcoal made from the burnt hair of all the people in the land, of which one thousand bundles would be needed.

This unique fire would need to be slaked with special water, in a hundred calabashes filled with everybody's tears.

The king gave orders for the people to shave their heads and prepare the charcoal, and the dreadful smell of burning hair covered the land. The king also gave orders for everyone to weep into calabashes, which they did until their eyes were red and raw. The volume of tears increased somewhat as they cried with laughter at how ridiculous they all looked with their heads shaved, but there was nowhere near one hundred calabashes full. Furthermore, their hair only produced two bundles of charcoal.

Even the king was not too stupid to realise that it would take at least two months for people to re-grow enough hair to make it worthwhile shaving. By that time the tears in the calabashes would have dried up, so the blacksmith's conditions would never be met. How relieved Walukaga was to be told that the king had developed other interests. After this, Walukaga visited his madman friend more often in the forest, and when they recalled this story their tears of laughter would have made an anvil sizzle.

DO YOU BELIEVE IN WITCHES?

DEMOCRATIC REPUBLIC OF THE CONGO/ CENTRAL AFRICAN REPUBLIC

As they were working on their small plot of land, a father was talking to his daughter: 'So you don't believe in witches you say? Don't tell me, too old-fashioned for your modern mind, I suppose. Well let me tell you, my daughter, if it weren't for a witch, I wouldn't have married your mother.'

At that remark, naturally the young woman, who had been so dismissive of the subject, was desperate to know more.

Her father began, 'There was, in a not so distant country, a circle of witches, with one more infamous than them all. You have to understand that what makes a witch, male or female, is not magic, but the practice of using magic to perpetrate the most evil of deeds. Sorcerers work alone, but witches work in groups, which is what makes them even more dangerous. Would you rather run from a charging elephant or try to escape from a stampeding herd? The witch I am speaking of had nine mouths on her body – sign enough, but ordinary people did not have the eyes to see them; only those involved in witchcraft could. Because of these nine mouths, she was the leader of the group but, of course, nobody knew who they were.

'She had been plotting to kill both her husband and her father-in-law and decided to do the deeds at the same time so that there would be less danger of the one avenging the other. Having gathered all the necessary poisonous herbs with the correct rituals and having pronounced her evil incantations over them, she put them into a delicious soup. So intolerable were her practices that even the utensils in her kitchen knew that somehow she must be stopped. Had they not been used time and time again to bring harm? Enough was enough. Perhaps it was their involvement in her evil spells that had also imbued them with power. When the two bowls were set before the men, one of them spoke, saying, "If I were you, I would cover me up, before the scent of this soup kills you even before you have a chance to taste it!"

'Not expecting a bowl to speak, each of the men thought the other had spoken, and each thought the other was making a joke about the woman's cooking. They burst out laughing, and the witch rushed into the room at this most unexpected of sounds. Seeing the men were unharmed, her face contorted with rage and fear as she wondered whether they too had magical powers that were stronger than hers. Alerted by this transformation in his wife, her husband heard the bowl repeat its warning. He took the bowl, and poured the contents over his wife's head. At that, all her nine mouths appeared and there she stood, revealed as the evil witch she was. Her father-in-law tried to seize her, but she spat in his face, and faster than a cobra, twisted in his grasp and fled. She was never seen again.'

For a moment there was silence apart from the crackling fire, then the young woman said, 'A wonderful story, Father, but what does it have to do with you marrying my mother?'

'Many years ago, I was a travelling merchant who was befriended by a family in that same village, as I often passed through it on my way to places large enough to have markets. After some months, an understanding grew between myself and the daughter of the house. However, when this incident happened, the scandal was through the village as quickly as a swarm of soldier ants. Knowing that this kind of witchcraft runs in families, I never returned to that village again. The young woman who had caught my interest was the witch's sister. So you see, if that had not happened, I would not have decided to only marry into a family I knew well, and I would not, therefore, have looked in your mother's direction.'

The light was fading, and work in the vegetable garden had finished for the day. The young woman's mother had come home and was singing in the house, and their daughter had affairs of her own to attend to.

A short way through the forest was another village in which lived the young man in whom she had a romantic interest. Being a modern young woman, she had decided that it was much too soon to tell her parents about this liaison. But you know what neighbours are like, full of gossip, so she was in the habit of slipping into the young man's house at twilight when she wouldn't be observed. On this occasion, he wasn't at home, so she decided to wait for him.

When he entered it was fully night, and he did not notice at first that he had a visitor. Instead of giving him a pleasant surprise, something made the girl hold back from her usual enthusiastic greeting. She watched him light a small fire and mutter angrily to himself as he unwrapped a small parcel in which was a human finger, which he began to crunch.

'Those witches think they can go on cheating me, I always get the smallest portion to eat. I will make them think twice about how powerful I am when I kill my girlfriend and only share her toes. Then I will devour the rest of her before their eyes!'

He then made up the fire and in the better light saw his intended victim. She was so frightened all she could think of was to feign sleep, hoping that he would believe that he hadn't been overheard. Not knowing whether she had succeeded or not, she heard him leave and was convinced that he was off to fetch the other witches in his coven. She was young, she was terrified, and she had nothing to lose if she could escape by running. In case her lover was thinking of waylaying her, she decided to take a circuitous route. This, however, did not help because the witches had a magical device, a fetish made from ivory, which could seek out whatever they were looking for. Roughly carved into a human figurine, it started to writhe with life as soon as it was in the witches' hands, and pointed towards the direction of their prey no matter how much she zigzagged or doubled back on herself.

As she neared her home at last, she could hear the group closing in on her. Silently she prayed to the Goddess Nzambi, the one who cherished kindness, and a startled antelope crossed her path and dashed off in the other direction. The male witches pursued it thinking it was her, and she managed to outpace the older women. Reaching her parents' garden, she only had time to throw herself under the pile of weeds she and her father had made the day before. The witches were almost upon her when a cock crowed and dawn broke. They would need to wait for darkness to pursue their evil intent.

Too weak to rise, the girl lay trembling under the vegetation until her mother found her. She managed to whisper her story but was otherwise unable to speak all day and barely had the strength to sit on a stool. As night fell, she saw a group of visitors coming towards the house. Among them was her lover and she knew they were the witches who had chased her. Her frantic gestures convinced her parents of this, but when they knocked on the door, their daughter was so overcome with terror that she died. Her father refused them entry and must have frightened them off when he asked which of the women had nine mouths. It was a long shot, but maybe that infamous escapee had taken up with these others.

At first light the parents rushed to the chief, whose soldiers rounded up the accused. In front of all the village they were forced to swallow the drink of judgement, which was poisonous for witches, but harmless to the innocent. The six crumpled lifeless to the ground. In a hut in the forest, an ivory figurine began to twist and turn. It writhed on the floor and beat itself against a pile of logs until first its arms broke off, then its legs, then its male member and finally its head.

THE STOLEN BABY

MOROCCO

Jamilla lived on a boat in a port that was visited by sailors from all over the world. There she could buy all kinds of exotic ingredients with which she would prepare the dishes that she sold to the sailors. How they marvelled at being able to eat the best of their native dishes so far from home!

One night, after she had been working especially hard, she must have been less careful when she tied her mooring rope. As she slept, the knot came undone, and her boat drifted. Tired from her long day, she didn't wake until the prow nudged against a distant shore. Jamilla found herself in a strange land where she knew nobody. The people around the port looked poor and too careworn to smile. At last, she sat down to rest in the dust by a broken door and was surprised to hear herself being invited inside. There sat one of the poorest people she had ever seen, surrounded by a multitude of children, with a toddler in her arms. Jamilla learned that her hostess had recently become a widow, and that she had another baby on the way. She apologised that she had no food to offer her guest, but at least she could offer a stranger shelter from the midday sun.

As Jamilla looked about her, at the half-starved children and their little dog who was hardly more than a skeleton wrapped in skin, she resolved to do something to help, but as yet she didn't know what or how. Thanking the poor widow and promising to visit again, she went on her way to discover more about this strange place. As her steps led her upwards and away from the port, the houses began to look like they belonged to wealthier people. This trend continued until she reached the top of the town and found herself standing outside a palace.

Lovely though the building was, the saddest of sounds emerged from one of the windows, and that was the sound of a woman weeping. Jamilla called out to her and asked her to share her troubles. A servant appeared and ushered Jamilla inside. The sultana found it easier to confide such a personal problem to a kind stranger than to family or servants. She was weeping because she had been unable to bear a child and feared that this sorrow would deepen if the sultan took another wife because she was childless. At this a plan began to form in Jamilla's mind – and what better plan can there be that solves more than one problem? She whispered the first part of it to the sultana. How hard can it be to pretend something you have been longing for? As Jamilla left, the news was flying round the palace that the sultana was pregnant.

Jamilla returned to her boat and cooked a small banquet, which she took to the poor widow. How everyone in that hovel rejoiced at the most delicious and plentiful food they had ever eaten. A special portion, mixed with marzipan, was given to the little dog. When the children were busy eating their desserts, the rest of the plan was whispered to their mother.

The next thing to happen was that Jamilla was installed in the palace as the sultana's special midwife and nurse from a distant land who brought with her skills unknown in her new country. Any questions or suspicions about her had been allayed by some of her most exotic delicacies, which, once they had been tasted by the court, the expectant mother couldn't be expected to do without. A special kitchen was built for her, any quantity of supplies was at her command, and she became the queen and terror of all the other servants overnight.

Every day she made food for the poor family and a marzipan treat for the little dog. However, each day he was fed this a little further away from his own home, and closer to the palace. This went on until he had been trained to come all the way to the palace's back garden gate himself. He had filled out, his coat was glossy and he had grown into his own strength. Time to increase the size of his marzipan treats, which Jamilla flung further and further from the gate. The little creature would leap up, catch them in his mouth and rush home to share them with his family. So far so good, everything was in place and awaiting the birth of the poor widow's baby, except for one thing. Just before the poor mother was due to give birth, Jamilla locked herself into her kitchen and prepared the most important marzipan dough she had ever kneaded in her life. Then she shaped it to look exactly like a newborn baby, and painting it with food dyes completed the picture to perfection.

The poor widow went into labour with Jamilla in attendance, and with good food and care, mother and baby were both healthy. Shortly afterwards, in the palace, the sultana pretended to go into labour and, with only Jamilla in attendance, she was safely delivered of a healthy marzipan baby. Surprisingly agile for such a new mother, she held the baby aloft to show her husband and the courtiers, who of course, would not intrude on her delicate state by coming too close. Then she declared that she needed fresh air and she, the baby and Jamilla, went into the secluded garden at the back of the palace.

Only one person saw Jamilla hurl the marzipan baby over the gate, but at her hue and cry many outside the palace saw a dog dashing along with a baby in its jaws. The courtiers and townspeople pursued the dog, jostling and falling over each other in their haste to save the child. The courtiers were just in time to see the poor widow wrest it from the dog's mouth and rush with it into her hovel for safety. By the time they reached her miserable dwelling, she was standing on the threshold singing a song of gratitude that the sultana's child had been saved.

What a heroine! She must be rewarded! And look how many children she has, she must be a good mother. A messenger arrived in haste from the palace. Would the baby's rescuer consider becoming nursemaid to the sultana's first-born son? Only if she could bring all her children. Of course, she must bring her own children. What woman could be trusted who would abandon her children? They refused to go without the dog and their mother refused to go without her children, so all were installed at the palace. The dog was given royal guard duties, which he relished, and the sultana blossomed like a new bride. The sultan was delighted, and the palace became a happier place, for the sound of children's laughter brings joy wherever it is heard.

THE TRICKSTER TORTOISE

CAMEROON

There was a time when Tortoise and Hawk were good friends and would often chat while Hawk was perched above. One day when she swooped down, Tortoise remarked that he hadn't seen her for a while. Hawk explained that she had been extra busy as her clutch had hatched, and she now had three fledglings to feed. Tortoise congratulated her on her new brood and said he must pay the new family a visit, as was the custom when new babies were born. Before she could stop herself, Hawk laughed and reminded Tortoise that her nest was at the top of a tall tree, and Tortoise could neither climb like a monkey nor could he fly like a bird. Although she had meant no harm, Tortoise felt very insulted and resolved to achieve with his wits what he could not accomplish with his legs.

He made his way steadily to a farm that had plenty of chickens and trapped one in his mouth. Although the chicken struggled violently, it could not get free, and, exhausted, spread out its wings over Tortoise's shell to rest. Hawk noticed the chicken, and just as Tortoise had hoped, swooped down to claim it as her own. How heavy this bird was, how fat this chicken must be! Hawk was delighted to be able to feed her young with it, and knowing that they had plenty to eat, rushed off to do another errand before they got hungry again.

Tortoise crawled out from under the carcass and patiently watched the fledglings devour it. Eventually their mother returned and was astonished to find Tortoise in her nest.

'You are most welcome, Tortoise, but however did you get here?'

'How indeed, dear Hawk, as I can neither climb nor fly?'

But Hawk was too concerned at having nothing to feed her guest with to pursue the matter, and flew off to find him some food. As soon as she was out of sight, he broke off one of the fledgling's legs and ate it. When Hawk returned, she felt a strange sense of dread. She could not understand how she had never noticed that one of her babies had only one leg. However, she had young, she had a guest, and they all had to be fed, so she flew off again. As soon as she was out of sight Tortoise devoured the entire fledgling. When Hawk returned, she was very anxious at its disappearance, and questioned Tortoise, who replied that he had thought the youngster was with its mother as it had flown off after her. Hawk knew that it was too young to fly, and peered below with her hawk's keen vision to see if she could see it lying wounded beneath the tree. Not being able to see it anywhere, she flew off to see if she could find it.

As soon as she was out of sight, Tortoise devoured a second fledgling.

After her fruitless search, Hawk was horrified to see that now two of her clutch had disappeared. Knowing who was to blame at last, she rushed at Tortoise, hooked her bill under his shell, and tumbled him from the nest. Down, down he fell, crashing against branches, bumping against the trunk, landing on his back and rolling over and over on the ground. A bush dog who had come to see what had caused the commotion righted him with his snout. From that day to this day, Tortoise still bears the cracks on his shell from that fall. From that day to this day, Tortoise no longer eats meat, thinking it safer to eat plants.

THE HUNGRY GHOUL

LIBYA

At the edge of the desert, Faisal lived with his twin sister Faisalla. Life was good for brother and sister. They had their own little oasis and Faisalla tended her fruit and vegetable plots with loving care, selling her produce, and visiting her friends in the market in the small town that lay within walking distance over the sand dunes. That was when Faisal would take his three saluki hunting dogs into the desert and catch the animals that provided the meat and skins that also brought them an income. As the sun was setting, Faisal would come home and feed the dogs with the food that his sister had prepared. Then he would carefully groom each one of them, brushing their coats and searching between their pads for thorns. How Biter, Gripper and Killer loved their owners, how loyal they were.

There was, however, a blot on the landscape of Faisal and Faisalla's contentment. Between their home and the edge of town lived a ghoul, a creature who, if he could get it, preyed upon human flesh, dead or alive. That is why he had settled in that spot, to be within convenient reach of the town cemetery, which, of course, lay just outside its walls. Only active at night, he would nevertheless lie in his lair during daylight hours listening to the prayers that were said at the gravesides of the beloved departed. If any mistakes were made, words omitted or stumbled upon, he knew that was his chance to defile the dead by eating their corpses. He seldom had an opportunity for this kind of feasting, so it was just as well that he had a taste for all kinds of creepy crawlies: spiders, centipedes, scorpions, and especially beetles. The sand dunes were frequented by large dung beetles, which he would crunch up with relish. Otherwise, the ghoul's life was taken up with speculating how he could devour Faisal and Faisalla – it had been some time since he had eaten living flesh.

To guard against this danger, the twins had come up with a little ritual that had ensured their safety over the years. At night the door was always barred from within. If one of them was alone in the house, as the other approached, he or she would sing out, so that their voice would be recognised, and the door could be unbarred without danger: 'Greetings Faisalla, it's only me, coming home to drink mint tea!'

To which the other would reply, 'Greetings Faisal, as it's you, come away from the cold night dew!'

Over the years the ghoul, despite his slow wits, had memorised this song. From time to time, when he was especially hungry, he would attempt to impersonate one of them, but was never successful. This was because his voice was as rough and gurgling as a camel's, and the door was never opened for him. At last, the ghoul had the idea of going to the local magician to ask for a spell that would change his voice into one that was as sweet as the cooing of the turtle doves in the palm trees.

'You get nothing for nothing,' said the magician. 'What will you give me?'

As it happened, all the ghoul had to bargain with was his pouch of provisions for the journey. The magician could see it quivering and stirring even before his customer revealed its contents, which were, of course, spiders, centipedes, scorpions, and beetles. These were useful ingredients for the magician's potions, so an agreement was made. Reluctant though the ghoul was to part with his lunch, even he realised that a tasty twin would make up for it. He was warned that the spell would not last for long, and not at all if he ate any spiders, centipedes, scorpions or beetles within an hour after swallowing the voice-sweetening potion.

That evening, when Faisal was looking after the dogs, the ghoul swallowed the potion and crept towards the house. Hiding in the lengthening shadows, he was waiting until it became quite dark and he would be at the height of his strength. As he sat there drooling at the thought of eating Faisalla, a large centipede twined its way through the dust. Irresistible. With one gulp the ghoul had swallowed it. Then he loped up to the door and started to say the rhyme he had been practising all day: 'Greetings Faisalla, it's only me, coming home to drink aargh, gulp, gag, gurgle, gurgle …!'

The only response from inside the house was the sound of Faisalla's giggle.

So back to the magician it was, with the whole process repeated. This time the ghoul managed to resist a centipede of even greater size, but when a huge spider dropped down from the palm tree, it proved irresistible once more. Stuffing its still waving legs into his mouth, the ghoul decided to lose no time.

'Greetings Faisalla, it's only aargh, gulp, gag, gurgle, gurgle …!'

Again, the only response from inside the house was 'giggle, giggle'.

On his third visit, the ghoul was told that the magician was fed up with time-wasters and that as far as he was concerned, this would be the last occasion when he would try to help him, no matter how many creepy crawlies he was offered. With a self-restraint that nearly made him burst, the ghoul resisted the procession of spiders, centipedes, scorpions and beetles that must have been sent to torment him.

The ghoul, his voice ringing out as sweet as a turtle dove, called, 'Greetings Faisalla, it's only me, coming home to drink mint tea!'

To which Faisalla replied, 'Greetings Faisal, as it's you, come away from the cold night dew!'

She opened the door and quick as a whip the ghoul was inside with the door behind him and his bony fingers around Faisalla's throat. Perhaps success had given life to his sluggish thoughts. Why be content with one twin when he could eat two? He ripped the headscarf from Faisalla's head and gagged her with it, knowing he would not have long to wait.

'Greetings Faisalla, it's only me, coming home to drink mint tea!' sang Faisal.

'Greetings Faisal, as it's you, come away from the cold night dew!' came the ghoul's reply, his voice still sounding as sweet as a turtle dove.

Now the twins were both inside with the ghoul between them and the door. Which one would he eat first? But Faisalla had been given time to think, and while her brother recovered from his shock, she said, 'You might be a monster, but you have terrible table manners, even for a ghoul. Don't you know it's rude to eat your dessert before the main course? I am fatter than my brother, therefore I am sweeter, so you should eat him first.'

'Quite so,' said Faisal, 'This is a respectable household. So you will start with me.'

The bewildered ghoul was looking from brother to sister and back again so quickly that they could hear his neck cracking.

'Well,' said Faisal, 'What are you waiting for?'

The ghoul let go of Faisalla's neck, which is what Faisal had been waiting for, and grabbed her brother's instead. Now that he was the target, and his sister was out of immediate danger, he said, 'I can see that you are learning some manners at last, and you were just about to grant me my dying wish.'

'What's that?' gargled the ghoul, whose voice had by now reverted to that of an enraged camel.

'To utter my last three words.'

'Well go on then, and be quick about it.'

'Biter, Gripper, Killer!' called Faisal.

When they heard the urgency in their master's call, the dogs rushed out of their kennel and hurled themselves at the door that the ghoul hadn't had the sense to bar. Biter bit, Gripper gripped and Killer finished him off. Faisalla and Faisal dragged his body to the sand dunes and buried it without even a marker for his grave, wondering why they hadn't done this years before. Even though the danger had passed, when one of them was home alone at night, they still called out, 'Greetings Faisalla, it's only me, coming home to drink mint tea!'

'Greetings Faisal, as it's you, come away from the cold night dew!'

Because you never know.

THE BLIND HUNTER

ZAMBIA

Reproduced here with kind permission from publishers Routledge & Kegan Paul from the International Handbook of Therapeutic Stories and Storytelling *entitled 'The Best Hunters', contributed by Sharon Jackstics.*

There was once a hunter, famed in the region for his skill. He would disappear into the forest for long periods, returning at last with his kills. His work was difficult and dangerous. His standing in the village was high and his wife respected him. As she was often alone, her brother came to stay to keep her company. He longed to be a hunter too, but his brother-in-law refused to let him accompany him into the forest because he was blind. It didn't matter how often he pleaded, the answer was always the same: 'What is the point of taking you? The game would flee and I would spend all my time looking after you. Stay at home where you won't be a danger to yourself and let others get on with their work.'

So he would stay sadly at home, helping his sister with the chores, milking goats or pounding meal. But every so often he would still ask to be taken into the forest. One day his sister took her husband aside: 'Husband, surely you could take Brother just once so that his longing would be satisfied. It pains me to hear him asking the same thing again and again. Let him go with you just once – maybe he will learn for himself what you have been telling him.'

'And maybe he won't,' said her husband.

Nevertheless, he told his brother-in-law to be ready before dawn for their trip. That night Brother taught himself to weave a net for the first time and was ready to leave even before the hunter, and so they set off together at last. The hunter was surprised at how quietly Brother moved. There was no sound of footfall, no rustling of branches as he crept through bushes, no stumbles as he glided over fallen trunks. If he kept still in the forest gloom, the hunter sometimes found it hard to see where he was. As they were skirting a pool, Brother suddenly laid a swift hand on his arm.

'Go another way, I hear a snake slithering down a branch towards us.'

The hunter, looking back, was astonished to see the coiled silhouette of a mamba swaying its head to seek them out.

Another time Brother paused, 'We should wait a while,' he said in that voice that was quieter than a whisper, 'I can smell elephant ahead of us. She is just finishing stripping a branch. Let her move on so we don't disturb her.'

The hunter knew how hard it is to see elephant in the forest for all her size, and how dangerous it is not to give her space to pass. As the day passed, he marvelled at how his brother-in-law was able to tell him things that were happening before he could know them himself – perhaps he had even saved his life.

At last, they came to a place that was ideal for spreading nets to catch birds for the bird market. People would pay a high price for ones that sang or those that had beautiful plumage. Although he had never done it before, Brother spread his own net as deftly as any girl stringing shells. They slept in their blankets, waiting for dawn to stir the birds into their trap. Tired out with the extra exercise, Brother was later to wake, and the hunter had already gone to see what they had caught. In the hunter's own net was a rather ordinary bird that would not find a good price, but in his brother-in-law's net was a rare and gorgeous bird that would fetch a high price. Quickly, the hunter swapped them over. When Brother appeared, each disentangled the birds, put them in their game baskets and turned back.

On their journey home, the brother-in-law was silent and barely responded to the hunter's attempts at conversation. The silence became more and more uncomfortable until, at last, the hunter blurted out, 'You are so quiet and it is so unlike you, I feel that there is something wrong. What is the matter?'

'Yes, indeed there is something wrong. I grow sad when I think that men are always so ready to be dishonest and to cheat each other whenever they have the chance.'

Now it was the hunter who remained silent and the tension increased as they neared home.

'Rather than return home dirty from my trip, I would first like to bathe in this pool. I can smell that the water is sweet and fresh.'

'As you wish, that is a good idea,' replied the hunter who had not yet noticed the inviting water.

When his brother-in-law was splashing in the pool, the hunter quickly swapped the birds around, so each had in his basket the bird that had originally been caught in his own net. For the rest of their journey, Brother chatted and laughed and even broke into song when they were too near the village to disturb any game. This change of mood cheered the hunter, who ventured to ask, 'You seem to be so much happier now. What is it that has lifted your spirits?'

'Yes, I am happier. My spirits lift at the knowledge that sometimes people realise that they have done wrong and take action to make amends.'

There were three happy people in that hut that night. Often the brothers would go hunting together. If anyone expressed surprise at a blind hunter, the husband would say, 'I don't know how I ever managed without him. We make the perfect team.'

If the women asked whether the wife was not too lonely with both husband and brother away in the forest, she would say, 'Yes, I am sometimes lonely. But at least I know that my husband will always return safely because he has my brother to protect him.'

WHY CROCODILE AND FOX NEVER MEET

Long time ago, Crocodile and Fox were best friends. One day, Fox went scampering to the river bank, full of excitement, calling for Crocodile. A great swirl of water and a gaping grin greeted her summons, and Fox explained that her sister was getting married and she wanted to borrow Crocodile's teeth so that she could sing at the wedding. Being a good friend, Crocodile readily agreed.

Equipped with Crocodile's teeth as part of her finery, Fox attended the wedding. First the feast before the entertainment, and now that she was wearing Crocodile's teeth, Fox could eat far more than ever before. How delicious everything was, how satisfying. Then came the music, the dancing, the storytelling, the singing. Full of confidence with her new teeth, Fox opened her mouth wider than ever to sing. How her voice rang out over the guests, bringing all chatter and gossip to a stop! On and on she sang to louder applause at the end of each song. When the guests had all departed, there was Fox, still singing to the moon!

It felt so good to have Crocodile's teeth that Fox never returned them. Crocodile would beg her to do so as Fox trotted along the river bank, but Fox never did. In time, Crocodile grew a new set, and Fox was extremely wary of going anywhere near the river bank again. That is why, from that day to this day, Fox never drinks from the river, only from puddles. That is why, from that day to this day, Crocodile is continually replacing her teeth.

WHO HAS EARNED THEIR WEIGHT IN GOLD?

TOGO

This chapter could not be complete without examples of 'dilemma tales', a feature of African storytelling in which listeners would be swept along with the action of a story that presented unresolved conflicts or decisions yet to be made. The storyteller would stop at a crucial point in order to leave the listeners, sometimes a whole village, to resolve the dilemma and create an ending by a process of consensus. A simple example could be as follows: a husband, his wife and mother were in a canoe that was overturned by a hippopotamus. He is the only one who can swim and can only save one of them. Which one should he save? So compelling was this form of storytelling that slaves brought it to the Caribbean, where it survives to this day. You can hear an example in this song created within living memory by a Jamaican band:

I heard some foolish guys around the corner
Say they'd rather their wife than their mother,
I asked them the reason, and this they answered:
You can romance your wife but not your mother.
My wife may be flourishing with gold and pearls,
But my mother comes first in this blessed world.
So I can always get another wife,
But I can never get another mother in my life.

The Jolly Boys, 1989

Perhaps if this narrative returned to Togo, a listener would say something like, 'Yes, but what if the wife happened to be pregnant, would the decision be different then?' And, in this way, the discussion would be continued.

There was once a powerful chief with an only daughter who refused to marry any of the eligible suitors who were presented to her. News of this spread until it became talked about in all corners of the realm. Overhearing some fishermen discussing this from their boat on the lake, a python who had the power to transform himself into the semblance of a man, decided to see if he could succeed where others had failed. Having shuffled off his serpentine coils, he presented himself to the chief. The young woman, who was sitting by her father's throne, raised her head and showed an interest for the first time. How lustrous his skin was, how elegantly he moved, what beautifully strange designs adorned his clothing. The maiden indicated to her father that she would like to become further acquainted with this stranger.

The custom was for young people in this situation to be allowed to pass the night in conversation on the flat roof of a relative's house, with attendant aunts and other female relatives close by, to ensure that no transgressions took place. All was soon arranged and the two were accompanied to the roof, where only two stools and no sleeping mats were to be found. The relatives then took up their positions. The night was exceptionally hot, and the gentle conversation between the young woman and man was a soothing background sound. Soon all the women fell asleep, including the maiden not long after. This was what her suitor had been waiting for and, under cover of darkness, he shape-shifted back into his true python form. He devoured the chief's daughter head first so that she could not cry out and, silent as a shadow, he slithered back to the lake.

On discovering the pair's disappearance, the chief immediately summoned help to trace them. He had among his retinue five faithful retainers, each one of whom possessed a special gift, and they were commanded to bring back his daughter. Whoever did so would be given their weight in gold.

The first possessed an extraordinary sense of smell. Her task was usually to check that the chief's food had not been poisoned by an enemy. She could tell instantly that they were on the trail of a python and followed it easily through the forest to the lake, accompanied by the others. The second retainer had an extraordinary ability to drink vast quantities – he was usually tasked to drink up all the beer at feasts when guests were lurching towards the wrong side of drunkenness. The lake was soon drained, revealing a thick layer of mud. The third had immense strength – this was usually deployed to dig the crop fields when the women refused to do any more work. Before long, he had dug out the lining of mud that formed the bottom of the lake, only to reveal a tunnel stretching deep beneath the lake bed. The fourth retainer had only a single arm, but this could be extended to any length. His usual occupation was to retrieve the chief's spear in hunting or battle, without endangering life or limb. His arm was inserted into the tunnel and the python was dragged out. All could see the human shape in the middle of its huge length. Docile as it now was in the midst of its reptilian digestive torpor, while some decapitated it, others slit open the skin and released the chief's daughter, who had been dead for some time. Then the last of the companions opened her medicinal pouch in which she kept the herbs of which she alone possessed secret knowledge. She sprinkled these on the corpse and restored it to life.

All six returned safely to the chief, and all of the five faithful retainers laid claim to the reward. Which one of them should have it?

AN UNEQUAL CONTEST

SUDAN

This is a well-known Aesop's fable, originating from Sudan. Aesop was a freed slave who continued to live and write among the Ancient Greeks whose captive he had been. Scholars have traced his prolific collection of fables to the oral literature of Sudan and neighbouring countries. Many of them have travelled all over the world, some even purporting to be Samoan (!), which were most probably missionary imports. I am fascinated by how they change according to the region in which they are told. Learned as a moral tale extolling the work ethic, in the English school's version the tortoise won because the hare kept taking naps instead of sticking to his task. It was rather a shock for me, as an adult, to discover this version in which the family helping out is the correct moral stance, but one that readers from my culture might call cheating. In Germany (Brothers Grimm) the tortoise becomes a hedgehog for greater credibility/familiarity and the incredulous hare runs himself to exhaustion (or even death as I have heard from an oral teller) as he repeatedly insists on re-running his part of the race. His insistence on re-running the race to exhaustion also travelled south and west to Mali, perhaps brought back by Sundiata Keita's entourage from their visit to Arabic-speaking parts of North Africa where these fables were also known.

Hare had made fun of tortoise once too often. Yes, she was the fastest animal for her size, but was that a reason to mock tortoise for his slowness? Tortoise challenged her to a race and Hare somersaulted backwards with surprise. Tortoise assured her that those beautiful long ears had heard correctly. They agreed on the course and were to start at dawn the next day.

Tortoise hurried home as fast as he was able, which barely left enough time for his relatives to carry out their instructions. They were to station themselves at intervals along the route and watch for Hare's arrival. When they saw her kicking up the dust as she ran towards them, they were to step out in front of her and give her a friendly wave. Tortoise knew very well that only a tortoise can tell one from another, and Hare would not be able to tell that she was up against a whole tribe of tortoises. It would appear that tortoise always managed to draw ahead of her. With these instructions in place, Tortoise made his way as fast as he could to the finishing line.

All went according to plan, and Hare was bewildered by Tortoise's ability to keep just ahead of her, even though she had just passed him. She had never realised until now that he was capable of sudden bursts of speed. There was the finishing line. There was Tortoise, who did not have to pretend exhaustion as he crawled across it, winning by a hair!

LION, KING OF THE BEASTS

CENTRAL AFRICAN REPUBLIC

There was Lion, lord of all who ran, hopped, swam, scuttled, flew, bounded, crawled or galloped, and it was time to make sure that all the creatures remembered this. Off he went at a pace that was more than a stroll, but less than a prowl. When he met giraffe, he said, 'I am Lion the magnificent, king of the beasts, ruler of all. Now tell me, who am I?'

Giraffe bowed her long neck and said, 'Majesty, you are Lion the magnificent, king of the beasts, ruler of all.'

And Lion rasped a grunt of condescension and continued his royal progress. Next he met Monkey and asked him the same thing, 'Majesty, you are Lion the magnificent, king of the beasts, ruler of all. Now tell me, who am I?'

'You are a cheeky monkey, now say it properly, or I will swipe you with my paw.'

'Majesty, you are Lion the magnificent, king of the beasts, ruler of all.'

With a warning look, Lion continued his royal progress until he met cheetah, who did not hesitate to reply, 'Majesty, you are Lion the magnificent, king of the beasts, ruler of all.'

Animal after animal gave the required response. The last one on the list was Bull Elephant, who wasn't hard to find. Now Lion was not strolling, he was definitely prowling towards him.

'I am Lion the magnificent, king of the beasts, ruler of all. Now tell me, who am I?'

Bull Elephant, flapped his huge ears and trumpeted at Lion to get out of his way.

'I am Lion the magnificent, king of the beasts, ruler of all. Now tell me, who am I?'

Bull Elephant curled his trunk around Lion and hurled him against a tree, before continuing on his way.

Lion slid down the tree trunk like a furry pancake from a pan. He shook out his four paws and looked around in case anyone else had been looking.

'Well now, you just have to feel sorry for an old animal who has become hard of hearing.'

THE MAN WHO CAME BACK

ESWATINI (SWAZILAND)

There was once a hunter with a cloak made not of one, but of many lion skins. Taking up his spear and saying goodbye to his wife and three children, he left for the hunt. That night he did not return, which sometimes happened. The next night he had still not returned, which seldom happened. On the third night when he hadn't come back, his wife told her eldest child that she would have to look for her father when it was light.

Older daughter returned from her search before dark without her father. When her mother commented on her returning early without him, she replied that she had heard roaring lions nearby and had become frightened, so she had come home. The hunter's wife then told the middle child that he would have to look for his father when it was light. The son returned from his search before dark without his father. When his mother commented on his returning early without him, he replied that he had seen a storm building and so had come home. The hunter's wife then told the youngest child that she would have to look for her father when it was light. Younger daughter returned from her search before dark without her father. When her mother commented on her returning early without him, she replied that she had heard strangers' voices speaking a language she didn't understand. She had become frightened, so she had come home.

After that, no one in the home ever mentioned the man who had disappeared. It was as though the hunter, the husband, the father, had never existed. Nobody spoke of him again. Meanwhile, the woman's belly was swelling. She had become pregnant just before her husband had left for his last hunt. When their baby was born, he was just like any other baby except for the fact that he was completely silent. He never cried, he never laughed nor made gurgling noises or baby babble, a strangely quiet child. When he was a year old, he pulled himself to his feet, looked around at his family and said, 'Where is my father?'

His mother and siblings stared back at him astonished.

'Tomorrow,' said his mother, 'We will all go to look for your father together.'

At first light they set off. They heard lions roaring, but they continued their journey. In the distance they heard thunder rumbling as a storm gathered, but they did not stop. Across the valley was another tribe with strange faces and speech, but still they went on. Then they were climbing out of the valley up a steep cliff. At the top of the cliff was a large flat stone. On it was a cloak made not of one, but of many lion skins. All around lay scattered bones, human bones. The hunter, the husband, the father had been found.

His older daughter stepped forward, and, stretching her arms over the stone said, 'Now that my father has been found, I will sing my song of power.'

As she sang, the bones began to shiver. The shivering turned into a trembling, and the trembling into rocking. The bones rocked until they upended themselves, fell flat and teetered upright again, and in that way they moved across the ground and up onto the rock.

Bone sought out bone and when Older Daughter had finished her song of power, each bone was lying next to its rightful neighbour and a perfect human skeleton was before them.

'Now I will sing my song of power,' said Older Son.

Holding his arms over his father's skeleton, he began to sing. Pink, pulsing muscle crept over the skeleton until all those dry bones were covered. The muscles became threaded with blood vessels, the brighter and the darker blood throbbing among the glistening flesh.

'Now it is my turn to sing my song of power,' said Younger Daughter

She waved her hands over her father's body as she sang, and that mass of flesh became clothed in skin. The skin sprouted hair and stretched and puckered into features. Every dimple, every scar, every whorl on each fingertip was present, even the seam of the closed eyelids with their curve of eyelashes.

The eyelashes trembled, the eyes opened. The man sat up on the rock. He looked at his family, he smiled at the son he had not yet seen, and, taking the baby in his arms, he stood up. Together they all went home.

All was almost exactly as it had been before, except that the man, the husband, the father, had rolled a large rock to the side of their hut. He had fashioned clay pots and into these he had put pigments that he had made from blood, ground stones and soot. By the light of the fire, he would make marks on the stone, but when his family tried to peer over his shoulder to see what he was doing, he would cover his work with his cloak. During the daytime, the stone was covered with animal skins, and although longing to, none of his children dared to look beneath it. One evening his wife said, 'Husband, you have been away from us for so long. You have been to the Other World. Few have ever returned from that place to speak of what they have seen, yet you tell us nothing. Will you not share the marvels of that other place?'

'Wife, children, I wish I could, but I do not have the words to describe the wonders I have seen. That is why I am making pictures of the Other World on this stone. When I have finished, I will give it to you. I will give it to one of you.'

At that the children all wanted to be the one gifted with the picture stone: 'You should give it to me, because it was my song of power that found all your bones and made your skeleton whole again.'

'You should give it to me because my song of power gave you the strength to move.'

'You should give it to me because my song of power gave you back your identity, otherwise you would have been a stranger to us.'

Their father looked at his children lovingly and praised them for singing their songs so well. Then he held up the picture stone, still wrapped in animal skins.

'I give this to you, my youngest child. I give it to the one who remembered.'

THE AMERICAS
AND CARIBBEAN

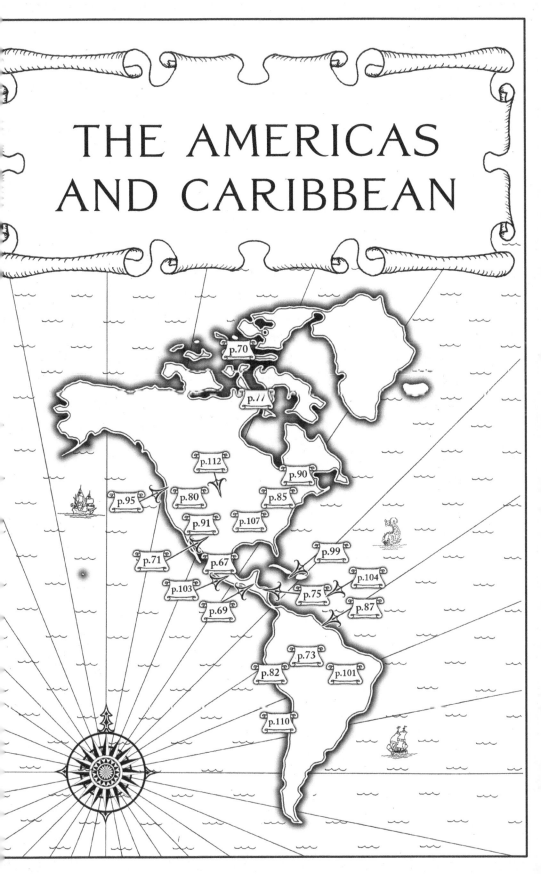

p.70

p.77

p.112

p.90

p.95

p.80

p.85

p.91

p.107

p.71

p.67

p.99

p.103

p.104

p.75

p.69

p.87

p.73

p.82

p.101

p.110

'When we talk about time, we describe it as grandparents of grandparents; the connection is strong, it is in the weaving and in the landscape all around us. The old knowledge is better – the textiles are stronger, the colours don't fade, just as we hope the memory of our ancestors doesn't fade either.'

Nilda Callañaupa Alvarez, Founder of the Cusco Centre for Traditional Textiles, Peru.

QUETZALCOATL, THE BELOVED AND DEFILED

The Sky and the Earth had been created, but who would populate the Earth? Quetzalcoatl, whose name means 'feathered serpent', was chosen to restore humankind from their remains, which mouldered from a bygone age in the realm of the dead. As he journeyed there he knew that the Age of the Gods was finite just as those people's had been. Divine though he was, he knew that his time would pass as it did for all beings.

The ruler of that realm was not going to surrender his treasures easily, even to one as divine as Quetzalcoatl. The first test was to produce a sound from a conch shell, which was impossible as it had no hole at the tip. The god-hero solved this puzzle by summoning a worm, who burrowed a hole for him. Then he summoned hornets and bees to enter and their buzzing made a tremendous sound. A trumpet to awaken the dead, indeed, as he went around the place of the dead four times, sounding the conch in every corner. Despite overcoming this obstacle, the ruler of the dead put many others in his way. It was only possible for Quetzalcoatl to seize the bones of one man and one woman – but these would be enough.

He brought them to the realm of Cihuacoatl, goddess of childbirth. There she ground the bones in a clay vessel. The god-hero then cut his own male member to shed fertile blood on the bones, and another race of humans was created for that cosmic age.

How he loved those humans, living among them in his palace, creating maize for them to eat, teaching them agriculture, writing, astronomy and many other arts – setting an example of how to live modestly, peacefully and, above all, forbidding human sacrifice.

But all things and all times must change. Tezcatlipoca, known as the 'God of the Smoking Mirror', was also deity of the night sky, of conflict and of hurricanes. He had grown jealous of how his brother was loved as well as revered. Moreover, he wanted to have the practice of human sacrifice restored. When his priests had failed to convince Quetzalcoatl to do this, the god himself appeared, bringing with him his smoking mirror. This was made of obsidian, black as the night sky, polished to shine like a mirror in which one could see oneself or which could be used for divining the future. Obsidian was also the stone, with a blade honed sharper than steel, that was used for sacrifice.

Probing for a week spot, Tezcatlipoca showed his brother god the mirror, and a weak, ugly and age-wrinkled reflection stared back. Then he reversed it and Quetzalcoatl saw a beautiful man, splendid in his many-coloured feather cloak and bright face paint. Flattered, he dropped his guard and accepted a fermented drink. Unaccustomed to drinking anything intoxicating, he drank it down in one go. By now he was too drunk to refuse another, or another and another … This was what Tezcatlipoca had been scheming for, when he led his brother to their sister's chamber, where he spent a drunken but incestuous night.

The next day Quetzalcoatl was horrified at how he had behaved. He decided that he was no longer fit to rule or be revered, and felt that he should be disowned by those who had supported him. Determined to leave, and knowing that his time and the age of peace had passed, he travelled east towards the light and disappeared into the ocean. Some say he did not go beneath the water but was borne away on a raft made of serpents. Others say that when he reached the shore, he immolated himself in his feathered robe and turquoise mask as an act of repentance. His shining ashes, as they floated heavenwards, were accompanied by all the brightly coloured birds of the land. When the ashes dimmed, his heart rose to heaven and he became the planet Venus, who, turn and turn about becomes the Morning or the Evening Star, marking the agricultural cycle for his beloved people.

THE MEN WITH FOG IN THEIR EYES

Before Time was new, sky and ocean existed, and the gods lay beneath the waters. They decided to make land, so islands and mountain ranges appeared, which they clothed with vegetation. As this new creation was too quiet, they made animals to provide sounds and the air was filled with the song of birds, the land was filled with the many sounds of mammals and the sea echoed with the calls of whales and dolphins. However, all these sounds were meaningless and, as the gods were now proud of what they had created, they wanted creatures that would praise them.

The first men were made from mud, but they slurred their words that, in any case, made no sense. As they were useless to the gods, they were washed away by a deluge. The second men were made from wood, which was much stronger and these knew how to use wood and make wooden houses. Their speech was intelligible, but although the gods could understand their praise words, they were uttered with no heart or soul behind them. The gods sent a tide of tree sap to wash them away, but because these men understood wood, they climbed the trees of the forest for refuge. There they were attacked by the elements and by wild animals. Those who survived this suffering became monkeys.

At last the gods created men from the dough made out of maize flour. Maize has been one of their favourite foods ever since and it was so easy to praise the gods for this gift that had not only made them but which also sustained them. Their praises became so eloquent that the gods decided that they had become too intelligent and might rival them one day. To prevent this, they blew fog into men's eyes, and their vision was limited. After this it was safe to create women so that people could multiply. Because women came later, and their eyes were not clouded with fog, many say that women are more observant and wiser than men.

SEDNA

The sea is the womb that cradles the grave
That rocks the tomb that births the wave
That slays the child that smooths the bed
Gentle or wild that lays the dead

Sedna was their only daughter and her parents wanted to see her settled
before they grew old. However, she refused all suitors without giving a
reason. Time went on with Sedna's parents ever anxious about what would
become of her when she was all alone in the world.

One day a stranger arrived among the people and was made welcome.
This was the man Sedna had been waiting for. How dark his hair was,
how feathery fine with a blue and green sheen like the colours beneath
the ice. How proud his curved nose, how glittering his eyes, so shiny that
you could never see into them.

When Sedna announced that she wanted to marry him and go to live
on his island, this news was like the same pair of hands pulling a rope
in opposite directions. Her parents were pleased that their daughter had
found someone at last, yet they were concerned that they knew nothing
of this stranger or his people. Sedna was as determined to go with this
man as she had been to refuse all others, so before long they waved the
couple farewell.

On the island, life was unimaginably different for Sedna and this was
because her husband was beyond recognising. Only the glittering eyes
remained of the man she thought she knew. The beautiful hair had become
feathers, the proud nose a hard, rapacious beak. She had been deceived
and carried off by Raven. Raven trickster, Raven shape shifter, Raven the
invincible, Raven who always got what he wanted. Nothing had been
provided for her in her new home – no tools, no hunting equipment – so
she was dependent on what her husband brought her to eat, which was
inevitably stinking carrion.

After many months, Sedna's father came to pay a visit, concerned that
his son-in-law had not brought his daughter back to visit her parents.
How shocked he was to see how she was living. He caught fresh food for
them, and while she built up her strength, he secretly plotted their escape.

The moment came when Raven hiked to the far side of the island. As soon as he had passed over the ridge, his father-in-law scuttled his boat. Then he and Sedna threw themselves into the one her father had arrived in, and paddled frantically for their own shore.

They were still in open water when the sky blackened, dark as a raven's wing, and then the storm struck. Raven did not need a boat, Raven could fly. Raven could summon a tempest that would blow the fugitives back to his island. Huge waves threatened to swamp it. Raven's malice gripped the father's heart; perhaps he would be spared if he gave Sedna back to him. He threw his daughter overboard. Sedna swirled, sinking, drowning in the icy depths, then, with the last of her strength, she forced herself upwards, broke through the skin of the water and grasped the side of the boat. Her father's panic at this further threat of capsizing made him seize his knife. One by one he chopped off Sedna's fingers, until she couldn't hang on any more and she sank to the ocean bed, never to return.

Her fingers became seals, walruses, fish, clams, whales, all the good things for people to eat. When Sedna, goddess of the sea, is calm, she sends plenty of food back to her people. When she is angry, she causes the waves to rise, lashing the shore and driving away all the food. The long strands of kelp are Sedna's hair. How she loves to have it combed and smoothed and plaited by anyone who dares.

COYOTE BRINGS THE SEASONS

ZUNI, NORTH AMERICA

There was Coyote, looking under logs for woodlice and beetles to eat as he always did. Eagle called out from above to tell him, yet again, what a bad hunter he was: 'We don't all have eyes as sharp as yours, Brother Eagle. If I had more light I would be able to see better and I wouldn't have to live on insects.'

Eagle swooped down and perched on a branch. How did Coyote know about more light? Had the Great Mystery spoken to him in a dream? In that time all was a twilit world, not quite dark and not quite light. Only Eagle knew that on the other side of the world, more light could be found. Now that Coyote had referred to it, Eagle felt obliged to tell him about it and explained that more light did in fact exist, kept by beings who walked on two legs but had no wings. When Coyote had finished laughing at the thought of creatures with only two legs and no wings, he asked Eagle to take him to where he could see more light. There were the two friends, one soaring high, the other running low, all the way to the other side of the world.

Before Coyote saw anything, he heard singing, and then he felt the ground beneath him pulsing. Lolloping over a rise he saw a circle of two-legged creatures dancing in a circle. In the middle were two baskets, one small, one larger. From time to time, one of the dancers would remove one of the basket lids. From the smaller basket, a gentle silvery light emerged. From the larger blazed a light so bright that it made Coyote's eyes water. At last, the dancers tired, lay on the ground and slept.

'Now is our chance,' hissed Coyote, 'You grab one basket and I'll grab the other and we'll make a run for it.'

Eagle was shocked at this suggestion. He had come to show Coyote the light, not to steal it. But Coyote whined and wheedled Eagle into submission until he finally agreed. Then he put the gentle and the bright light together in the same basket to make them easier to carry. The two made their way back to the other side of the world, with Eagle flying ahead and Coyote running below.

As soon as they were out of earshot of the creatures who had kept the light, Coyote called to Eagle to let him carry the basket. As far as Eagle was concerned, this was certainly not going to happen. But before long, Coyote had whined and wheedled Eagle into agreeing. The mighty bird flew down and placed the basket on the ground. It was only when Coyote had promised not to open it that Eagle flew off, guiding Coyote back home. Carrying the basket made Coyote run more slowly, and without his burden Eagle flew faster. The distance between them increased, and as soon as there was a hill hiding him from view, Coyote stopped running and lifted the lid.

A gleaming silvery sphere bounced out of the basket. It was irresistible – Coyote patted it with a paw. That made it bounce even higher. Coyote chased and swatted it and the silvery sphere bounced back and away, each time bouncing further and further up into the sky, where it stayed.

Coyote threw back his head and howled at losing his bright bouncy ball, but there was still something left in the basket. This time the dazzling light was so powerful that it flew straight up into the sky, further and further until the blazing golden light hovered higher than the silver one. It was so hot when it emerged that it singed Coyote's fur, which still has black tips on it to this day.

As soon as the blazing golden light flew further from the Earth, a change came over it, and Coyote did something he had never done before: he shivered. Now that the sun was far away, cold had come into the world. Coyote sniffed; there was a different smell in the air. Then all the leaves turned brown and fell from their branches, drifting like feathers. That was the first autumn. High in the sky, Eagle too felt these changes and knew instantly that the promise had been broken. He wheeled around and flew back. As he landed by Coyote, something followed him from the sky, pure white, soft and silent. Snowflakes were falling. The first winter had arrived.

Now that the moon and sun had escaped from Earth there were tides in the oceans, and as the silver and golden spheres bounced closer and further there was more light, or less, more heat or more cold. Coyote is still yearning for his beautiful silver ball; you can hear him whining and wheedling for it to return whenever the moon is full.

FIRST MAN MEETS FIRST WOMAN

AMAZON RAINFOREST

First man had not been in the forest for long. How exciting it was to discover all its plants and animals, sights and sounds. One day, when he was exploring, he came across a creature very much like himself. At first, he was delighted to find a being so similar and who could speak the same language, but his initial enthusiasm soon gave way to concern. He noticed that First Woman had something missing, and not only that, but where the missing piece should have been, there was a wound instead.

Eager to help, First Man ushered First Woman to his shelter and told her to wait. He hurried off to a clearing in the forest where he had made a shrine to the gods and asked them how he could cure her. The gods told him about all kinds of medicinal herbs and how to collect and prepare them. He then rushed about and did not rest until he had collected all of them. He boiled them until they were almost solidified into a thick paste. When First Woman tried to swallow it, it tasted so vile that she spat it out in disgust and refused to drink any more.

Undeterred at this setback and still full of good intentions, First Man returned to the shrine in the clearing and asked the gods for another suggestion. Directions for administering a massage were given, and implemented with enthusiasm. After an overly thorough massage, which left him covered in sweat, and her covered in his sweat, there seemed to be no improvement in First Woman's condition.

Again First Man returned to the shrine and asked the gods for another suggestion, and this time it was to play her music. They explained how to make a flute, a rattle and a drum and soon First Man had his orchestra ready. After listening to the cacophony for a whole afternoon, First Woman announced that she had had enough of being poisoned, pummelled and deafened, and stalked off.

Yet again First Man went back to the gods to ask them what he should do, but by now they had had enough, and turned their backs on him. Feeling abandoned by the gods and by his new friend, First Man was disconsolate that his efforts had gone unappreciated and that her wound still hadn't healed. He also missed having someone to talk to and felt lonely. As he wandered forlornly through the forest, he heard a commotion in the branches. The monkeys seemed exceptionally excited so he stopped to see what the fuss was about. He noticed that they too were different in a similar way to how he and First Woman were different. He also saw that the female monkeys were not behaving as though they were wounded at all. Then he realised that their differences might look strange when they were apart, but made rather a good fit when they were together.

Next time he met First Woman he was able to show just how much he appreciated all of her. While this was happening a wind passed over them and was able to spread the news all over the world that Man and Woman had discovered love.

THE GIRL WHO DANCED WITH THE SUN

MAYAN, HONDURAS

There was once a chief whose only child was the loveliest of daughters. How he dreaded the day when some young man would steal her heart, and thereby steal her away from her doting father. As she neared womanhood, the chief forbade her to go out during the daylight so that her beauty would be hidden. Hers became a twilit and starlit world, yet in the sky the Sun, whose bright eyes see all, had noticed her in her youth and still remembered her.

How Sun longed to see her again, but she was a dutiful girl and obeyed her father even though she longed to run free in the forest as she had before. One day, Sun looked into the clearing where the chief's village lay and saw him mustering his men. They were going to trek through the forest for a meeting with another tribe. As soon as they set off, Sun knew what to do.

He reached an arm-shaped ray of sunlight down through the forest canopy to the leaf litter beneath. From there he took up an empty tortoise shell and held it towards his face. Slowly, slowly he drew the shell across it, so that the world gradually became darker. Some say that when Sun covered his face in this way, Earth saw the first solar eclipse. That was why the chief's daughter was surprised that dusk had come so early – had she slept without knowing it? Glad that the tedium of her day had passed so quickly, she ran out of the hut and across the clearing.

Squinting from behind the rim of the shell, Sun just caught her darting shape reaching the trees. It was then that he wove with his other hand a ladder of sunbeams, which he dangled down among the tree trunks.

The young woman was astonished to see these shining, dancing lianas before her. She couldn't remember when she had last seen anything so bright – and they were such fun to swing from. How strange that they seemed to have no roots, but they were so easy to climb! Up and up she went, brighter and brighter everything became, because she had now reached the Sky World. Here was more space and light than she had ever encountered. She danced around and around with joy at this unexpected taste of freedom. Sun was delighted to have her near him at last, and the young woman did not want to return to her old life, so there she stayed.

When the chief returned, he was furious to find that his daughter had disappeared. When he ordered a search some of the young people were almost too frightened to tell him that they had seen the silhouette of their former playmate dancing across the face of the sun. This enraged the chief even more. How dare Sun steal his daughter as soon as his back was turned. He would teach that coward a lesson!

The men of the tribe were ordered to cut down a swathe of the forest. Women were ordered to hollow out all the felled trees. Children were ordered to scoop great quantities of mud from the river bank and shape them into huge balls, which were left to harden in the heat. When these tasks had been accomplished, a path was cleared to the top of the tallest mountain and the hollow trees and hard-baked mud balls were hauled or rolled to the summit. The chief ordered the trunks to be joined together, and now the giant blowpipe was ready.

The chief loaded the pipe with a mud ball, determined to knock Sun out of his orbit. The first blow fell short and the second ball shot beyond him. The third blow reached Sun just as the chief's daughter was dancing past and instead of striking Sun, it knocked her out of the sky. Down, down she fell into the ocean with such force that her body was shattered and scattered in many pieces.

All the creatures of land and air and sea had been horrified at this spectacle, and now the body of this wonderful young woman was spread across the surface of the ocean. All the fish rushed to gather up the pieces before they could sink without trace. So many and eager were they, that not a single part of her was lost. Together they tried to refashion her beauty, but being fish they could not recreate a human shape and the many parts would not hold together. Slowly at first, then quicker and quicker they began a great whirling, flashing swirling dance, in which their scales stuck all that remained of her into a huge silver ball. Then the fish made a raft of their own bodies that flexed and straightened with the silver ball bouncing higher and higher. Moving as one, all the fish gave a mighty leap and the silver ball was hurled into the sky. She is still there. We call her Moon. From that day to this night, Sun and Moon follow each other across the sky in their eternal dance.

SKELETON WOMAN

INUIT, CANADA

The stranger paddled his canoe across the bay with its calm waters sheltered by high cliffs. Before casting a line, he could see huge fish shoaling around the prow. He did not wonder why there were so many of such size, and no one else fishing for them. He did not notice that no birds flew across the water or nested in the cliffs. Even the wind was subdued in its passing.

Long ago, but not so long ago that people couldn't remember, a young woman had disobeyed her father. In his anger he had tied her arms and legs together and flung her over the cliff. When she had sunk to the sea bed, the creatures of the ocean had picked her body clean, and nibbled at the knots that tied her limbs. The tides had caressed her, their toing and froing turning her in her endless sleep. Since then, her people feared to go near that place. Even the birds remembered her last cry, more piercing than any gull's, as she fell. That is why nobody saw the stranger arrive and there was nobody to give him a warning.

He cast his hook over the stern, noticing that these huge fish seemed to show no wariness of his canoe. It would not be long before he felt his line grow taut. Down, down sank his hook and then he felt it bite. He could feel the weight as the catch resisted. It would take some playing before he could get it into the boat. Turning away, he made to fasten his tackle more securely, but when he turned back, he gasped with fright. There, fastened to the rim of the stern by its teeth, was a skull. Forcing himself to approach, just as he was about to swing at it with his paddle, he saw that the skull was still attached to its skeleton. Horror weakened his blow. All he wanted to do was to get away from that place as quickly as he could. He turned to the prow and paddled frantically for the shore.

He wanted to believe that the whistling sound behind him was the wind, but the only movement on the water was caused by the paddles and the prow as the canoe shot forwards. He didn't want to see what was behind, but he had to. There was the skeleton, half out of the water, arm bones flailing towards him, skinny bone fingers outstretched to catch, and the wind caught in the grinning mouth, whistling through the gaps in the teeth. All he could do was make for the shore, hoping that land would be an escape from this nightmare from the sea. At last, the boat grated on shingle. Not daring to look behind him again, he grabbed what he could of his supplies and rushed up the beach in the gathering dark. There in the gloom, he saw what could be some kind of shelter. Behind him he could hear the rattle of shingle as the skeleton pursued him. He made for that solid shape at the top of the beach where shingle met boulders, desperate for a refuge. There he found a little hut made from driftwood. He tore open the door and flung himself inside.

Lying face down on the floor, he listened for sounds of pursuit. At first his heaving breaths were too loud for him to hear anything else. When they calmed at last, all was silence. Night had fallen and it was quite dark in the hut. Slowly the man groped for his fire bow. He had done this so many times, he could do what was needed in the dark without being able to see. He gripped one end of the spindle in his teeth, and shuddered as he remembered the skeleton with its teeth clamped onto the stern. Then to the business of making fire, the soothing effect of this familiar task. When the moss had caught, it was a matter of moments to set the oil lamp with its wick at the ready, to pour the whale oil from the sealskin pouch, to see light bloom in the little vessel.

Holding the oil lamp like a torch, the man rose and held the light up to see what was there. This truly was a refuge. There on the shelves were more lights, stores of blubber and oils for fuel, fishing tackle, piles of folded skins. Here he would be safe, could survive for weeks if he needed to.

His gaze slipped back to the floor where lay his own muddled gear, which he had snatched up in his panic. Something gleamed among it. He nearly dropped the lamp in fright. It was the skull staring up at him. Shadows shivered and danced on the walls as his hand trembled. The dead and the living stared at each other. All was quiet, nothing happened. Then the man let out a great sigh. In his fright he had forgotten to breathe. Now, he was not only looking, he was also seeing. There, caught in the breastbone, was his fishing hook. All the time he had thought he was flee- ing he was dragging the skeleton behind him. Nothing was chasing him except his own fear. As fear moved away from him, pity stepped into its shadow. He did not know who this person had been, how they had come to be lying beneath the water or how long they had been there. Kneeling, he gently disentangled the bones from his belongings, coaxed the limbs into their correct positions, closed the gaping jaws. When it lay, smoothed and whole, the man was overcome by fatigue. Blurred with exhaustion, he drew down a pile of skins, rolled onto them and fell asleep.

When he was breathing deeply, Skeleton Woman stirred. She sat up, looked about her, knelt by the man. As the lamp dimmed, she peered at him with her empty eyes. In the last of the flickering flame, she saw something shining squeeze itself from beneath an eyelid and run down his face. It was a tear. She put her bony mouth on his cheek and sucked it up. She could not stop drinking; although it was just one tear she drank and drank until she was no longer thirsty. Then she stretched out her sharp bony fingers and sliced into his chest. She made a long gash and, pulling apart the skin, she reached deep inside and pulled out his heart.

Skeleton Woman stood up on her teetering bony feet, still holding the heart. Then she began to beat upon it like a drum. As its music filled the hut, she began to dance. At first a shuffle, then firm strides as long as that small space would allow. As she played and danced, she began to sing. As she played and danced and sang, flesh clothed her bones. Skin clothed her flesh. Hair and features clothed her skin. When she was whole, she knelt beside the stranger and slipped his heart back inside his body. At her touch, the wound closed over. Then Skeleton Woman lay beside him and slept. When the man awoke, he was no longer alone.

THE STORY STONE

The eldest of three, it was she who hunted for the family, her arrows seldom missing their mark, always bringing back enough food for all of them. That day she had walked along the shore without having found any prey. On she went, until she had walked beyond further than far, and reached a part of the river she had never been to before. There she saw a large rock rising midstream, and on it two great white birds. Creeping among the sedge, she notched an arrow to her bowstring. With one movement she rose and let it fly. So true was her aim that it pierced both birds through the neck and they lay dead on the stone. Older daughter waded out to the rock to retrieve her quarry, but now that she was there, how pleasant it was to feel the warm sun on the stone, the cool water caressing her feet with its flow. She had meat enough for many days. No need to hurry back. Sitting there drowsily, she heard a voice: 'Would you like to hear a story?'

There were none there who could have spoken. The birds were dead; the water gurgled past. Then the voice spoke again and this time she knew it came from beneath her. The stone itself was speaking.

'Would you like to hear a story?'

'What is a story?'

'A story is something that speaks of all that has happened and is yet to happen. A story is something that takes you to where you have never been and shows you places that you have never seen. A story is something that makes you believe what you could not even begin to imagine.'

'Yes! I would like to hear a story.'

'Good, but you get nothing for nothing. If I tell you a story, what will you give me?'

Elder sister had no gifts with her. Much as she wanted to hear a story, she could not afford to give her bow and arrows, as then how would she feed her family? But she could give the birds she had just shot. Replacing the arrow in her quiver, she smoothed their feathers tenderly and gently laid them on the rock as her gift.

Then there was a trembling, a stirring and a rocking. Stronger the movements grew until the birds had tilted themselves upright and great webbed feet were trampling against the stone. Huge white wings stretched and flapped. The birds rose up, their wings beating in time as they soared into the air and flew away. Elder sister spent the rest of the day listening to a story. When she returned to her family that evening, it was the first time that she had brought nothing to eat. Their bellies stayed empty, but their ears were full as she told them the story she had heard.

Knowing that some mystery lay behind this, the mother told her middle child to secretly follow his sister and find out what she was up to. Happy to avoid the chores around their camp and to practise the tracking skills that the elder sister had taught him with such expertise, brother followed elder sister without being detected. He saw her pause opposite the rock with the two great white birds. He saw how a single arrow pierced both their necks. He could hardly believe what happened next as those dead birds rose and flew far away. It was then that he came out of hiding and joined his sister on the rock. For the rest of that day brother and sister listened to a story. That night, the family's bellies stayed empty once more, but their ears were full.

The following day, her mother sent the younger daughter to follow the others as they left hastily at first light. All passed as it had before and she joined the others on the rock. Yet again, that evening, bellies remained empty while ears were filled. Then it was left to the mother to follow her children, which she did the next morning. All happened just as it had before and she soon joined them on the rock.

Now that the family knew what to do to hear another story, they moved their camp nearer to the rock to make time for hunting both for themselves and for a gift for the story stone. Whatever they brought would be restored to life before the story began, and they sometimes found themselves carrying animals that couldn't swim or fly back over the water to release them on dry land. As time went on others passed the story stone on foot or in canoes. Noticing the family sitting there, they too crossed the water, clambered up beside them and listened to a story. More and more people kept coming and sometimes the rock was entirely covered so that you couldn't see what people were sitting on in the middle of the river. So many came that everyone had to stand and even carry the youngsters so that all could get close enough to hear a story.

One day there was a great cracking sound, and the people felt fissures running beneath them across the stone.

'Now I have told you all the stories I know. There will be no more from me!'

With that the story stone split apart and broke into many, many fragments. All the listeners were hurled into the river. Some dived deep and brought up many pieces of the stone; others were only able to snatch one or two. Far more pieces were washed downstream to find their way at last to the sea, where they washed ashore on different lands. From that day to this day, we love to pick up stones on the beach. From that day to this day, fragments from everybody's stories can be found all over the world.

THE POTATO FARMER
AND THE STAR MAIDEN

PERU

A farmer lived with his old mother on his mountain farm. As the soil was so poor, all he could grow was potatoes. This meant that he was poor too, so he was especially dismayed when he went to work in his field and discovered that some of his crop had been stolen. He waited in the field to catch the thief, but he fell asleep and when he awoke, more potatoes had gone. The next night he did not allow himself to sit down in case he slept again, but this time he fell asleep standing up leaning against a wall. In the morning, even more potatoes had been stolen. He wondered all day what he could do to stop the thief, and then he had an idea: of course! The thief only came when he slept, so all he had to do was to go to the field and pretend to be asleep to entice the thief, and he could be caught before the farmer fell asleep for real.

That night, when the farmer went to the potato field, his hid his eyes behind his hands and snored loudly while peering between his fingers. He soon forgot these pretences after what happened next. The sky suddenly bloomed with balls of light that grew larger and brighter as they floated nearer to Earth. By now he could see that in each ball of light there was a maiden. The maidens were dancing, and as they danced their stars twinkled. Then they landed on the ground and began to collect his potatoes. With a shout of rage the farmer chased them away, and they rose effortlessly back into the sky; all except for the youngest one, who tripped over a potato – allowing the farmer to seize her. But now that she was in his arms, he forgot his anger and could only think of how happy he would be if this beauty would stay with him forever. He begged her to marry him, but the star maiden replied that she could never stay on Earth because her starlight dress made her too light and she kept floating back into the sky. That was why she and her sisters came to steal his potatoes, as their weight allowed them to explore the Earth when they tired of the featureless sky.

The farmer replied that his mother would give her an ordinary dress, so they returned to the farmhouse and there she was given a potato sack to wear instead. Hers was hidden away in the furthest corner of a dark cupboard. The couple lived happily together, the star maiden fascinated by ordinary domestic life, while the farmer worked his potato patches.

One day, having seen her mother-in-law using a broom, a most curious object, the star maiden decided to try it herself and soon found herself poking about in that cupboard where her dress was hidden. She drew it out and her heart lifted when she saw that half-forgotten shimmer. As she touched those beams of starlight, she felt so light that she floated from the floor. The dress slipped over her and she floated out of the open window. As she flew back into the sky, her shadow passed over the field where the farmer was working and he looked up to see his beloved leaving. He raced after her as she flew ever upwards, running up the mountain slope to keep her in sight. When he was at the summit, he crouched down to catch her as she floated past, but just as he sprang towards her, a sudden gust of wind snatched her away and his arms closed on emptiness. He watched her disappearing light until he could see it no more, put his head in his hands, and wept.

Soon he heard a sound like distant thunder and felt a wind swirl around him. Then a harsh voice spoke: 'I know where your Star Maiden has gone: to the other side of the sky. I can take you there on my back, but it is a long way and I will need meat for the journey.'

Hope conquered fear as the farmer looked at the giant bird with its huge curved beak that had landed beside him. He ran down the mountain, grabbed a few saved coins from the farmhouse, rushed to the market and bought two deer carcasses. These he hauled up the mountain to where the bird was still waiting for him. He climbed onto its back, dragging the carcasses with him, and the bird wheeled into the air. Higher and higher it flew until Earth looked like a small blue potato beneath them. From time to time the bird would say, 'I am hungry, give me meat!'

Then the farmer would tear flesh from the carcasses, inch his way along that huge neck and shut his eyes as he offered it to that deadly beak.

At last, the farmer needed to tell the bird that all the meat had been stripped from the bones and there was none left to give him.

'Then I will grow weak and fall out of the sky!' came the harsh reply.

At that the man rolled up his sleeve, crept along the neck and offered his own arm for the bird to feed from. The sharpest of beaks dug into his vein and the brave farmer's blood sustained the bird for the rest of the journey.

At last they reached the Palace of the Sun, and as it was night time, Sun was rolling home to rest. The Star Maidens, who slept in the palace during the day, were streaming out through the windows and spreading across the sky. The farmer wondered how he would recognise his own Star Maiden and the bird told him that, being the youngest, she would be the last to float past them. He told the farmer to grab her and swing her behind him and they would return to Earth together.

'And make sure she doesn't look back or I will fall out of the sky!'

The moment came, and this time there was no wind to snatch her out of his grasp. But when the other Star Maidens saw her leaving, they cried out, 'Do not leave us again Little Sister!'

At that, the Star Maiden turned to look back and the great bird fell from the sky. As she floated back towards her sisters, the farmer fell down, down, down until he landed with a huge bump in his potato field. Bruised and sorrowful, he crept home. The next evening he noticed, shining above his roof, a star that had never been there before. All night it shone in the same place, never wheeling about the sky like the others. The next night it was there again, and the next and the next. Years passed and the farmer's bones grew stiff and the frost in his hair would not melt with the rising sun, but that star shone as brightly for him as it had when they first met.

BEAUTIFUL BROTHER

Mother was telling a story to her nine sons and one daughter. It was from the time when Great Eagle had told his own son and daughter to fly down to the Earth so that the Eagle People could live there. When they had obeyed their father, the brother suggested to the sister that they lie together to create more beings. At first she refused, but then she saw that otherwise they would be the only people and that when they died there would be no more, so she agreed. Their children spread over the Earth and when it was populated, brothers and sisters no longer lay together.

When the story ended, and the children were asleep, Mother and Father talked again about their concern for their eldest son. Even as a young child he was so beautiful they knew that he would attract too much attention, and they did not know how to protect him from danger, so they had decided to live far away from other members of their tribe. Now that he was older, they told him to spend more time with his grandparents, which he often did. Furthermore, in those days, the Sky People and the Earth People often mingled, travelling up and down the sky pole, which was easy to find. Eldest Brother would often do this on his way to and from his grandparents, and soon he fell in love with one of the Sky Maidens.

His only sister was a solitary child, seldom seeking to play with her younger brothers. When her moon bleeding started, she had her own little hut for these times, built beside a pool. When her father and brothers finished their sweat lodge, they too would bathe there. One night she was swimming alone and she felt the tender caress of something winding around her body. She caught it and when she emerged, discovered that it was a long black hair, exactly the same length as hers, but too coarse. How she longed to know whose it was. That night, as Mother told them stories, she combed her brothers' hair to match theirs to the one she had found. They were all too short.

Her parents had begun to speak about her taking a trip to the valley to make friends and see if there were any young men she might be interested in marrying. She knew that there would be none. That night she was about to swim in the pool when, in the moonlight, she recognised her eldest brother, not knowing that he had just returned from the Sky People. He dived into the pool and when he had finished swimming, disappeared again into the darkness. Then she slipped into the water and again felt the same caress from a long, thick hair. It matched the first exactly.

The next day she consented to the trip to the valley as long as her eldest brother accompanied her. Her parents were reluctant for him to go, but at last they ran out of excuses and brother and sister set off together. When they camped that night, on the other side of the mountain, she breathed a sleeping spell over him so that he slept as deeply as one who had drunk medicine. Then she crept into his shelter and embraced him. Thinking in his half-awake, half-asleep state that she was his Sky Maiden lover, Eldest Brother did not push his sister away, and made love to her. Upon waking before her, he was horrified to realise what had really happened. His turn, now, to breathe a sleeping spell so that she would not wake until late in the morning. He also took a log from the fire that was still warm and wrapped her arms around it. Then, silently, he ran back to his parents' camp.

They had been full of foreboding for so long that they were hardly surprised to hear what had happened. Their son urged them all to climb up the sky pole and take refuge among the Sky People. Father agreed but insisted that his daughter should be utterly abandoned and that no trace of their home or any possessions should be left for her. All would have to be burned, and that would take time. Back in the shelter, Sister had stirred in her sleep, but did she not feel a warm body between her arms? If Elder Brother had not woken, then neither need she.

At last the family had burned everything they owned. On the other side of the mountain, Sister had finally woken and was enraged to discover that her brother had tricked and abandoned her. Fury whipped her legs as she pursued him. Already he could hear her calling out with a sound that put fear in his heart; shrieks of rage, bubbling sobs, and crazy bursts of laughter.

Eldest Brother urged the others to follow him as he ran for the sky pole. He told his mother to climb behind him and his younger brothers climbed after her with his father coming last. Eldest Brother was at the rim of the Sky World when Sister arrived at the bottom of the pole. Rage made her do a clumsy, lurching dance and still those bubbling sobs and crazy laughter forced their way out of her mouth as she called out to her family to wait for her, not to leave her alone.

Mother, high up the sky pole, looked back down to Earth – perhaps she should not abandon her only daughter. Looking down made her dizzy and she lost her grip. As she fell, she took all of her sons and their father with her. Down, down they plummeted toward the fire, which was still hot enough to burn them all to death. Only Eldest Brother escaped to the Sky World.

There was Sister, still dancing with rage, still calling that strange, chilling sound. Only now she was raking in the fire, pulling out ten white skulls, white of ash, white of bone. There she was, stringing them into a necklace on two beautiful, long, strong hairs. You can still hear Sister with that flesh-creeping cry, and you can see her do that clumsy lurching dance, her only ornament a necklace of white skulls. Today we call her Loon Bird, lonely as a Loon Bird.

HOW THE BIRDS GOT THEIR COLOURS

GUYANA

Long time ago, the birds had no colours, they were only black or white. The forest and riverside were full of birds in those days. On the shore of the great river was a village of huts whose people lived by fishing and hunting. Their houses, made from palm leaves and vines, were raised up on stilts to be clear of snakes and the river's risings.

One day, the chief's son was hunting alone when he saw a bird, which he shot. Seeing where it had plummeted from its perch, he found the corpse only to retrieve his arrow, leaving the dead bird where it had fallen without taking it for its meat or feathers. This was the first time that such a thing had happened. When his father asked whether he had found any prey as he had been away all day, his son replied that he hadn't. Next day he returned to the forest and the same thing happened, except that this time he shot two birds. The chief was surprised that his son returned without anything to show for his efforts, especially as he was such a good shot. Day after day the young man went alone into the forest. Looking and listening carefully, he made sure that he hadn't been followed before shooting more and more birds, only pausing to pull out his arrows. Because he had shot so many there were fewer birds to be found and he needed to go further from the village. By now the surviving birds had become more wary and were proving harder to find. Further and further into the forest he went, returning home later and later, but still empty handed. The chief didn't ask his son what he had been up to, and so the young man continued unchecked.

There came a day when it had been so hard to find a bird to kill that the sun was already sinking beyond the tree canopy before he needed an arrow. He was about to reach to his quiver when he found that he couldn't raise his arm. It seemed to be stuck to his body. He tried with the other, but that too was impossible to move. Trying to take a step forward, he lurched and fell. His legs had fused together, and he found himself lying full length on the leaf litter. Now he had no limbs at all, they had been absorbed into a body that grew longer and longer as it grew a skin patterned with every colour of the rainbow. His eyes slid round to the side of his head and his nose and ears disappeared. His mouth now stretched around what had been his face and when he opened it to call for help a flickering forked tongue emerged and the only sound he could utter was a hiss. The chief's son had become a snake.

He slithered into the undergrowth looking for prey, his rippling progress bringing both beauty and death. The more he ate, the bigger he grew. The bigger he grew, the hungrier he became. The hungrier he became, the more he ate. He grew to a monstrous size, and still he was hungry. All the animals in the vicinity had been eaten, but his hunger could not be satisfied. There remained one place where he could continue to eat and still remain hidden, which was the great river, and the villagers were to become his prey.

By now the size of a small river himself, it would be easy to hide in the larger one that flanked his village. Soon children who swam there started to disappear. The hungrier he became, the more he ate. The more he ate, the bigger he grew. The bigger he grew, the hungrier he became. The surviving children had been forbidden to go near the river, because, by then, a river monster had been seen, covered in beautiful colours the like of which had never been seen before, but vastly powerful and terrifying in form. Now even men and women were being attacked on the shore if they were fishing, moreover, they were no longer safe in their canoes. People had seen these being overturned by the monster snake, who would wrap their occupants in his coils before drowning them and swallowing them whole.

The monstrous snake had appeared at the same time as the chief's son had disappeared, but if he connected the two, the chief never mentioned it. If anyone else had noticed that coincidence, they were too frightened to say anything. However, the surviving villagers demanded that their chief do something about this calamity before they all perished. The chief proclaimed that whoever could kill the snake could have its skin as a reward. However magnificent and precious that skin was, all the villagers were too frightened to attempt to kill the monster. There was just one creature who was brave enough to try, and that was Cormorant. How was such a small bird going to succeed where a whole village was too fearful to take on the task?

Cormorant dived into the river where the snake was lurking. A little dark shadow, not worth chasing to eat. With his sharp, curved fisherman's beak, the little bird pecked out the monster's eye. When the snake had finished roiling and thrashing in his agony, Cormorant swam along his blind side. Choosing his moment, he dived beneath the enormous head and shot up beside the remaining eye. This was pecked out like the first, and now the snake was completely blind and at his attacker's mercy. Blows without number were aimed at the great neck, gouges beyond counting were inflicted by that determined little beak. At last it severed through the head, and the dead body of the monster rolled up onto the shore.

Exhausted, Cormorant went to claim his reward and asked for the snake to be skinned. But the chief wanted the beautiful skin for himself and tried to think of a way of wriggling out of the bargain. He pointed out that the agreement had said nothing about skinning the snake and that if Cormorant wanted the skin, he would have to strip it himself. Cormorant pleaded with the chief to help him, but the man refused. Understanding that he was going to be cheated, the little bird threw back his head and gave a great cry that soared above the forest canopy and beyond.

The sky began to darken even though there were no clouds, and a distant clamouring grew louder and louder as the darkness deepened. The villagers covered their ears as countless birds from all over the forest landed on the snake's body. Then with beaks and claws each one of them tore off a piece of skin and flew away. Whatever scrap of colour each bird managed to tear off, became the colour of their new plumage. Some birds managed to carry off multicoloured strips, which you can see today in the glorious feathers of birds like the cotingas and the macaws. As for Cormorant, he decided to remain black because he wanted to be recognised not for what he looked like, but for his brave deed.

TRAPPED IN THE ICE

QUEBEC/NEWFOUNDLAND, CANADA

This event was documented and reported at the time. Were it not for a similar incident reported decades later, it would have remained a historical story and would not have claimed the status of legend.

The ship's passengers had given up all hope of rescue. They had been trapped in the ice for many days far from the Newfoundland coast, and provisions were low. They feared thirst more than any other privation as the ice was frozen sea water and too salty to drink. Perhaps it was due to the effects of thirst, or hunger, or cold, that one of their number fell into a strange sleep in which it was as though he had left his body, but nevertheless had boarded a ship sailing in their direction, entered the captain's cabin, and written a message on the slate he had found there. When he had come to, so certain was he that this had been no ordinary dream, that he had gone to his own captain and assured him that rescue was on its way.

Meanwhile, on a trading ship sailing from Quebec to Liverpool, the first mate and the captain were plotting their course. With his head bent low over the charts, Mr Bruce did not notice that the captain had left the cabin and assumed him to still be there, especially as he heard the unmistakable sound of someone writing on a slate. However, Mr Bruce did look up when he received no reply after repeatedly mentioning their course – and found he was looking at a stranger. The first mate was so discomfited that he rushed out to find the captain to tell him that they had a stowaway on board. The captain was near the cabin entrance and had seen no one leave, so the man must still be inside, but, on re-entering together, they could find nobody. There, however, lay the slate, with the message, 'Steer to the Nor'-West', which would have been in the wrong direction. First the captain tested Mr Bruce's handwriting, which bore no resemblance. Suspecting a prank played by an undisciplined crew member, the captain then tested theirs, which didn't take long as few of them could write. The mystery persisted, so a thorough search was made for a stowaway, which yielded no result.

Extremely disturbed by this bizarre event, and trusting his first mate implicitly, the captain was intelligent enough to know that there are more things 'twixt heaven and earth' that can be explained, especially if they occur at sea. He gave the order to steer 'Nor-West!' and the relief in Mr Bruce's voice rang clear as a bell when he responded 'Aye, aye Captain!' The ship changed course, and later that day came across the passenger ship that was caught fast in the ice.

All were rescued, and as each climbed aboard, Mr Bruce scrutinised every man among them. With absolute certainty he was able to point out the stranger he had seen in the captain's cabin. Instantly, the captain placed the clean side of the slate in front of him and told him to write 'Steer to the Nor-West'. It was identical to the writing on the other side. Although the stranger could not recall writing anything, he did remember that in his dreamlike state, he had been on another ship that he felt sure would rescue them. The captain of the stranded vessel confirmed that the same man had told him that a rescue would happen that day, which, at the time he had put down to a fevered and wishful imagination. Fortunately, the captain's trust in his first mate and in his intuition ensured that this strangest of visits was not in vain.

JOHNNY APPLESEED

MASSACHUSETTS, NORTH AMERICA

Born Johnathan Chapman on 26 September 1774 – right in the middle of the apple harvest – Johnny Appleseed's life was well documented until his death in 1845, a ripe old age for those days, despite the physical hardships that he took upon himself. He could certainly be described as a legend in his own lifetime. The descendant of an immigrant farmer from England who arrived in North America in the seventeenth century, he grew up in a country that was what we might describe today as a wilderness. Losing his mother at an early age, he was raised with many half-siblings from his father's second marriage. He grew up at a time of armed conflict with the indigenous tribes known by their aggressors as the Indian Wars, and his father had fought in the American War of Independence. A lover of animals, Johnathan Chapman also became a devotee of the teachings of Baron Swedenborg, a Christian mystic and proselytiser whose interpretations and preaching from the Christian Bible emphasised loving acts and the sacrifice of physical comforts.

Johnny Appleseed, Johnny Appleseed,
Chief of the fastnesses, dappled and vast,
In a pack on his back,
In a deer-hide sack,
The beautiful orchards of the past,
The ghosts of all the forests and the groves –
In that pack on his back,
In that talisman sack.

Vachel Lindsay

Everyone loved Johnny, with his gentle and hard-working ways. That is, everyone with the exception of the trappers, whose snares were dismantled, or, if he discovered them too late, from which trapped animals were released. He never outgrew this compassion for animals, rather it increased as he grew older. Reputed to have a pet wolf that he had released from a trap, and which followed him everywhere, Johnny Appleseed even stopped lighting his campfires during his travels, to prevent insects from being consumed by flames or smoke. As it was fire that kept wild beasts at bay in the wilderness, it must have been his wolf or a reciprocal respect from the animals that kept him safe. He was safe too from the indigenous war parties whose territories he travelled through but who never harmed him, even though he would warn settlers of their imminent ambushes. In later life he became mostly vegetarian, only accepting meat that he had not killed himself.

Whilst still a young man, Johnathan Chapman left home with his copy of the Swedenborg Bible and a sack of apple seeds he had acquired from the local cider mills. He had already learned how to plant orchards, the craft of raising seedlings and saplings, and the skill of grafting. His mission was to plant apple orchards in the new lands that settlers were claiming for their own as their wagons rolled ever westwards towards the sunset.

In keeping with Swedenborg's teachings, he led an austere life; walking barefoot, eating and dressing sparingly. Perhaps it was his faith that enabled him to survive these chosen hardships. Settlers were few and far between in those days and apart from the difficulties of establishing farms and becoming self-sufficient, they lived or died with the threat of reprisals from those who saw their lands and their freedom taken from them.

Using his money only for the barest necessities and to buy up tracts of land for his orchards, Johnathan Chapman was always on the move, digging and planting whatever the weather or season until heavy snow prevented him. To the poor and sick he brought not only the Christian teachings of kindness, but practical help too. Spending so long in the wild, he had learned about medicinal plants and herb lore from the indigenous tribes, and was able to use this skill to tend the sick in remote areas far from the reach of any doctor. He also had a supply of buckskin pouches full of apple seeds, which he left with poor families so that they could start their own orchards. Toing and froing across the land, he would teach the new farmers how to prune and graft and make brakes of brush to protect their saplings from rabbits and deer.

By now he had become a familiar figure, and his distinctive silhouette with his cooking pot hat and his sack of seeds on his shoulder made certain that he would be recognised from afar. The travellers would haul in their wagons alongside and call out to offer him a seat as they rode westwards. But Johnny Appleseed, as everybody now called him, would always refuse, saying that he needed to feel God's good earth beneath his feet to know which were the best places for planting his next orchard.

Seasons passed into years and years into decades. Johnny Appleseed continued to plant and heal, preach and teach, retracing his steps some of the way to check how seedlings had become saplings and saplings had become orchards, and then pushing ever further westwards.

They say that you can't do countless good deeds without the Almighty getting to hear of it. Word had got about that a man was imitating the Creator not only in image, but in actions. The Almighty called together a host of angels and requested that one of them go to Earth and see whether or not these rumours were true. If they were, whichever angel found Johnny Appleseed was to become his guardian. Unsurprisingly, there wasn't a stampede of enthusiasm for searching this enormous territory for a single individual among a population that, since the origin of the human race, had never shown much interest in angels anyway. Many of that glorious host remembered that they were just about to go into moult, pointed out that they were already moulting, or explained that they were still recovering from that particular millennial ordeal.

At last, however, one was found and this angel's goodwill was rewarded with an easier task than expected. It happened to be springtime in North

America when s/he rolled back the clouds and peered down to Earth below. There was a flush of apple blossom winding its way like a pink river from east to west. Surely Johnny Appleseed would be found at the end furthest from the sea, where the pink had petered out, planting his way towards the setting sun? And so it was, and the story does not tell us whether or not our hero ever knew that he had a guardian angel for the rest of his days, but even as an old man he was still planting apple trees.

There came a winter that seemed longer and harder than usual, or was it just that his skin was thin with age, and his joints aching and twisted with years of labouring? He had recently turned three score years and ten, and, as far as he was concerned, that was no reason to hang up his spade and sit in a rocking chair on the porch. Come the middle of March there was still no sign of a thaw and Johnny Appleseed had returned to the orchards he had planted some time before, to see to their pruning. The snow still lay deep and, that day, he hadn't seemed to be able to travel as far as expected. Realising that he would not be able to reach one of the homesteads where he would receive a warm welcome for the night, he knew that he would have to spend it outdoors.

For the first time he was ill prepared, with no fuel for a fire. How had that happened? He stumbled gathering fallen twigs to brush away the snow, but it lay too thick, and why were his careful hands now so clumsy? What to do? He looked up into the branches of a tree he had planted long ago. When that was, he could not rightly remember. The tree held out its branches wide in welcome and Johnny Appleseed climbed into them. Pale gold in the moonlight, some autumn leaves were still clinging, shivering in the bitter breeze, just as he was. Then it seemed that there were more leaves, shimmering gold against restless branches. But they weren't leaves, they were feathers, and for the first time, Johnny Appleseed saw his guardian angel.

'It's time to come with me now, Johnny, I've come to take you home.'

'This is my home and I'm not going anywhere until I've finished planting my orchards, and that's not going to be any time soon seeing how much land there is to cover.'

The guardian angel hadn't been expecting any resistance. Somehow s/he felt that the role would be compromised if Johnny Appleseed didn't come willingly. And what to tell the Creator if s/he returned to heaven without him? Then the angel had an idea. 'You've done enough, old man, and it's time for you to meet your Maker. Haven't you prayed for this moment all your long, hard life? In any case, you're needed in heaven to plant some apple trees, because we don't have any.'

'What? No apple trees in heaven? How can that be? How can heaven be heaven without apple trees?'

'Well, it all started with a certain unfortunate incident a long, long time ago. The Creator and Adam and Eve had a major disagreement over an apple tree, and since then there have been no apple trees in heaven. Not God's favourite tree, you understand. But, as I say, that was all a long time ago, and I think you are just the fellow to change the Almighty's mind. So why don't you hurry on up with me and carry on doing what you do best?'

The guardian angel enfolded the old man in golden wings and in a moment the tree stood empty-armed and bare-branched again with just a few golden leaves clinging on until spring. But as for Johnny Appleseed, he was on his way to make heaven a better place.

Without a hope of recompense,
Without a thought of pride,
John Chapman planted apple trees,
Preached and lived and died.

Johnny Appleseed monument, Dexter City, Ohio

MOMO

NORTH AMERICA? URBAN LEGEND SPREAD ON THE INTERNET

Retold here with kind permission from storytellers Amelia 'Ace' Armand, Jason Buck and Aaron Oliver from their digital theatre series entitled 'It Came from the Internet: Myths of Modern Monsters' and told and broadcast online by Aaron Oliver. Urban legends are a type of story that often have a scary or cautionary content or can be elaborate jokes, stretching the listener's credulity until it snaps. Rather like those pet alligators released into New York's sewers when owners become tired of them. Growing to a huge size on a diet of sewer rats, they force themselves up the U-bends of domestic plumbing in an effort to find their way home again, or raise drain covers to roam the streets at night, searching for larger prey.

Knowing that stories are constantly being shaped and reshaped to accommodate our concerns and interest, I was curious about the impact of the most important cultural development of our times – the internet. Apart from its benefits, many adults know the threats it can also pose to us all, ranging from fake news and AI content that prevents us from being able to tell computer-generated material from 'real' sources, to the horrors of the dark web. Many of us are concerned about the addictive effects of internet games, especially on young people, and how social media is used for cyber bullying, resulting in a surge of self-harming and even suicide among children. This particular urban legend caused so much concern among educators, social media content monitors and law enforcers that several international agencies were involved and declared 'the Momo Challenge' to be a 'worldwide moral panic'. Warnings were issued to family organisations and schools before it was eventually discovered to be a hoax, alias an urban legend. I have included Momo's story as an example of an internet phenomenon expressed through narrative, and to demonstrate how we create or adapt stories to explore the new challenges brought on by profound technical and social changes.

Of all the different gaming names that he used on the internet, nobody knew that Cool Blue was his favourite. His friends at school had nick-named him 'Cool' because of his readiness to be the first to take on a dare, and because he always kept his nerve when their pranks were discovered. He chose 'Blue' himself because, not only did it seem to fit with 'Cool', it referred to his favourite pastime, which was to play internet games long into the night, caressed by his screen's flickering blue light. Cool Blue shared a bedroom with his little sister. Perhaps that blue flicker was such a familiar part of her night time that she never mentioned it. Tucked in with her teddy, any blue light playing against closed lids as she fell asleep was as normal as the distant buzz from her brother's headphones. As soon as she was asleep, he would take one of his covers and roll it up against the bottom of the door so that his parents wouldn't see any telltale flickers through the crack underneath. If they had ever noticed the blue bags under his eyes, they were now part of his everyday appearance, and nobody remarked on them as he listlessly spooned his breakfast cereal before rushing off to nearly miss the school bus.

At school he heard a rumour that there was a new game circulating that was so scary it had to be kept a secret not just from parents and teachers, but from any social media watchdogs or content monitors. Annoyed that he hadn't been the first among his circle to discover it, Cool Blue was somewhat mollified to learn that none of his circle had been brave enough to play. To make amends for this lapse, he boasted that he would be the first to play the Momo Challenge. As he was the daredevil trailblazer among them, his friends were glad that he was going to do exactly what they had been secretly hoping for.

For someone of Cool Blue's skill it wasn't too hard to find and download the Momo Challenge app. Although he was accustomed to some pretty scary stuff on the internet, nothing could prepare him for the horrifying face that introduced the game. The impact of that image was far worse than being told that he had to adhere to absolute secrecy about the challenges. The first of these was to watch an adult horror movie, which Cool Blue had never done before. It was really frightening, so he was quite glad that he wasn't allowed to mention it and was able to avoid admitting this to any of his friends. Next day he received a message from Momo telling him to spend an hour in his front garden from three in the morning. He was too preoccupied with how not to get caught to wonder how Momo knew that he had a front garden. With great stealth, and wearing clothes that would camouflage him against any casual glance from a passerby at that early hour, the challenge went off without mishap. It was soon followed by a congratulatory message from Momo at his having passed his initiatory tests, accompanied by a warning that the real tasks would begin soon.

The first came with a reminder that he was not to tell anyone about the challenge – which was to tear off the head of his sister's teddy bear. Cool Blue typed back that he didn't want to do this and immediately received another image of Momo, the face distorted even more horrifically into an expression of omnipotent menace. This was accompanied by a message that if he didn't do it, his sister's face would be damaged instead.

In the hurry to get ready for school the mutilated teddy wasn't noticed straight away. Cool Blue spent all day worrying about what would happen when it was discovered, and when that did happen he was compelled to deny his guilt. His parents and sister found it hard to believe that the boy could have done it. He had never shown any jealousy to his sister, nor any signs of violence. Yes, he could be impulsive and risk-taking, but weren't many young boys? He managed to convince everyone that his sister must have done it in her sleep during a nightmare. At school his friends kept asking him when he was going to do the Momo Challenge, but as he couldn't talk about what was involved, he invented some lie about why he hadn't started it yet. When some of them teased him about 'being chicken', he had to put up with the humiliation, and secretly feared that he would lose his reputation for fearlessness.

The next message was to praise him for having succeeded in the challenge and averting the harm that would otherwise have come to his sister. Now that Momo was being so threatening, Cool Blue was dreading the next notification but, of course, it came, this time with the instruction to stretch a cord across the top of the stairs at ankle height. Again, he typed back that he didn't want to do that. Somebody could get badly hurt. Didn't people sometimes die from falling down the stairs? Well, that was a risk he would have to take, came the reply, because the alternative was Momo telling his parents who had torn the head off his sister's teddy. Cool Blue hoped against hope that someone would notice the cord before anyone tripped – surely that was much more likely. The crash and howls of pain came in the middle of the night; his father had fallen and broken his ankle. The boy was told to look after his little sister while his mother took him to hospital.

Cool Blue was just about to comfort his sister when he heard another notification arrive. This time he was being told to climb onto the roof and walk along the ridge tiles. How did Momo know that he had a secret fear of heights? He had always managed to hide this. 'Slides are just for little kids,' he used to say, or 'I'd rather spend my money on a game,' if anyone suggested he went on the roller coaster at the fun fair. So he knew that if he even managed to get up there, he would definitely fall. Momo had tried to get to his sister and had succeeded in harming his father. Now Momo was coming for him. He had nothing to lose. He deleted the app.

Brother and sister decided to snuggle up together to watch one of her favourite films on YouTube. He connected his computer to the television so that they could see it on the big screen, then he brought his duvet downstairs and they cuddled up under it on the sofa. Animation images chortled and frolicked across the screen, and for a while, the children were lost in that idyllic world, worries about their father forgotten. Suddenly the images warped, a high-pitched, searing noise came from the television and Momo's face appeared, distorted with viciousness. Cool Blue turned off all the devices and started to cry. His sister kept telling him that it was only a horrible story, it wasn't real, it couldn't get to him. He didn't need to be frightened of stories. If he was scared of something, he could tell a friend. As soon as he started telling someone about what frightened him it wouldn't be so scary any more. Holding her tight, every pore of his being drank in her words.

When he finished crying, he told his sister that he had been scared by a game he had downloaded on his phone. As he spoke those words it seemed to him that in his mind's eye, in the secret chambers of his heart, in his churning stomach, Momo, who had utterly consumed him, was beginning to shrink. Now featureless, inanimate, and unable to resist, Momo was small enough to be held in the palm of his hand. Cool Blue got up and flushed his phone down the toilet. Momo was dead. Whatever he told his friends, however they reacted, it would be much easier to bear than what he had already gone through.

NO MOUTH WOMAN

JAMAICA

Ananse is a spider, Ananse is a man
Ananse is West African and Caribbean
Ananse he leave Ghana on banana boat
When the people see him they all give a shout:
'Ananse! magic spider man, Ananse! he do what he can …'
Ananse reach Jamaica on banana boat
When the people see him, they all give a shout:
'Ananse! magic spider man, Ananse! he do what he can …'

Traditional children's song

It didn't take Ananse long to make a name for himself after arriving in Jamaica from Ghana. Indeed, so clever was he that he managed to appear on several Caribbean islands simultaneously, thus ensuring that his numerous exploits would be spoken of far and wide. He soon became famous for his tricks and his teachery, all motivated by the greed that expressed itself in his penchant for fine clothes, fine food and fine women. Perhaps of all his exploits, the envious Ananse liked to speak of those in which he was bested, especially as these were few and far between.

Now that he was settled and had created a reputation he needed to live up to, Ananse decided that it was time for him to get married. Of course, no ordinary woman would do, and he thought hard and long about who among the 'fairer sex' would be good enough for him. Eventually he decided that he would only marry a woman with no mouth – a wise choice as she wouldn't be able to answer back and he wouldn't need to feed her. Surprisingly there wasn't a tidal wave of replies to the advertisement he had grudgingly paid for in *The Daily Gleaner* newspaper. One woman did present herself, and it was instantly obvious that she had no mouth. As the only candidate, she would have to do. Being unable to speak, she nodded her head vigorously at the right moments for her wedding vows. Charging *The Daily Gleaner* for the publication of the most unusual wedding photos ever, easily recompensed Ananse for the advertisement fee, which he still resented paying.

Married life proved most satisfying for him, especially as the happy couple was invited to dinner all over the island, so eager were people to see No Mouth Woman with their own eyes. Although she didn't eat a thing, she was always eager to help with the clearing away and washing up. She didn't monopolise any conversations, express ideas beyond her station or opine about politics or religion. She was the perfect dinner guest. Their island tour consisted of Ananse eating his fill of the very best free meals, and resembled a royal progress. Before long, however, fame was to be followed by rumour. Wherever the couple had been invited, large quantities of food were subsequently found to be missing from larders, pantries and store cupboards. How could this be? Ananse was waited on hand and foot, so he never left the table, and his wife would have no use for food.

Soon after they had finished their honeymoon tour, it happened to be Ananse's birthday. As a precaution against him playing any of his tricks on her, his neighbour would bake him a lavish birthday cake every year. Having been presented with it as usual, Ananse decided to eat it that evening, having various schemes to set up during the day. On his return, to his horror, he discovered that there was only one piece remaining. How could this be? Incomprehensible as it was, there could only be one prime suspect. That night, the remaining piece of cake remained on his bedside table where he could keep an eye on it, under a net cloche to protect it from cockroaches. All night it tormented him with its sticky sweet scent. The following day he scuttled off on his round of errands as usual, but instantly doubled back to the house and put his eye to the keyhole.

He could just see No Mouth Woman seating herself at the table with the last slice of cake in front of her. The sight of her removing her blouse while being spied upon could have completely distracted him from his purpose, were it not for what happened next. On raising a plump and beautifully rounded arm, Ananse could see something stirring in her armpit. As she raised her arm higher, Ananse could see that it was a great hairy mouth with flashing white teeth and a curling red tongue.

The divorce settlement was generous and, for the rest of her days, Ananse's bride could afford more cake than even she could manage to eat.

JORGE PLAYS FOR THE GIANTS

BRAZIL

The Portuguese had colonised Brazil for centuries before this folk tale was recorded. Its storyline is a composite of those that can be found all over Europe, and incorporates, in particular, Portugal's tradition of processional giants. Here the reader can see how it has been adapted in its adopted country.

Jorge was an unusual young man, not sharing the same interests as his fellows. The only thing he ever wanted was a violin, but he and his father were poor, and he had been told that they didn't even have enough money to spend on what was useful. Jorge was an only child, so he helped his father on their small plot of land until he died. Then he sold everything he could, and bought a violin. This was to be his travelling companion, and he listened to the violin as he had to his father.

Soon he came upon a *fazenda* (a cattle ranch), which was full of cattle grazing where the forest had been cleared. He asked the gauchos for work but was told they didn't need any extra hands. Jorge slipped among the trees where the forest began and started to play his violin. Deeper and deeper he went and at first the gauchos tried to discover where that exquisite music was coming from, but they became frightened of getting lost and of all the wild animals that lived there. However, when they had taken their eyes off the cattle, many of the herd strayed into the forest to get closer to the music. They did not have the same fears as the gauchos and followed the beautiful sounds deeper and deeper as Jorge went on his way.

Now that he had company, the young musician felt more cheerful and started to play jollier tunes. Soon the cattle were dancing along as they followed him. Moreover, the forest animals started joining in and tagging on behind as they wound their way through the rainforest. The tapir was skittering about on his tiny hooves, and the anaconda, despite having no feet, was slithering along and waving its tail in time to the music. Monkeys were dancing along the branches, macaws were flapping and squawking in time, and even the jaguars were dancing along on their hind legs.

On and on went this happy procession until they reached a great wall that stretched as far as they could see. They had arrived at the citadel of the giants, and their sentry roared with laughter at the sight. At that, the trees thrashed about as if in a storm, but Jorge kept on playing and soon even they were swaying in time to his enchanting music. The king of the giants heard its sweet strains from inside the castle, along with the sentry's laughter, and he came out of the battlements to see what was happening. When he saw the spectacle, he too started to laugh, as much with joy as with mirth. The king of the giant's laughter was like thunder bouncing between the citadel's walls, and now the sound of drum rolls joined the violin, and the animals danced even faster.

It so happened that the king of the giants had an only daughter who was very melancholy and never smiled. Her father was so worried about her that he had declared that anyone who cured her of her sadness would be allowed to propose to her. So far, all had failed, but perhaps now was a chance for her to join in with the merriment. The princess was sent for and climbed up onto the battlements with her father. As soon as she saw the merry procession, she clapped her hands before seizing the king's and whirling him round and round in a dance. Her delighted laughter rang out over the violin like silver bells.

When Jorge stopped playing, he was invited to propose to the princess, who accepted him because he had brought her such joy. The king of the giants was so pleased that he also gave Jorge half his kingdom. Jorge ruled without any difficulty, and if his huge subjects ever became threatening, all he had to do was play his violin and they started dancing, all evil intentions banished. As for the animals that had followed Jorge, they refused to be parted from the violin and laid siege to the citadel. Jorge gave orders that they be allowed in to live in his part of the kingdom. There they grew to giant size, perhaps not as tall as this tall tale, but just imagine a giant anaconda and a giant jaguar!

UNHOLY MEAT

OTOMI TRIBE, MEXICO

Stories absorb all kinds of influences from other cultures and some are born because of this interaction. Here is an example of these phenomena, a meeting place for pre-conquest tribal beliefs and those of the Old Testament in the Bible introduced by Europeans.

A farmer tried to prepare his land to make it suitable for planting. However hard he worked in the day, overnight all the brush and scrub that he cleared had re-rooted itself. Suspecting that some evil spirit was responsible, he decided to wait and watch in the night. From his hiding place, he saw a rabbit with a magic stick. When the rabbit brandished it at the cut vegetation it rose up as though it had never been cut down. Fearlessly, the farmer confronted the rabbit and remonstrated with him. The rabbit replied: 'Your labour will come to nothing because the world is coming to an end. Do not continue to try to work this land. Instead, you should make a wooden box, large enough to fit all your family in. Make plenty of tortillas for them to eat – I will manage on beans and grasses.'

The farmer believed the rabbit and did what he was told. They all squeezed into the box, which was then sealed, leaving just enough holes for air and to look out of. At that moment a deluge arrived and the box floated up until it reached as high as the sky. Eventually it came to rest once more on dry ground, which was covered in the corpses of the men and animals that had drowned. The rabbit found enough to eat from the surviving plants, but the tortillas were soon finished, so the farmer and his family started to cook the carcases that were lying about.

In the sky, God noticed their smoke and instructed some of the smaller angels to go down and see what was making the smoke and the smell. As they prepared to fly, he told them not to eat anything down there. They arrived as the family were offering the rabbit some of their cooked meat, which he declined. However, the angels were tempted and enjoyed eating their fill. They cleaned and preened their wing feathers so that God would not detect the smell of meat, but however well they groomed themselves, the smell still clung on.

As soon as they returned to heaven, God asked them what they had eaten. They kept preening and beating their wings to get rid of the smell as they lied and said, 'Nothing!'

'Very well,' said God, 'since you have eaten "nothing" you can go back and eat even more "nothing". And on Earth is where you will stay.'

When the angels returned to Earth they became vultures and from that day to this day they continue to feed from carcases. Perhaps as they wheel so high in the sky that we can scarcely see them, they are remembering their first home in heaven.

MONKEY SEE, MONKEY DO

SINT MAARTEN/SAINT MARTIN, CARIBBEAN

When I first heard this tale, told as a Caribbean story, I was surprised to learn that there were monkeys on such a small island. Having researched further, I discovered that Vervet monkeys had been introduced from Africa. Perhaps they were stowaways on slave ships or had been brought over as pets and escaped into the wild. If either of these explanations are true, this tale must be a comparatively recent addition to the island's folklore.

Raoul lived with his mother at the edge of the forest, where the open land with its tall, rough grasses gave way to the treeline. His mother was a skilled weaver and made the best hats on the island from the grasses that grew all about them, and from the straw that was left when their crops had been gathered. As she worked, she sang, and Raoul's favourite song was 'Monkey see, Monkey do, Monkey do like we do too!' He still wore the hat she had made him when he had been sturdy enough to toddle after her in the fields. Worn for years, and by now much too small for him, it had long lost its brim and its different coloured grasses had faded into the same pale yellow. So fond was Raoul of this hat that he even slept in it and wore it when he bathed. People joked that it had become like a second skin, and his mother merely smiled and waited for the day when it would split like a snake's and he would be ready for another.

As for the other hats, she would take these to the market whenever she had made enough to make the journey worthwhile – it was a long trek to the nearest town, which had to be made through the hot jungle, where the gentle sea breezes never penetrated. One day she told Raoul that he was now big enough to make the journey without her, and that he was to go to the market the next day all by himself. Raoul was so excited at the prospect of this adventure that he could hardly sleep and was up before first light to get ready.

There seemed to be more hats than usual and he was having difficulty finding a container for them. Just as his mother wove excellent hats, so too did she make baskets of all shapes and sizes, but, somehow, only one was large enough to take them all, and this was too big for him to manage. As he was still quite small, he could only drag it on the ground and that would be impossible for that distance. This being the first time he was given adult responsibility, he was too proud to ask for help, and so he wrestled with the problem alone. How to carry the hats? But of course, one carries a hat on one's head! All he had to do was to was to carry them all on his head, starting with the smallest and gradually increasing their size so that they would all nestle one inside the other until the largest was placed at the top. Raoul swelled with pride at this solution, which fortunately didn't reach as far as his head, and so he was able to set off with a precarious, teetering, tottering tower of hats.

Progress was hot and slow. The light was dim amongst the trees and he couldn't turn his head to make out the twisting path in the gloom. Having heard the stories of how people had become lost in the forest, the plants growing over their trail so quickly, that only dogs could follow their scent to find them, he knew how dangerous it was to lose the path. Sometimes he had to swivel his whole body to be sure he didn't stray. As he picked his way along, he had the sensation of being followed and heard curious rustlings in the leaves above, but of course he couldn't tilt his head to look. The weight of the hats was pressing them down over his eyes, and the inevitable happened when he tripped over a tree root and fell, the hats rolling off his head. All that was hurt was his dignity, which soon mended as he realised that there was nobody to witness this mishap. Jumping up, he looked for his spilled wares and was astonished to find that they had disappeared. How could this be? He looked along the path, behind the nearby bushes and behind tree trunks. Nothing! Then he looked up to the branches. There staring down at him was a troupe of monkeys, each one wearing one of his mother's hats.

Raoul called out, 'Give me back my hats!'

The monkeys called back in their chittering snickering voices, 'Give me back my hats!'

This was because, just as the song tells us, 'Monkey see, Monkey do, Monkey do like we do too!'

'They're not your hats, they're my hats!'

'They're not your hats, they're my hats!' came the mocking reply, because 'Monkey see, Monkey do, Monkey do like we do too!'

Now Raoul could see that he had quite a problem, and suddenly he didn't feel quite so grown up anymore. He inspected the tree and knew that even if he could climb it, the monkeys would be long gone.

'Please give me back my hats,' he beseeched them, clasping his hands and kneeling on the ground.

'Please give me back my hats,' came the mocking response as each monkey contrived to mimic his posture because, 'Monkey see, Monkey do, Monkey do like we do too!'

At that, Raoul burst into tears and was soon accompanied by howling and hiccupping from above, because, 'Monkey see, Monkey do, Monkey do like we do too!'

Humiliated and despairing, the little boy was now furious that he could be so unjustly treated. He leaped to his feet, snarling with rage. His fingers reached to his head as though to tear out his own hair in frustration. However, they only found the old hat his mother had made him so long ago, still sticking to him like a second skin. Nevertheless, they clutched and they tore, and for the first time it was dragged off his head.

Raoul flung it to the ground, screaming, 'All right, keep my hats then!'

The monkeys reached up to the hats they were wearing and chittering, snickering as loudly as they could, they hurled them to the ground, 'All right, keep my hats then!' because 'Monkey see, Monkey do, Monkey do like we do too!'

Faster than a tide of land crabs rushing to the sea, Raoul picked them all up and resettled them on his head. By the time he reached the market it was late, and the midday sun was burning down. How the people needed those hats! Within minutes he had sold them all. His return journey was so much faster, his only burden jingling in his pockets and dragging at his trousers. When he reached home, his mother asked him how his day had been.

'Not so bad thank you Mother,' came the modest reply, and there was all the money to prove it.

'I see I have another hat to make, one that may reach the market but will never be sold,' said the woman to her son, who had all of a sudden become quite a little man, as quickly as a snake sheds its skin.

THE DEVIL'S DULCIMER

It was unusual for a young girl to be living alone, but Annie was tough and Annie was independent. She couldn't remember what life was like when her parents had been alive, and the aunt that had taken her in had also died of the plague fever when it had returned to the valley some years later. If she had any brothers or sisters, she hadn't heard of them, and so from a young age she had learned to live from her own resources.

Given how poor and how proud she was, it was a marvel that she managed to survive, but she had one great talent that always saw her through: she was a superb musician – the best in the district, the county and the entire state. Annie made a scratchy living by playing her dulcimer at parties, weddings and wakes. If these were few and far between, she would be tossed some coins when she played outside the saloons. Music was her passion and her only love. She never felt lonely, and she had never needed friends.

Great was her excitement when she heard that the state music competition was to be held in her town that year. How she had longed to compete, but could never afford the travel as it moved each year from place to place. Now she would be able to enter, but there was still a difficulty. Her old and only dulcimer was long past its best. Constant use had worn it down beyond repair. Annie needed a better one, and she couldn't afford it.

She knew that with a better instrument she stood to win every category of the competition she entered. She had no friends, so there was no one to ask for help. But there was, perhaps, just one person she could go to.

Desperation drove Annie to the wise woman who lived at the edge of town. Everyone was wary of her. Many wanted her advice but at the same time they resented and feared her special powers. Annie's hard life had taught her that you get nothing for nothing, so she was not surprised to be asked, 'Tell me my child, what would you give for the sweetest-sounding dulcimer?'

'Oh, please Ma'am I'd give anything!'

'Have a care my dear, those who would give anything, can end up giving everything.'

The wise woman then told her that she would have to leave town that night when the full moon was at its zenith. She would have to cross the graveyard and follow the road beyond it. Then she would see what she would see. Annie didn't want to walk alone at night under the full moon, and she certainly didn't want to walk the road that stretched beyond the graveyard into the mountains. Nobody walked that road, day or night, because it led to the deserted village where everyone had died of the plague fever. But she wanted the dulcimer.

The gate into the graveyard creaked, 'Go back! Go back!' The gate out of the graveyard creaked, 'Too late! Too late!' The clip-clop of her footsteps on the milk white, deserted road sounded, 'Go on! Go on!' And there was the village, looking as though it was full of life. The gardens were tended and full of flowers, the smallholdings were thriving, the houses were in good repair with lights in the windows. Amazed, she walked down the village street, and was just about to pass the last house when the door opened and a figure beckoned her in.

Annie stood on the threshold. The man was now inside the living room by a blazing fire. He was the handsomest man she had ever seen, but even handsomer was the dulcimer set on a table, with the firelight playing over its rich varnish and stroking flashes of light from its strings. She hesitated no longer and went in.

The stranger told her that if she wanted the dulcimer, she would have to give him a kiss. Well, that wouldn't be so difficult, seeing that he was so handsome, and it was quickly done. For all the blazing fire, his lips were the coldest thing she had ever touched. Her hand strayed to the dulcimer, but he caught her wrist and his grasp was like a bracelet of ice. He said that if she wanted it, she would have to give him her red petticoat. How did he know what colour it was? Well, there was nobody else to see, so nobody to tell and nobody else to know. She slipped out of her petticoat and handed it to him. Without even looking at it he threw it behind him into the fire. Now she was allowed to touch the instrument and the sweetest sound she had ever heard swelled through the room. Even the fire stopped crackling, its flames turning towards it to listen.

Then her blood ran as cold as his touch when she heard him say that if she wanted that dulcimer, she would have to give him the head of the one she loved the best. At first her mouth was too dry to reply, but that gave her a moment to think – and it came to her in a flash that she could outwit him. She was an orphan with no relatives and no friends. There was nobody that she loved at all! The bargain was struck and she took the dulcimer. She hastened through the village, but, at the last house, she could not resist looking back. There were no lights in any of the windows. A few broken doors swung, creaking on rusty hinges. The gardens were overgrown and weeds straggled up between the broken slabs of the road. By now it was dawn and already the sound of carts and buggies could be heard as people poured into town for the music competition.

Annie played in the dance music category, and her playing was so lively that people danced through their shoe leather, danced through their stockings and begged her to stop before they danced through the skin on their feet. She won that one. Then she played in the slow section and her music was so sad that neighbours who had been feuding for years wept in each other's arms and even the hogs in their sties wallowed in their own tears. She won that one. Then she played in the lullaby competition and people crumpled to the ground where they stood and snored. Even the daisies closed up their petals as though it were night-time. She won that one too. The competition was over, and Annie had won every event. She would have enough money to last her the year, and without needing to look for work, she would have plenty of time to practise. No time like the present, Annie returned to her little shack to play some more.

The next day she was due to play for the dancing at a wedding, but she didn't appear. This was most unusual; Annie never missed a chance to play. After waiting for some time, the best man went to her shack to remind her about her commitment. The curtains were still closed. He knocked on the door but there was no answer. However, he could hear the squeaking of a rocking chair so there had to be someone in there. Growing anxious, he fetched some of the wedding party and together they broke down the door. There was Annie rocking in time to music that only she could hear. Her fingertips had been worn away from playing all day and all night, and on her shoulders there was no head.

THE OLD COUPLE AND THE VOLCANO

CHILE

An old couple lived on the slope of a volcano. Every night the ground beneath their little house rumbled and shook, and their walls shook too. Sometimes their possessions would fall and break. Everything would be covered with black grit or thick dust, which penetrated their clothes, coated their food and even got in between their teeth and into their eyes. After years of this, they finally decided that enough was enough and decided to take action. But what to do? They had no idea and did what I hope you will do too if you need help – they went to consult the sorceress in the nearest village, which was, as you can imagine, some distance away.

She asked them if they had ever tried being nice to the volcano and the couple replied that they had not. They hurried home to remedy this. The next day they toiled up the burning slopes to the crater's rim. There they threw flowers into the furious red mouth, recited praise poems and sang songs composed in its honour. That night the volcano behaved exactly as it always had, albeit slightly more violently. The disappointed couple returned to the sorceress, who did not look surprised to see them.

'I never said that this was going to be easy. As that didn't work, maybe you should tell the volcano how angry you are with it.'

Somehow, they didn't think this would be so difficult. They were hastening up those baking slopes before dawn. When they could go no further, they shouted their rage, shook their fists, screamed curses and even spat into that huge red mouth. That night, if anything, the volcano behaved even worse. The elders wasted no time in returning to the sorceress.

'I feared it would come to this,' she said with a sigh, 'We will have to do the very thing I was trying to avoid because it is so dangerous. I will have to teach you a magical dance, which, if you get it right, will move the volcano. However, if you get one step wrong, or get tired and finish too early, great harm will befall you. Oh, and you have to do it wearing a blindfold, and don't let me forget to tell you that the whole thing must be done backwards.'

Deciding that they had nothing to lose, the old couple spent the rest of the day learning the dance. Exhausted, they returned home, sleeping soundly that night despite what the volcano got up to. In the morning, they packed what they could carry on their backs in case the volcano decided to destroy their possessions in revenge at being tamed by a dance. Then blindfolded and bent double with their packs, they started the dance as soon as they stepped outside. Down those slopes they danced, never missing a step, always moving backwards …

At last, the valiant pair had to stop. When they removed their blindfolds, they rubbed their eyes in astonishment. There on the distant horizon was the volcano, still spitting fire. But the magical dance had worked, they had moved the volcano! True to its inconsiderate nature, however, it had taken their house with them, so they needed to build another. This didn't take long, as, to their surprise there were all kinds of building materials lying around, such as logs and branches that they had never noticed before.

Soon others noticed the new arrivals and were told the tale of how the old couple had moved the volcano. From time to time, they would repeat the magical dance, which their new neighbours were eager to learn. News spread and others came to live there too, because everyone likes to be near those who have the power. If you go to that place in Chile today, you can still see the villagers dancing their traditional backwards dance.

THE OLD WOMAN AND THE SOUP

WHITE RIVER SIOUX, NORTH AMERICA

When we talk about time, we describe it as grandparents of grandparents, the connection is strong, it is in the weaving and in the landscape all around us. The old knowledge is better – the textiles are stronger, the colours don't fade, just as we hope the memory of our ancestors doesn't fade either.

Nilda Callañaupa Alvarez,
Founder of the Cusco Centre for Traditional Textiles

We know that somewhere there is a well-hidden cave, maybe people have forgotten how to find it now. It is where the prairie meets the dry and rocky places. But some say that it is deep in the darkest woods. If you near it you will know because of the smell of soup. The people who live on the prairie say it is berry soup and those who live in the forests say it is meat soup, but your nose will tell you. Follow it and you will see the tunnel that opens out into the cave. You will need to stoop as you go down and soon you will see the flicker of firelight licking the walls. The tunnel opens into a cavern with a fire burning. On the fire is a clay pot in which the soup is bubbling. By the light of the fire is an old, old woman, so bent over with age that she does not need to stoop when she uses the tunnel. Her eyes are pale with age like the ice in midwinter, and her skin is wrinkled and cracked like the canyons. Lying beneath her feet is an old dog with not much fur and only two teeth left in his head. He groans with pleasure when she changes the position of her feet, otherwise he sleeps and snores.

By the light of the fire, Old Woman is making something with porcupine quill beads. Her twisted fingers search in the bark basket where the beads of every imaginable colour are waiting for her touch. When she pulls out the right colours, she stitches them onto a hide. If you could look over her shoulder you would be able to see that it is a picture of the whole world. As the firelight and the shadows play across it you would see all that has already happened, all that is happening now, and all that is yet to happen. When Old Woman finishes the picture, the world will come to an end.

From time to time her nose twitches because she can smell that the soup is sticking to the side of the pot and is about to burn. Grumbling, she heaves up her old bones to stagger over and give the soup a stir. When the old dog feels her getting up, he lumbers up too and when her back is turned, he unpicks some of the beadwork with his two teeth. That is why the world has never ended. Perhaps you sometimes forget things for no reason. You go to get something important and suddenly you can't remember what you went to fetch. A child puts up his hand because he has the right answer in class, desperate for the teacher to choose him and when she does, he can't remember what he was going to say. All those things are because Old Woman's dog has just unpicked that part of the picture. We must be patient with ourselves when it happens because those moments help to stop the world from ending.

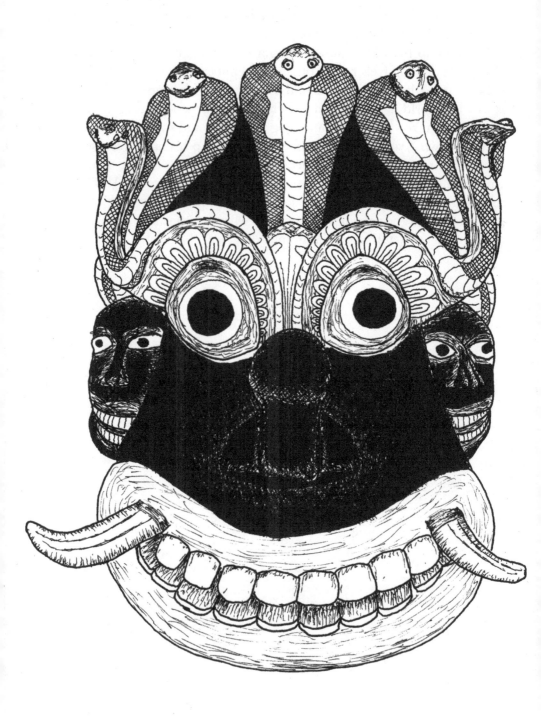

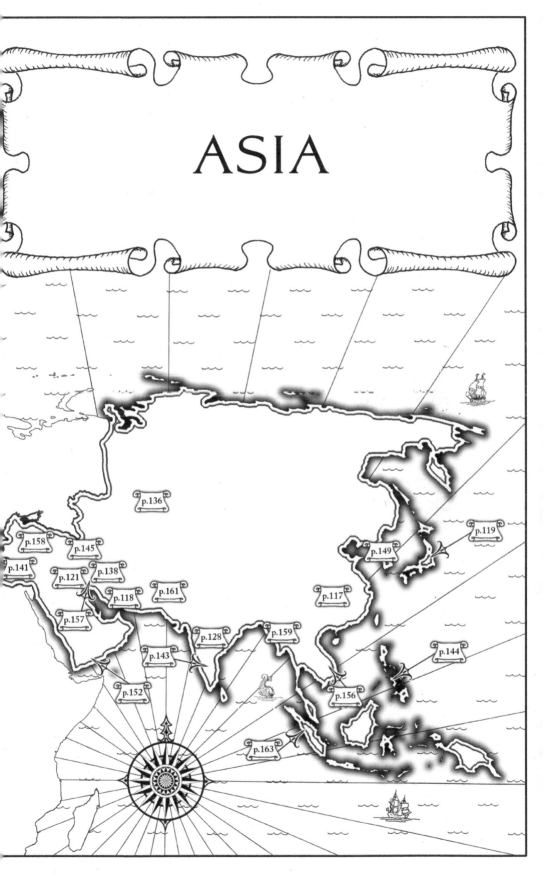

ASIA

p.136

p.158
p.145
p.141
p.121
p.138
p.157
p.118
p.161
p.143
p.152
p.128
p.159
p.163

p.149
p.119
p.117
p.144
p.156

'Words are the voice of the heart.'

Confucius, Chinese writer, teacher and philosopher.

HOW THE WORLD WAS MADE

In the very beginning all that existed was a huge egg-shaped stone. Inside it slept a being, growing slowly larger with each aeon. This giant, Pan Gyu, grew so large that his body started to press against the sides of his prison and it was this chafing that woke him. All was dark and silent. His mighty hands groped about and found a lump of stone that had broken off the wall. Pan Gyu sharpened it on his teeth and made an axe. With his great strength he managed to swing it despite his cramped position. The egg shape split into two and the larger piece, being heavier, sank, while the smaller and lighter piece floated upwards.

Pan Gyu did not want to be imprisoned again so he stood upright for the first time and kept these pieces apart with his arms upraised. One became the vault of heaven and the other became the Earth. Further and further they floated apart until the giant knew that they would not touch each other again. By now very tired, Pan Gyu laid himself upon the Earth for his final sleep.

As he died, one eye leaped into the sky and became the moon and the other became the sun. They shone their light on what became of his body as his blood poured from the empty craters left by his eyes. His skull became the caves and his blood became the rivers and the oceans. Hair became the first forests and plants. Flesh became soil and bones became mountains and rocky places. Those teeth that had sharpened the axe were now the Himalayas, the highest mountains of all. The world had been born.

THE FIRST SACRIFICE

IRAN (ZOROASTRIAN, ANCIENT PERSIA)

Reproduced here with kind permission of The History Press, from Myths of Gods and Goddesses in Britain and Ireland *by Sharon Jacksties*

Before Time was new, there was on Earth a perfect being, one of righteousness and love. Sun God sent him an instruction through his messenger, the raven. When Mithra heard this message, he was appalled because it was telling him to kill the most beautiful creature on Earth. Mithra struggled with himself; he was not able to bring himself to do what he must do, which was to follow Sun God's command. How could the source of all goodness and life itself be telling him to kill White Bull? Why kill a creature of power and beauty, one whose immense strength was never measured against the weak, White Bull, who would nuzzle from Mithra's hand, who loved and trusted him?

Mithra could not pretend that he hadn't heard that command, nor that he hadn't understood or remembered it. As his knife sliced into the bull's neck, he turned away from the sight of his blood. But even through his closed eyelids he could see a great light that forced him to look around to see what it could be. Now there was no blood or body of the animal to be seen. White Bull had become the moon and was rising into the sky. A wind came and tore away Mithra's cloak, which rose up and beyond the moon, becoming the firmament in which planets shone and stars twinkled. Then to each heavenly body came their own dance. At different speeds they wheeled and criss-crossed the sky, encountering partners at times, disappearing over the horizon edge of Mithra's cloak, but always to return sooner or later, because Time too had been born and all now danced to Time's measure.

Only White Bull's tail and genitals had remained on the ground. From his tail corn and grapes sprouted and spread across the Earth. Sacred seed seeped from his genitals and Mithra collected this in a bowl. From then on, all the animals were shaped with a mixture in which this seed had been blended. Sun God was so pleased that he alighted on Earth in his chariot. There he feasted for the first time with his beloved son Mithra, on meat after the first killing of an animal, and on wine and bread after White Bull's gifts. Together they rode over the ocean, across the sky and onward to the furthest reaches of creation.

But the light of the moon, rising from the ground, had awoken creatures of darkness, who now crept out of the soil to steal the gifts that White Bull had left. Snake was seeking to lick any spilt blood and scorpion to seize the sacred seed. Then began the conflict between light and dark, good and bad. From that time to this time all people have had that conflict mirrored in their lives, teetering between or choosing to take action towards good or evil.

FROM THE DARK COMES LIGHT

JAPAN

The union of two deities had resulted in the conception of another, and this was the god of fire. However, he burned his mother so severely as he passed through her birth canal that she died and disappeared into the Underworld. Her consort, Izanagi, followed her there into the darkness, hoping to entice her to return. She warned him not to try to look at her, but Izanagi disobeyed and lit a torch to see his beloved. In so doing, she was startled by the very element that had so wounded her, and Izanagi saw, not the beauty he had so loved, but the hideousness of a decaying corpse. Furious that she had been disobeyed, his wife sent demons to chase him from the Underworld, from which Izanagi barely escaped. To prevent further pursuit, he rolled a boulder in front of the entrance, and his wife remained in her new realm, as goddess of the dead.

From death comes new life. After ritually purifying himself in the great river, Izanagi wiped his left eye and found that his hand held a being of such dazzling beauty that he placed her in the sky as the sun, where Amaterasu gave gladness and growth to all the Earth. On wiping his right eye, he found he was holding another bright being, this time with a gentler, calming light. He placed Tsukuyomi in the sky near his sister so that he could be the moon, bringing both dreams and time to the people on Earth. Then he noticed that, due to his immersion, his nose was running. In wiping away the snot, there was another being between his fingers. This was Susano-o, so different from his sister and brother, restless, turbulent, uncontrollable. Susano-o rushed off across the sky to become the storm wind that whipped up the ocean into an angry frenzy. However, this disturbance was not enough for him and wherever he went he stirred up trouble and discord until his travels over the Earth and through the heavens became one long journey of destruction.

Meanwhile, Amaterasu, beloved by all creatures, had taught people the art of agriculture and cloth making. In one of her temples, she was teaching weaving to her acolytes and lesser deities, when due to a previous unresolved dispute, Susano-o hurled a horrifying object that came crashing through the temple roof. This was a sacred heavenly horse that had been flayed alive, and this act of sacrilege caused a goddess, some say it was Amaterasu herself, to be wounded between her legs with her loom shuttle. If this dreadful act was not enough, Susano-o then defecated on his sister's throne. It was not in Amaterasu's nature to retaliate and even at this outrage she was too wise to allow herself to be provoked into doing so. Instead, she retreated down a tunnel into a cave, sealing the entrance behind her with a boulder.

How the people mourned her departure. Their world was now dark and cold and all joy had seeped from their lives. At last, the other deities intervened and pleaded with Amaterasu to reappear. When she didn't, they tried to entice her by placing a decorated tree outside her entrance. On its trunk hung the first mirror ever seen. Still there was no sign of the sun goddess. The others started to play music, to dance and to sing, and deep in her cave, Amaterasu heard their distant joyful sounds. She began to feel the way we can when others are having a party to which we have not been invited. Then Uzume, goddess of laughter and entertainment, started dancing on the upturned tub that had been used to dye Amaterasu's weaving silks. This humble tub gave rise to another art, that of taiko, Japanese drumming; it was the first drum ever heard. By now they were all dancing with lighted flares, and the caged cockerels they had brought with them started to crow as their light was magnified by the mirror.

Hearing this deep in her cave, Amaterasu wondered at their sound. How could cockerels be crowing as she had been the only one to make that happen? Overcome by curiosity, she rolled the boulder away, far enough to look out and ask what the party was about. She was told that they were celebrating the finding of another sun goddess as an equal substitute to herself. At that Amaterasu emerged to see this impossible rival, and there she was. The two radiant goddesses stared at each other – one not understanding that the other was a reflection of her own beauty. Closer and closer stepped Amaterasu to this shining vision, brighter and brighter it grew as the mirror reflected even more of her brilliance. By now she was so close that the entrance to her cave was unprotected. The god of strength seized her while another tied a rope of straw across the entrance. It was Amaterasu herself who had taught how to weave straw with a pattern that showed a holy place lay behind it, indicating that nobody could transgress by passing the rope. What she had taught others, she too had to abide by, and now she couldn't go back to the darkness.

Her return to the sky was gently welcomed by her serene silvery brother and she ignored any further troubles that her stormy brother created. All the earthly beings rejoiced that light and warmth had returned at last, as we still do to this day.

GILGAMESH, DEMI-GOD, TYRANT, HERO, MORTAL

IRAQ (ANCIENT MESOPOTAMIA/SUMERIA)

Many scholars agree that The Epic of Gilgamesh *is the oldest written story in the world. Written in poetic form, it is located in Uruk, one of the world's most ancient cities, so old that it has had many names in many languages. First translated into English in the nineteenth century from neglected cuneiform tablets in the British Museum, there is as yet no complete written record of this huge poetic work, nor is there likely to be, given the centuries-old ravages of war. I remember taking an Iraqi family to hear an oral storytelling performance of Gilgamesh in England, as they too were survivors of the latest wave of destruction in their country. Steeped in knowledge and pride in their ancient culture, even they marvelled to hear episodes they had not heard before. Apart from their formal education familiarising them with this work, they grew up listening to Gilgamesh's stories from their own oral tradition, which had thrived from earliest times. Who knows what episodes have been preserved in this way and which have not been found in written form? We know that most traditional narratives were written long after they were first told, and that particularly in the case of epic heroes, episodes have been added to them over time, so it is impossible to know how old the story of Gilgamesh is. Some claim it to be over 10,000 years old, which is credible given that its written form can be dated to 7000 BCE. Its story of a great flood is both confirmed as a physical event and contemporaneously consistent with geological records. Its narrative ripples have spread through the ocean of time to find their way at last into the Old Testament. Composed in an era when cities were developing in Asia Minor, much of the text celebrates the 'subduing' of Nature. So many thousands of years later, some episodes may be heard or read with rather different thoughts in these ecologically sensitive times. It is perhaps these that have informed my choice in this brief and partial retelling, which I hope will entice readers to inform themselves further.*

The river rises, flows over its banks
and carries us all away, like mayflies
floating downstream: they stare at the sun,
then all at once there is nothing.
Translated from The Epic of Gilgamesh by Stephen Mitchell

Mighty ruler of Uruk, greatest of cities, the man-giant, demi-god, Gilgamesh, strode through his palace and, at each step, walls and people trembled. Who could match him in war, in hunting, in games, in his conquest of women whether they were willing or not? Because none could challenge him, he took to increasing the numbers of his feats, having long given up the search for harder ones. More animals were massacred in the hunting, more young men were wounded in the wrestling bouts, broken beyond their destinies' calling as warriors and heroes, more young women were seduced or violated, and still he could not be satisfied.

At last, his people prayed to the gods to release them from Gilgamesh's tyranny. The clamour of their complaint reached the heavens, borne upon the smoke of incense and the sacrificial fires, lit from fragrant cedar wood. Anu, Sky God, mightiest among the many divinities, heard their prayers, and summoned a council. Among those gods and goddesses was Gilgamesh's mother. Reputed to have a temper like a raging bull, her vengeance was faster than the strike of a serpent. When she spoke, all listened.

Keen to protect her son, she quickly proposed a solution. This was to create another being, one who also surpassed mortal strength, who could become Gilgamesh's companion and temper his excesses. To flatter the mightiest of the gods, he would resemble Great Anu himself.

Divine hands reached down into the mud that flanked the vast Euphrates river. Divine palms shaped a being from that clay, almost as tall as her own son. Divine fingers sculpted each shape, each feature of that magnificent body. Divine breath gave it life. So vigorous was this new being, Enkidu, that he sprang away from his goddess creator before she could place him in Uruk. Before she could even clothe him, Enkidu had run naked into the wild. There he thrived with the animals and the elements as his companions. Birdsong, the roars of beasts, running water and racing wind were his only language.

In time, rumours reached the villages and eventually the city of a strange creature seen by hunters. Too huge and beautiful to be a man, but surely not a god to be sometimes running on all fours like a beast – and why would one such as this be found among the gazelles as though he were part of their herd? How could they know that Enkidu ran with the fastest, climbed with ibex, the most agile, and wrestled with lions, the strongest. The wild beasts were his only family and he protected them as best he could, dismembering traps with his skilful touch, or freeing animals from pits and snares. He was spoiling the hunters' livelihood and something would have to be done about it. However, with the speed and strength of the beasts and the cunning of a human, it was impossible to catch him.

But there exists a snare that can entrap most men. Waiting for him by the waterhole where he and the gazelles drank was a creature the like of which Enkidu had never seen. The gazelles fled, leaving him to stare at the loveliest of beings whose delicious scent made his eyes brim and his limbs weaken. There, on a rock, sat Shamhat, priestess of Ishtar, goddess of love and fertility. To behold Shamhat's beauty was to see the goddess herself through a veil. To touch Shamhat was to shiver as though the goddess's sighs of desire raised the hairs on her lover's skin. Shamhat had come from her temple to teach this wild man what no animal could. The priestess's sacred act of love, freely given to those on whom she chose to bestow this blessing, would be his taming. There she sat, her robe raised to her thighs, her legs apart, and their lovemaking lasted for seven nights.

When Enkidu tired before she did, she returned to her temple and left him asleep, to be found by shepherds. Weakened and hungry, he allowed them to lead him to their camp. It was there that he ate bread for the first time and drank great quantities of beer. He had made love to a woman, eaten cultivated food and drink, and when he tried to return to his wild companions, they fled from him just as they had from her. It was then that he cursed Shamhat for causing him to lose everything he had known. It is not wise to curse the priestess of a goddess, Ishtar's dearest handmaiden. That and another offence would cost him dearly. Now more man than wild man, his place would be with people, and they were to be found in the city. Enkidu made his way to Uruk.

He followed the thronging people to a great house. There the crowd clustered and made ugly sounds with their mouths. The wedding party had turned to an angry mob as Gilgamesh, their king, having not long since defeated the bridegroom in a wrestling bout, was now going to satisfy his lust with the bride on their wedding night. The groom, who had tried to defend her, lay against the wall where Gilgamesh had thrown him. No one else dared to take on this man, who was at that moment more monster than king. Suddenly the crowd fell silent and Gilgamesh turned to see why.

There, crouched beneath the lintel, was a man too tall to stand upright. For the first time Gilgamesh did not have to bend to look into someone's eyes. Enkidu strode across the courtyard and barred the way to the bridal chamber. Bereft of his animal companions, here was something else he could protect. The crowd swayed with tension. Gilgamesh lunged, grappled and was thrown down. People scuttled out of the way like insects as those two mighty beings fought. Neither could win and neither could lose. Then Gilgamesh threw himself on his back, limbs splayed, defenceless, and began to laugh. He laughed until the walls shook, he drummed his fists on the floor with joy – at last he had found an equal! Now his arms were around Enkidu not to squeeze the life out of him, but in a tender embrace. He kissed his cheeks, buried his face in the unkempt hair, wept away his loneliness, for now he had a brother, a beloved, a friend. From that moment Gilgamesh and Enkidu were inseparable.

What great deeds could they not accomplish together? To the west lay vast cedar forests. This precious, sacred wood was used for ritual fires, its scented oils for anointing the bodies of the priestesses dedicated to the worship of Ishtar and all her rites. But what if they could obtain it in huge quantities, adding wood to their building materials of mud bricks, increasing Uruk's size and splendour and its fame throughout the world? The companions set off on this quest, undaunted by the certainty that they would bring down the wrath of the gods for whom this forest was a sacred place.

These immense cedar forests were under the special protection of Enlil, God of the Winds and Storms. Only he had the right to bring down trees with those elements at his command. To make sure that no one else attempted it, he had appointed the monstrous Humbaba to be its guardian. This creature was himself guarded with seven layers of magical protection. Some say that it was Enkidu's cunning that suggested a way of tricking Humbaba into exchanging these protective layers for luxuries that could only be found in the cities – luxuries that included two of Gilgamesh's sisters. Without these, Humbaba was easily slain. Others say that it was a weapon of power loaned by yet another deity that ensured Humbaba's death in a physical fight. Despite his scaly body and fiery breath, he was overpowered by the heroic efforts of two against one. It was then that Gilgamesh and Enkidu destroyed the sacred cedarwood forest, while Enlil looked on with rage.

It was Enlil who, not so long ago, had been the first of the gods wanting to destroy the human race. He, along with others, had objected to all the noise that people were making. Having become so numerous, the humans' cacophony had been disturbing the gods' rest, and it was decided to wipe them out. Several attempts had failed, and the last was to send a great flood that would drown everybody. How Enlil wished that the flood had succeeded as he saw the destruction that these two had wrought. Was there nothing that humans would not now attempt in defiance of the gods that had created them? As he ground his teeth, he remembered how the great flood's purpose had been subverted by a single mortal helped by a single deity.

While some of the gods and goddesses were bewailing the fate of the sacred cedars, Ishtar looked down from the heavens with a lustful gaze at this superman Gilgamesh. How mighty he was, what courage, what strength! How she longed to celebrate her lustful attraction by entwining her body with his! She presented herself in all her beauty, expecting him to kneel adoringly before her, never for one moment thinking he could refuse. However, the same defiance that had helped to slay Humbaba now said 'No' to the goddess of love herself. Gilgamesh knew how Ishtar treated her lovers, how her lust sucked them dry and how soon she tired of them, leaving them where they lay like discarded husks. He had heard the story that she had turned her father's gardener into a mole for not responding to her advances. And what need did he have of that kind of dalliance now that he had discovered true love and loyalty in his friend Enkidu? In shock and fury at being spurned, Ishtar turned her gaze on her rival.

Her eyes narrowed as she remembered his cursing of Shamhat, that insult to her devoted priestess.

She stormed back to the heavens, where she asked her father, Anu, father also of all the gods and goddesses, to lend her the Bull of Heaven, which she would unleash on Gilgamesh and Enkidu. At first Anu did not want to do so because he knew that the Bull of Heaven would trample down the cities, drink the rivers dry and eat all the crops. Ishtar knew that it would cause so much destruction that Gilgamesh and Enkidu would need to subdue it and that they would be destroyed in the struggle. Her father gave in to her request when she threatened to break open the gates of the Underworld, releasing the dead so that they would rise up and devour the living. Knowing that the dead outnumbered the living, Anu agreed.

The Bull of Heaven was released onto the Earth, where it behaved as destructively as anticipated. When it had been provoked into attacking Gilgamesh, Enkidu threw himself at his tail. As he pulled it like a rope in a tug of war, the beast spun round and round trying to dislodge his assailant. Enkidu, his head spinning, held fast until the monster began to tire. He was slowing down just enough for Gilgamesh to cut his throat with one slash of his sword. The Bull of Heaven, symbol of the power of the gods and goddesses, was being butchered in the city of Uruk. There stood Ishtar on the town wall cursing Gilgamesh, whereupon Enkidu seized one of the beast's legs and hurled it at her. Her robe streaked with blood, Ishtar rushed back to heaven demanding revenge once more, and this time, she was not alone.

Another divine council, another decision: to take the life of Enkidu or Gilgamesh or both? Eventually it was decided that Enkidu must die. Perhaps they thought that for Gilgamesh life without Enkidu would be an even worse punishment than death.

Beloved Enkidu sickened and was dead by the twelfth day. Cradling his corpse in his arms, Gilgamesh howled like a wild beast and wept like a man. He would not allow his servants to take away the body to prepare it for the funeral rites. By the fifth day he refused to acknowledge the smell of corrupting flesh that came from that beloved body. It was only on the seventh day, when he saw a worm crawl from a nostril, that he surrendered Enkidu's corpse. It seemed to Gilgamesh that he had lost everything dear to him and that there was only one last thing to conquer, and that was death itself. It was then that he remembered the story of the only people who had defied death; surely he could persuade them to share their secret with him?

There were only two people still alive from the family that had survived the great deluge. At first there was fury from Elil that there had been any survivors at all from that noisy, intrusive race. Fury because one of the gods had told his devotee, Utnapishtim, how and when to build a boat for his family and all the animals and plants that would be needed after the deluge. When this god was challenged about having defied the council, the reply came that he had only been speaking of the imminent destruction to his house: 'Oh! Reed Walls, if you had the ears to hear. Oh! Reed Fence if you only had the ears to listen...' How was he to know that his acolyte could hear him on the other side of the wall? How could he be blamed if those words had found their way into Utnapishtim's dream, and he had acted accordingly? He hadn't broken his oath not to warn anybody. Enlil was enraged at this trick, but his voice had been drowned out in the clamour, far surpassing that of the human race, that now came from the gods and goddesses who were regretting their decision to wipe out human existence. Was it pity, compassion, or the need to be worshipped? Most of the deities were by this time glad that humans had survived and Utnapishtim and his wife were rewarded with eternal life. Now semi-divine, they lived together in the Other World. If anybody had the secret of eternal life it would be this couple.

Many were the hero's adventures to find Utnapishtim, and too numerous his encounters with beings from the Other World to write of here. Fuelled by his customary defiance and empowered by the grief that still burned within him, he was not to be dissuaded by obstacle or counsel. He was taken in by the old couple at last, and Utnapishtim's wife took pity on him. She persuaded her husband to compromise, by showing Gilgamesh a magical plant that would restore him to his youthful self. It grew deep down on the ocean bed, and, in the last of his superhuman feats, Gilgamesh tied weights to his body so that he could reach it. Now he had his antidote to death quite literally in his grasp. If he grew the plant in his own land, he could continue to eat it whenever signs of ageing appeared and, in that way, gain immortality. Perhaps he could cultivate it to share it with his people so they would not have to suffer the indignities of old age.

On his return journey, he set the plant carefully on a rock while he washed off the grime from his travels. A passing serpent scented something new, and the strange smell came from that object on the rock. Was it edible? In one gulp it was gone. Instantly, the snake shed its skin. Serpents have been shedding their skin from that day to this. When Gilgamesh turned to retrieve his magic plant, all he found was a scaly scrap of withered skin. He had held the promise of eternal life between his fingers, and now it had vanished. Only then could he accept that eternal life was not for him, nor for any others of his kind that came thereafter.

This story was first written on tablets of clay, about a city built of clay, about a beauteous man who was made of clay and an idolised hero who had feet of clay. One day, we too will all return to clay.

'Gilgamesh, where do you wander? The Eternal Life that you seek, you shall not find. When the gods created people, they set aside Death for humanity, keeping Life in their own hands.'

THE TALE OF DRAUPADI IN *THE MAHABHARATA*

INDIA

The Mahabharata *is the world's longest written epic poem, comprising approximately 100,000 verses. Composed in the fourth century BCE, its narrative centres on the intertwined fates of two sets of cousins who become embroiled in a great war. A jewel in the crown of world literature, it has never ceased to be studied throughout the centuries. Among the most splendid examples of how mythology entwines the lives of mortals and deities, this work also includes aspects of the protagonists' lives from previous incarnations – re-incarnation being a fundamental belief in Hinduism, the religion that this epic celebrates. Deeds from former lives influence the twists and turns in the plot during the listeners' or readers' immersion in the unfolding narrative. Written and told in a slower age, without the distractions of screen-dominated technologies, its telling would take several days or nights. One form of traditional performance took place with a khavad, a storytelling cabinet on which would be depicted images from the major episodes of the story. During the telling, which was often chanted or sung, the cabinet would be opened to reveal more images according to the relevant part of the narrative. Khavads were placed on a cart and taken from village to village. In this way the epic was able to reach the remotest parts of India. Translated into countless languages,* The Mahabharata *has been written, recited, told, painted, danced in Indian classical and Western contemporary styles, turned into world-touring theatre pieces, and made into films and animations.*

Being lucky enough to have Indian adoptive family, I have been indulged by their kindness and humour at my attempts to retell episodes from this sacred work. My journey with this immense story, made up of so many tangled tales, continues to present ever increasing complexities. Many scholars and ordinary listeners believe that the Princess Draupadi's story is the fulcrum on which the epic balances and inexorably turns.

Drupada had inherited a throne and was now a king. How fortunate he was, how powerful, how proud of his great status. However, although he was in the best position to be generous, he dishonoured his position by refusing help when it could most easily have been given. Moreover, he refused this help to a boyhood friend, with whom he had grown up and been trained. Drona was the son of a wise man, a sage who taught Drupada alongside his own son. Drupada made the childish promise that if he ever became king, he would share half his kingdom with Drona. A childish promise is one thing, a king's decision is another. Drona had led an abstemious life, continuing to train in martial arts and the ways of wisdom. This poverty led to his son being taunted by bullies when he couldn't afford to buy milk, and Drona had come to his old friend to ask for financial help for old time's sake. The king arrogantly refused him, disdainfully telling him that now that he was a king, Drona had no right to think of him as a friend as their situation in life was so unequal. Leaving Drupada's palace in a cold fury, the spurned friend was already plotting his revenge.

In time Drona succeeded in acquiring a position as the greatest teacher of martial arts ever known. The best in the land could count themselves lucky if they were trained by him. Princes and nobles from far and wide came to his school. Among his students were two sets of cousins, the Kauravas and the Pandavas. The most gifted of all of these was one of the Pandava brothers, Arjuna. His feats as an archer exceeded any imaginable accomplishment, his arrows finding their mark even in the dark. Perhaps this is where the seeds of rivalry were sown, as the cousins tried to outdo each other, brother supporting brother.

Eventually, when the young warriors' training was complete, Drona was able to ask for his fee. It was agreed that it would be paid by all these young men being in service to him. In this way was Drona, who had once been too poor to buy his son milk, now able to gather an army. Drona was at last able to be in a position to make war on Drupada, but was at first unable to win. Another attempt was made, this time with Arjuna and his brothers, who succeeded where an entire army had failed. Drupada was brought back as a prisoner. His kingdom was then divided according to his child-hood promise – a high price to pay for a boy's drink of milk and an insult to one who should have been treated as a friend. An old score had been settled and Drona declared that he harboured no more enmity towards the king. That may have been true on his part, but whether from fear or from a thirst for revenge, Drupada was not prepared to leave things as they were. He determined to ensure that Drona could be beaten in battle and requested certain holy men to intercede with the gods on his behalf, so that he could have a son who could either take back the kingdom he had lost or defend what he still held. At first the sages refused – perhaps they foresaw that this would lead to even greater strife. However, they were persuaded at last, and the king immersed himself in holy rituals and practices to ready himself for their successful intervention.

During a ceremony over the sacred fire, a figure appeared from out of the flames. This was the son that the king had prayed for. Not only was his prayer fulfilled, but another figure appeared, a daughter, Draupadi. She was dusky skinned, beautiful as the black lotus. Starlight trembled in the deep-est night of her dark eyes. She was known as Draupadi, meaning daughter of Drupada, but her given name was Krishnaa, meaning the dark-skinned one. No one could have known, unless it was the holy men whose fire brought her into being, what power that name would invoke, now that she shared the name of the dusky blue-skinned god Lord Krishna. Moreover, the sages predicted that this girl would bring about the deaths of many great warriors.

Draupadi's reputation for beauty and righteousness spread far and wide. When the time came for her to marry, her father arranged for the cer-emony, during which the bride-to-be chooses from among the invited suitors. There were many hopefuls – kings, princes and one suitor that Draupadi rejected immediately as he wasn't of noble birth. Perhaps her decision was based on what was considered proper for those times, but Karna took it as an insult that would not be forgotten. He had been born out of wedlock, and although his father had been the sun god Suriya, and his conception had been immaculate, his mother had not wanted to keep this unexpected child. She had placed him in a box and cast him into the river. The box had come ashore and the baby had been rescued and adopted by a charioteer's family. It was this that had determined his caste as being inferior to that of warriors and princes. Nevertheless, through his own efforts, he rose beyond this strangest of beginnings, becoming one of the greatest of warriors. Beloved foster son to the Kaurava court and foster brother to the Kauravas of his generation, he swore undying love and loyalty to the eldest of the brothers.

Meanwhile, King Drupada had devised a contest for the suitors to show off their prowess. A mechanical device had been installed above a pool of water. From a pole whirled the shape of a fish. Round and round it went, its reflection caught in the water below. The test was to take the bow and arrow that had been placed by the pool and shoot the fish, not by looking at it directly, but only by looking at its reflection.

At first there was a throng of suitors eager to try the challenge. Now they had seen that her beauty far exceeded even her reputation, who among them was not desperate to win the hand of Draupadi? Moreover, there hung about her an alluring air of mystery and power. When she walked in the palace gardens, birds would fall silent as she passed and the breezes would cease to play. Even the blades of grass turned to follow her passage, and the fountains would cease their murmurings. It was as though every-thing held its breath lest they miss any aspect of her presence. One by one those eager suitors seized hold of the bow, but were not even able to lift it. At this spectacle, the line of contenders soon dwindled to nothing. The king roared out his disappointment, asking if there was not one among them who could even attempt the challenge, and the suitors, ashamed, were only able to look down at the floor.

Suddenly a young brahmin approached the pool. How could a priest pre-vail when the mightiest of warriors had failed? A priest was good for reciting prayers, tending sacred fires and burning incense, not for feats of arms. Little did anyone realise at that moment that the young brahmin was Arjuna in disguise. As he had been the one to capture Draupadi's father he feared he would not have been welcome at his court, far less as a potential son-in-law.

Everyone gasped as the young priest lifted the bow as though it were no heavier than a newborn baby. As he notched the arrow to the bowstring, many guessed who this young brahmin really was. With barely a glimpse at the water, he shot the writhing fish in one movement, so swift it was hard for the eye to follow. They say that thought is the fastest thing in the world. Now that they had witnessed something faster, their thoughts were not far behind. As the sound rang out at the arrow striking its target, everyone knew the identity of this man. And there was Draupadi, standing, her voice clear and steady as the pool, 'I choose Arjuna for my husband!'

The rejected suitors would have needed to be saints not to feel bitter envy as they made their subdued farewells, knowing that they would only be returning to the court as guests at Draupadi's wedding. There was among them, however, one whose love for his namesake was of a different kind. Not everyone had the eyes to see Lord Krishna as he watched serenely, as though he were looking through three eyes. The first saw how actions in their past lives had created the many twisting paths of their destinies – destinies that all converged in King Drupada's palace. The second eye saw, in the minutest detail, all that was happening in the present. The third saw the paths of everyone's future from the moment they would leave the palace; how they diverged, re-joined, separated and disappeared over the horizons of incarnations yet to come. The path of the Kaurava cousins was now paved with the smouldering coals of jealousy, fanned by yet another Pandava triumph, but this time their prize would be beyond price.

After many adventures, the six of them at last reached the brothers' home, where their mother, Kunti, lived. The young men, alerting their mother to their arrival, called out to her that they had brought a blessing with them. Delighted that they had returned, but still at her prayers, she called back to tell them to share the blessing equally between all of them – this always having been her approach to raising five boys. Great was her consternation when she realised what she had done, but there was no taking back those words, and perhaps they had not only come from her, perhaps another was using her well-worn phrase to fulfil a destiny that had been seeded in Draupadi's previous incarnation. As a young woman in another time, she had prayed to Lord Shiva to send her a husband with five particular qualities. How well the gods know the imperfections of men – Lord Shiva knew that these virtues could not all be found in the same individual. Now, in Draupadi's lifetime, she would at last find all these five virtues, but they would manifest separately in five husbands. Curiously enough, Kunti too had had five successive consorts, four of them divine.

A local sage advised that sharing Draupadi could be so divisive that it could bring disaster upon the Pandavas. It was therefore decided that their wife would spend a year with each husband in turn, in their separate households. It was also forbidden for any brother to visit the one in which Draupadi was staying. To do so would incur the punishment of being exiled for twelve years. On one occasion, Arjuna needed to enter one of his brothers' homes where Draupadi was staying to retrieve his weapons. Circumstances had forced him to make that difficult decision as he had to defend a brahmin from thieves. Not to do so would have been to also break his oath as a warrior and upholder of the law. Nevertheless, even though his brothers and Draupadi begged him to forego his punishment as the situation was not of his making, he chose exile as a matter of honour.

Thus did all six of them manage to lead virtuous lives, free from conflict, and the marriage was blessed with a son born to each of the brothers.

The fortunes of the Pandavas prospered to the extent that they were able to found a new city. They then decided to perform a ceremony that would declare them to be the high kings above all other kings, demanding allegiance from all the royal houses in the region. Those who accepted their new status were invited to the event, and those who did not were subjugated by means of arms. However they may have felt about it, the Kauravas were to attend, as, being cousins, they were seen as being close family. Lavish preparations were underway, with a new palace constructed with connecting assembly halls. Built to impress, one of the floors was entirely made of glass, a most costly material in those times.

Finally all was ready and the guests were welcomed. The last to arrive were the Kauravas, striding in as family rather than subservient royalty. The eldest, Duryodhana, preceded his brothers and hesitated only for a moment, dazzled by the light bouncing from the floor of the first hall. Thinking that the brightness was reflecting off the surface of a great pool of water, he was not deterred, and, making ready to splash through, he lifted his robe to avoid it getting wet. Instead of walking in what he expected to be an ankle-deep pool, he slid and skittered on glass. Then, clear as glass, there came a sound. It tinkled like a cascade of broken glass. It bounced off the glass floor and echoed around the chamber. It was the sound of Draupadi laughing. Duryodhana's face may have darkened, but he was determined not to show his humiliation, and onward he strode. There was the next assembly hall, but now he was prepared. He lowered his robe, and, supple warrior that he was, padded leopard-like onto the next glass surface. Only this time, it wasn't glass, because the second assembly hall really did have a pool of water running down its entire length. Duryodhana fell into it with a great splash. This time a fountain of laughter burst from Draupadi. Higher and higher mounted that fountain of sound as Draupadi laughed in delight at the ridiculous spectacle. This was an insult that Duryodhana would not forget or forgive. His plan for revenge was laid before the ceremony had even begun.

As the gods well know, no one is perfect. There is always at least one flaw in the best of us, and Duryodhana knew that his eldest cousin's great weakness was gambling. When Yudhishthira received his invitation to play at dice, he was troubled. It was against the code of honour for a warrior to refuse any contest, but at the same time, Yudishthira mistrusted the invitation and believed that no good would come of it. On consulting a sage, he had been told that a thirteen-year period of war and destruction was imminent. This was extremely distressing news and Yudishthira didn't know what to do for the best. Would refusing to play be interpreted as yet another insult? Above all he wanted to keep the peace. If any of his brothers had played that fateful game, the outcome would have been different. Not only was Yudishthira a bad player, he never knew when to stop. As soon as he heard those dice rattling, he was like a man possessed. It was as though their jostling shook him away from his power of judgement and rolled away all sense of reason and proportion. Their sound and motion held him like a helpless moon trapped by the relentless spinning of a planet of evil omen, and he lost all control over his actions.

What inexorable forces were at play to render that gambling game so catastrophic? There sat the Kauravas and the Pandavas opposite each other in a great gathering of royal houses and noble warriors. The atmosphere was so charged and so hostile that no women were present. Draupadi, in any case, had withdrawn to her own chambers for her period of monthly seclusion. The game unfolded with Yudishthira losing hand over fist. No matter how many times he lost, he would not give up. Instead he gambled away his treasures, his weapons, his horses and chariots, his houses, his lands, the list went on and still he would not stop. Now that he had lost all his material possessions, he could only gamble with his subordinates. Slaves, servants, even his own brothers were won by his cousin Duryodhana until there was only one person left to lose and that was Draupadi. Despite the hurtling speed of this wheel of misfortune, the Pandavas never for one moment thought that their eldest brother would bet their beloved wife. But the wheel did not slow down and there was still another person to crush in its wake. Four Pandava brothers bowed their heads in shame, now subject to their ruthless cousin. They could not even cast a warning glance in his direction as they heard Yudishthira stake Draupadi.

'Surely,' he was thinking, 'This has all been to test my courage. Surely the gods would not let me, a virtuous man, lose everything? This is the final test and if I keep my nerve and put my trust in the gods, I will win this final round and win everything back.'

How we can deceive ourselves, even to the point of explaining away addiction as a virtue. Yudishthira staked Draupadi and lost.

Triumphantly, Duryodhana broke the shocked silence, 'Bring my slave Draupadi to me now!'

Draupadi was just about to attend to her toilette when a warrior burst into her chamber, seized her by the hair and dragged her to the hall, where the assembly seemed to have turned to stone. The spectacle of her arrival was in itself an insult. A married woman's hair is sacred; the only man permitted to touch it is her husband. There she stood in her blood-stained sari, trembling not with fear but with anger at this outrage. But things can always get worse. Duryodhana slowly raised his robe, not to avoid wetting it this time, but to reveal his thigh, a most sexually offensive gesture. At this Bhishma, one of Draupadi's husbands, regained his speech and swore that he would drink his cousin's blood and break that thigh. Draupadi, however, was well capable of speaking up for herself. She demanded to know how she could be lost in a betting game by somebody who was already lost himself.

The only answer she received was from Karna, the suitor whose presence she had forbidden at her groom-choosing ceremony. He called out that she was a whore for living with five men. Who knows what Kunti, Draupadi's mother-in-law would have thought, she whose instructions her five sons and new daughter had obeyed. Abandoned at birth, perhaps not even Karna knew that he was Kunti's natural son and that he was insulting his sister-in-law and his blood brothers.

But Karna hadn't finished. He demanded that Draupadi be stripped naked in front of everyone and seized the hem of her bloody sari. So fateful was that gesture, sealing as it did the deaths of so many thousands of righteous warriors, that it was a miracle that the stain did not transform into the shape of India herself. Maybe it did, but the thousands of eyes would not have noticed, so quickly did Karna jerk the sari away. There it lay in folds around her feet, yet Draupadi remained fully covered. Realising that no mortal present would rise to protect her, Draupadi was praying to her namesake god, her revered Krishna.

As she prayed, more and more of the sari played out, its billowing folds settling like drifts of sand on the floor. On she prayed, and on and on looped the sari throughout the hall, as Lord Krishna responded to her supplication to protect her.

The silence that accompanied this miraculous sight was not one of shock, but one of awe, and for some, one of fear. When Draupadi stopped praying, her words became prophetic as she cursed those who had insulted her and declared that her honour would be avenged by war. The Pandavas left the palace, and she and her five husbands went into exile to prepare themselves for the most terrible conflict of India's ancient history.

KOBLANDY, WARRIOR, SUITOR, PROTECTOR OF HIS PEOPLE

KAZAKHSTAN

While hunting with his uncle, the hero Koblandy heard voices on the other side of the hill. Fearing an ambush, he asked his uncle to listen, but the older man denied hearing anything. Koblandy persisted and his uncle admitted that those were the voices of men competing for the hand in marriage of the local chief's only daughter. Rumour had it that any who failed the test were beheaded, but so great was her beauty, so strong was her spirit, that no man could resist the attempt. As his uncle had feared, Koblandy instantly wanted to win the maiden's hand and could not be prevented from taking on the challenge. When he saw that he could not change his nephew's mind, he armed him with a supple and slender bow, chain mail so fine it whispered like the dawn wind of the steppes when he slipped it on, and lastly, a sword made of Syrian steel. Then, with three kisses, he gave him his blessing: 'Let your heart never know fear, may your secret dreams come true, whatever your adventures, may you always return home safely.'

Koblandy then presented himself to the tribe's chief. When he saw the daughter, Kortka Slu, he knew why he had defied his uncle. When she saw Koblandy, she wished that her own secret dream would come true, and she also knew that it was no longer a secret because he shared it. The challenge was to shoot a golden coin suspended from a pole so high it seemed to pierce the very clouds. With his first and only arrow, the coin was hit and split, its two halves falling to the earth like autumn leaves. Although Koblandy was from a different tribe, Kortka Slu's father was true to his word and he gave orders for the wedding preparations to begin.

However, there was one who did not agree with the chief's decision and Koblandy received an invitation, in the most insulting of terms, to fight this rival who had suddenly announced himself. However, when the hero presented himself at Kyzyl-Er's yurt, the bully would not even rise from his bed to meet him. So used was he to intimidating everyone that he did not even bother to sit up for the man he had already turned into an enemy. There he lay, a huge fat giant, calling out taunts and insults. Realising that he would not confront him outside, man to man, Koblandy rushed into the yurt, where Kyzyl-Er continued to make fun of his eagerness to fight.

Tauntingly, he lifted his huge leg in the air and suggested that Koblandy have a battle with it, as he waved it about like a tree trunk in a storm.

The furious Koblandy noticed a horsehair rope hanging from the door post, which he seized and tied around his enemy's leg. He tied the other end to his horse and set off at a gallop. Kyzyl-Er was dragged off his bed and along the ground, where his huge bulk gouged a furrow as he was pulled along. A yellow cloud of dust rose high above him and marked his ignominious journey. First Koblandy drove his horse through thorn thickets, where strips of fat were torn from Kyzyl-Er's body. Then he rode up and down mountains, shaking loose boulders to break every bone in his body. Finally, he uprooted trees that not even a hurricane could loosen, with which to crush what was left of his enemy. At last Kyzyl-Er was dead and Koblandy's father-in-law rejoiced, knowing that he had been a treacherous man plotting to oust him as chief.

When it was time for the young couple to start their journey to Koblandy's people, the chief gave his daughter many costly gifts. He told her new husband that he loved him like a son and that he also had gifts for him. Pointing to the sky, he told Koblandy that he was giving him the clouds. Too polite to question his father-in-law and suspecting that perhaps his wits were less certain in old age, Koblandy said nothing. However, the chief went on to explain that the four clouds he was pointing to were no ordinary clouds and that they had special powers. One would appear in the summer and protect him from the burning heat of the sun. Another would appear in the winter and protect him from the blizzard's rage. The next would fly towards him from the direction of any enemy to warn him of their approach. The last would be a faithful sign of the friendship and unity between his and his wife's people.

So, just as his uncle's third blessing had stated, Koblandy returned home safely. Only now he also had superb weapons, a glorious reputation and magical clouds at his service. But best of all these put together was his wife, Kortka Slu, who would help him in so many of their adventures yet to come.

A HERO HUMBLED

Many important historical figures collect pre-existing stories that are subsequently attributed to them. Like barnacles clinging to a keel, these tales adhere with a tenacity strengthened through telling and retelling over time – even if these stories existed before their actual protagonist was born. In this way the powerful become heroes and heroines whose lives are a pageant of triumphal exploits beyond the aspirations of ordinary mortals. How poignant then, and how much easier it is for the listener or reader to identify with these paragons on those rare occasions when he or she is shown to be as flawed and vulnerable as anyone else. Such a one is Bharam Gur, who ruled 398–420, a famous Persian king mentioned in Iran's great works of literature. His name is a composite of meanings, 'Bharam', referring to the ancient Zoroastrian god of victory, and 'Gur', referring to the wild asses (onagers) he delighted in hunting, as different from our domestic donkey as a domestic cat is to a snow leopard.

We are told that Bharam Gur was still completing his studies when his father was assassinated. He hurried home to lay his claim to the throne against those of his rivals. This involved a contest in which the crown was placed between two lions, the heir proving his worth by being able to retrieve it. The prince's rivals withdrew when he realised the danger, but Bharam Gur killed both lions and claimed the crown. Flawless warrior, famous hunter of the fleet and fiercely untameable wild asses, fond husband of seven wives, Bharam Gur was brought low by a slave girl. Azadeh was a court musician whose duties included composing songs praising the king's exploits of the day. The court would listen to her exquisite voice and musicianship as she sang of their ruler's mighty deeds. Sometimes the king would playfully suggest that she set a challenge for him that he would not hesitate to tackle, so that he and everyone else would soon hear his deed being immortalised in song.

Whenever he could escape his duties at court, Bharam Gur loved nothing better than to hunt. It was not practical for his wives to accompany him, those most favoured of women who lived in their own palaces with a different day of the week, planet and colour assigned to each. But his other beloved, the slave girl Azadeh, could accompany him. At the end of each day, she composed a song celebrating the hunting achievements of her king and lover, and he and his retainers would hear these set to verse around the camp fire, desire smouldering as he listened to her soaring voice.

On one of these expeditions, the king invited Azadeh to set him a challenge. Faster than a warrior can draw their sword, she told him to pin one of the wild ass's hooves to its ear using but a single arrow to touch the beast. A hard task indeed. A herd was sighted, an animal singled out. Bharam Gur let fly an arrow that did not touch the beast but which came so close that the wind of its passing tickled the hairs inside the onager's ear. The agile animal lifted its hoof to scratch and no sooner had it touched the ear when another arrow pinned them together.

'How was that!' demanded the king triumphantly.

There was a pause before the lacklustre reply: 'That was alright.'

Puzzled, the king repeated his demand: 'How was that?'

'That was alright.'

Now there was threat in his voice: 'I said, how was that?

'And I said, that was alright.'

Then all his lust and passion turned into rage as Bharam Gur ordered his beloved to be beheaded. His bodyguard led her away as the king rode furiously back to the palace.

As soon as they were alone, Azadeh reminded her executioner that the king often regretted his hasty temper. He was bound to do so on this occasion and then where would that temper be redirected to when he discovered that his order could not be rescinded? The bodyguard saw the sense of this and his captive suggested that they journey to some distant part of the country where she could remain hidden.

Just as she had predicted, the king soon regretted his outburst and fell into convulsions of grief. Even the skies joined in with his weeping, raining torrents until the rivers broke their banks and the land flooded. At last there were no more tears left to shed and he fell into a decline, taking no pleasure in any of his previous pastimes, only attending to the necessities of kingship. He was now a more measured man, solemn in company and sad when alone.

Meanwhile, the two travelling companions had reached such a remote part of the country that it was almost uninhabited. In the past two days they had only seen one group of herdsmen and their cattle. The terrain had become mountainous, and, looking up towards one of the crests, Azadeh noticed an abandoned stone palace with a great number of steps leading to its ruined entrance.

'This is the place I have been seeking. Before you leave me here, return to those herdsmen and buy me the smallest of their weaned calves.'

The bodyguard did as he was told, returning with a young animal whose satin coat glowed like the setting sun. Making his farewells to the slave girl, his last sight of her was as she stood on those rocky steps, an arm around the calf's neck. Then he made his way back to the palace, where he kept a low profile until better times would come.

As soon as he had gone, Azadeh lifted the calf upon her shoulders and slowly climbed the one hundred and one steps to the palace entrance. At the top, she steadied herself, turned around once, sunwise, and descended, still carrying the calf on her shoulders. She did this at every dawn, spending the days searching for grazing and forage so that the beast grew as large as any of its kind. The herdsmen, who brought her supplies, marvelled at her strength.

Better times came at last. One day the king asked for his old bodyguard and the two men, greyer and grizzled, looked quietly at each other. Bharam Gur said that he had neglected his kingdom for too long and wished to travel its length once more, particularly to those places with which he was least familiar. He had long lost any yearning for pomp and excitement, so the two men left all others behind as the bodyguard led his king on a meandering journey, with no apparent destination in mind.

At last, just as the bodyguard knew they would, they reached the distant mountains where the abandoned palace was to be found. The king looked at that deserted place that once must have been alive with splendour. The empty-eyed windows and crumbling pillars reminded him of his own loneliness, but still he was curious about anyone causing a building like that to be built in such an inaccessible place.

'Who would want to climb so many steep steps?' he murmured out loud. His companion replied that it was indeed a strange place with an even stranger story about it. The local tribespeople said that each morning a woman would appear, carrying a red ox on her shoulders and, thus burdened, she would climb those steps to the top.

'That is something I would very much like to see,' said the king, and his heart started to pound and the blood rushed into his ears without him knowing why.

They rose in time to see dawn's golden touch climb those steps, where it was not alone as it drew fire from the coat of a great red ox draped across the shoulders of a slowly ascending figure. Although robed and veiled, it was unmistakeably a woman. Steadily she climbed, turned sunwise at the top and steadily descended. This time she did not release the ox as soon as she reached the ground, but continued to carry it as she walked towards the two men. Only when she had drawn close did she set it down. Then, drawing back her veil, Azadeh looked at her old lover and said, 'How was that?'

Bharam Gur looked into the eyes he had lost all hope of ever seeing again. 'That was alright.' And so it was.

WHY THE ROMA KEEP MOVING

ROMA (GYPSY)

The centurions were happy: a whole half day just to buy three nails! No need to hurry, and so much money for such a small purchase, nobody would miss the change if they spent some of it on drinking, or even a spot of gambling. Late in the day they tore themselves away from their amusements to get the task done, but it didn't prove to be as easy as expected. The blacksmith knew what this request meant and asked who they were going to crucify this time.

'The King of the Jews,' came the sneering reply.

'You must mean Jesus of Nazareth. Some say he is a prophet, some just a storyteller, but if so, a storyteller of the best kind. Sorry, my fire is too low and it's not worth the fuel to build it up again just for the price of three nails. You'll have to go elsewhere.'

The centurions considered threatening him to make him change his mind, but he was a blacksmith, hugely strong, and they were drunk. It would be less trouble to find another. They didn't notice the blacksmith's lad running past them up the street, sent on an errand to another of their trade. When they reached the next forge, the blacksmith told them that he had run out of raw metal and had no materials to make the nails with. It was getting late, the centurions were sobering up and didn't dare to return without the nails. The next smithy was closed – it seemed to have shut up shop early. What to do? By now they were near Herod's gate and the sun was setting.

Then they heard the sound of music and singing from beyond the city walls. It was coming from the gypsy camp. They were among the best of smiths and always needed work. Living outside the city, they may not have heard who these nails were for, and wouldn't be asking any awkward questions. At sunset, the gates were locked and guarded; only the centurions would be able to get through. They signalled to the soldiers on guard to open up and as they passed through, one of the gypsies slipped in to get some last-minute supplies from the town.

As the centurions had hoped, the gypsies were willing to make the three nails and they waited for the fire to be made hot enough for the work to begin. At last the nails were ready, and were paid for with three bronze coins, all that was left of the soldiers' drunken spree. The smith was not best pleased with the payment – one had a piece nicked out of it, one was smaller than the others and the last was crooked – but he knew better than to complain to the centurions. Just as Herod's gate was being opened for them again, the gypsy was returning from his errand, and slipped back to his camp. He was in a ferment about the news he had heard. Everybody was talking about preparations for the crucifixion that would take place the next day. Apart from two thieves, an innocent man was to die. A prophet, perhaps even the Messiah, it was to be the man they called Jesus of Nazareth, a man whose teachings had spread throughout the land.

That name went around the camp as quickly as a desert wind. Now the gypsy smith knew why the centurions had come so far for their three nails. The three bronze coins weighed heavier than lead on his palm. It was too late to do anything about the nails, but at least he could refuse to keep any payment for them. With a curse uttered from the depth of his soul, he flung the coins after the soldiers as hard as he could.

Their chief was already giving orders for them to strike camp and move away from that cursed spot. They managed as best they could in the dark, moving westwards, only stopping after midnight. In the morning light, the smith gave a cry of dismay. There in the sand on the edge of camp were those three same pieces of bronze with no footprints leading to or from them. The cursed coins had followed them. Again, the chief decided to move his people on. Who knows how many times those coins reappeared, but from that time to this time, the Roma people like to keep moving in case the curse of the three nails catches up with them again.

THE PARSEE'S ARRIVAL IN INDIA

ZOROASTRIAN/INDIAN

Times had changed in their homeland of Ancient Persia. The Zoroastrians had created one of the world's oldest religions in which they had united beliefs in several deities under the one all-powerful god Zarathustra. But now a new religion had come, and one that was inimical to theirs. Many of the Zoroastrian priesthood decided that it was time to find a new homeland and, over a period of two hundred years, many of their community sailed to the coast of India, where they had been trading for hundreds of years.

During one of these voyages with the most numerous of the Zoroastrian community, a terrible storm arose that threatened to drown them all. They prayed to the Almighty that if he saved their lives, they would light an eternal flame to him – a promise that they kept as they landed safely on the Indian coast at a place that is now part of the state of Gujarat.

News of the largest landing of these religious refugees soon reached the local king, Jadi Rana, who was concerned at such a numerous, powerful and different group of people arriving in his domain. How would his country accommodate them? What influence would they have over the population? All questions, which are, of course, alive today in different regions of the world. An emissary with a royal entourage was sent to the sands where the strangers had landed.

With due ceremony, a courtier appeared before Dastur Naryosang Dhaval, the priestly leader of the Zoroastrians, bearing a vessel full to the brim with fresh milk. Its recipient bowed low at this diplomatic gesture, well aware of its multiple symbolic significance. First, any traveller must be welcomed according to the laws of hospitality, hence the refreshing drink. Secondly, the richness and purity of the milk showed that the country lacked for nothing. Thirdly, the vessel was brim full to show that there was no additional room in the country for such a multitude of people.

Dastur Naryosang Dhaval gestured to another of his party and after a rapid whispered conversation, a bowl with a silver spoon appeared on a cushion. Holding the Indian emissary's eyes in his gaze, the Zoroastrian lifted its lid to reveal the purest of sugar crystals. Slowly, gently, without spilling a drop of milk or a grain of sugar, spoonful by spoonful, the sugar was added to the milk until the bowl was empty.

Nothing of the greatly symbolic significance of that diplomatic gesture was lost on the king's emissary either. First, the newcomers were not without wealth of their own. Secondly, they were prepared to share it. Thirdly, even if they were as numerous as grains of sugar, they could be absorbed into a new culture without causing any upset. At this, the new community was given the right to settle in this new land, subject to certain conditions with which they had no difficulty in complying. In gratitude for being saved from the storm, they lit their sacred fire, a feature of all Zoroastrian temples and a symbol of the purity of their religion and faith.

THE TEARS OF A GIANT

PHILIPPINES

In the Filipino archipelago, made up of over seven thousand islands, lies Bohol, unique in the Philippines and the rest of the world. Its curious hill formations resemble an endless landscape of upturned conical egg boxes, so uniform in size and shape that you would imagine them to have been man-made. But this completely natural landscape is a place where folk tale and climatology meet, creating a legend that Bohol could not share with any other part of the world.

The geology is limestone, created by innumerable corals that once formed the seabed. Due to seismic activity caused by the friction between tectonic plates, this entire area was raised above sea level at the same time. Being limestone, it is easily eroded by water, and this process is especially rapid in a tropical climate, creating the phenomenon of cone karst erosion. Bohol also experiences two monsoons a year, resulting in 10ft of rainfall. These factors combine to produce this multitude of over seventeen hundred uniform cones stretching as far as the eye can see.

But the eyes that produced them, according to ancient belief, were so full of tears that the Giant Arogo was blinded with grief. How he wept at the death of his mortal lover, Aloya. Although immeasurably huge, he was gentle and loving and so Aloya had loved him in return but, of course, their love, being subject to a human lifespan, was doomed. As he wept, his tears solidified into those many rounded hills – each one we see today, one of his tears. His sorrow was so affecting that even the rain goddess, Anitun Tabu, joined him in his grief, weeping torrents that we now call the monsoons. When the rains come, we know that she is remembering Arogo and Aloya's story.

WATERMELON

ARMENIA

There was once a young king who needed to make a long journey across a desert. He took no servants with him – it would be an adventure! Where the scrub gave way to sand, there sat an old woman selling watermelons, which the prince thought would be ideal for sustaining him during his hot, dusty ride. Because of their weight, he decided to buy no more than three and as he paid for them, the old woman warned him to make sure that he only opened them when he had completed his journey. The king thought this a very strange injunction: surely he wouldn't need them then, when he would have reached water, surely it was for the journey that they would be needed! However, out of respect for her age, he didn't argue.

As the sun beat down, he became thirstier and thirstier and sliced open one of the melons. Out stepped a lovely young woman, as naked as the day she was born, because, of course, that was the day she was born. Stretching out her hands, she begged him for water, but he had none to give. With horror he watched her burn and shrivel in the sun until she lay like a twisted husk at his horse's hooves.

He rode on with the memory of what had happened until he was so feverish with thirst that he wondered whether it hadn't all been a bad dream. But he couldn't continue without some moisture, so he sliced open the second watermelon. There was another lovely maiden, beseeching him for water, and again he could not help her. Transfixed with guilt, he watched her shrink and wither under the sun until she was just a scrap of brittle skin in the sand.

After this he was determined not to open the last watermelon, no matter how he suffered. As his horse stumbled on, his vision blurred, and his swollen, blackened tongue could no longer be contained by his cracked and bleeding lips.

At last, when he could not bear to believe that it was anything other than a mirage, he saw in the distance the city that marked the end of his journey. But before that lay a pool of pure water, next to which grew a luxuriant tree. King and horse drank deeply. Then he slit the last watermelon, and as the two halves sprang apart, out stepped another young woman, lovelier than the others. This time he was able to help her, bringing her water as she sat in the shade. As he had brought her into the world, the maiden asked if he would like to marry her, and the king could hardly believe his good fortune.

'But you can't get married like that! You have no clothes on! I will ride into the city to buy you a wedding dress and I promise to marry you when I return. In the meantime, you had better climb that tree and hide among the leaves in case anyone sees you. Oh! and, by the way, what's your name?'

Watermelon, for that was her name, climbed into the tree and waited for her beloved, but she was not alone for long. Hidden behind a sand dune was a hut from which emerged the most hideous creature you can imagine. Sliding along on a trail of her own slime, she reached the pool to fill her pail. She bent over the water as Watermelon peered out from her hiding place. Ugly, for that was her name, thought she was seeing her own reflection as she looked at the image of a face lovelier than the full moon. It was only when a leaf drifted down that she looked up and saw its true source. Seeing Watermelon among the branches, she climbed the tree, disappointment, anger and envy roiling inside her.

Straddling the same branch, she set her back against the trunk and asked the maiden who she was and what was her story, and Watermelon told her everything she could. Now you will know why Ugly was so named, not because of what she looked like, but because what she was really like on the inside had found a way to show itself on the outside. She reached a massive hairy arm behind Watermelon, gripped the branch with her seven-fingered, talon tapered hand, and snapped it off. Down, down fell Watermelon, but instead of drowning in the pool, just as she touched the skin of the water, she turned into a little white bird and flew away.

The king returned with a dress of white silk, a gold embroidered sun on one breast, a silver embroidered moon on the other, and all over sprinkled with diamond and pearl stars. He looked up into the tree and thought how much Watermelon had changed as those hideous hands reached out and a voice that could grind stone ordered him to hand over her dress. He tried to fit it over her huge bulk, but in the end, he had to rip it into pieces, and tie it round her in strips. Thus bandaged, his horse staggering under her weight, they made their way to the city. How his heart sank at the prospect of marriage, but a promise is a promise even if you are a king. A promise is a promise, especially if you are a king.

As for the new queen, the first order that she gave was that no watermelons were to be grown anywhere in the land. From his wedding day, her husband was the most miserable man and monarch to be found. Ugly harried and hectored him so that he never had a moment of joy. With the excuse that he needed to sign state papers, the king would retreat into his study, where he would try to stay for as long as possible. As these visits increased, Ugly grew suspicious, and one evening she set her eye to the keyhole. There on the windowsill, she saw a little white bird alight, open its beak, and sing a song so sweet it made every wart, wrinkle and scale on her body shudder. But what of the king? There he was, listening with his eyes closed, tears glistening as they squeezed beneath his eyelids and ran bitter salt into a smile as sweet as the singing. Ugly ordered the gardener to shoot the little white bird, and an arrow pierced it through the heart. The moment a drop of its heart's blood touched the ground, bird and arrow disappeared and there instead was a graceful pear tree, with blossom as silvery white as the full moon. The astonished gardener had carried out his instructions and decided to say nothing about the tree.

With no reason to linger in his study, the king took to wandering in the garden and came upon a tree he had never noticed before. How soothing was its shade, how gentle the murmuring of its leaves. He took to leaning against its silvery trunk whenever he could, his only moments of gentleness and comfort. Suspicious Ugly spied on him, and seeing his peaceful expression, ordered the tree to be chopped down when the king was elsewhere. The deed done, the troubled gardener could not resist taking some of its wood. How sweet the sap smelled, how smooth the grain. In his cottage, where he lived alone at the edge of the palace grounds, he carved a wooden spoon from it.

Great was his surprise when he returned from work the next day to see smoke rising from the chimney and, where his curtains used to hang, lit lamps glowed at the windows. Wafting through the door came the scent of delicious cooking. All had been neatened in the cottage; everything sparkled with tenderness and care. On the table was a white silk table-cloth, a gold embroidered sun at one end, a silver embroidered moon at the other, and all over sprinkled with diamond and pearl stars. How the gardener rejoiced in his enchanted home before he left for work the next day. When he returned all was as it had been the previous evening, but now the windowsills were full of pots overflowing with the most beautiful flowers he never had time to grow for himself.

In the morning he left for work as usual, but doubled back secretly and peered through the keyhole. He could see the tablecloth, and, lying on it, the pear wood spoon he had carved. Just then a tremor ran through it and it began to shiver and shake, tilt and upend itself. Then arms and legs grew from its handle, and in no time, a naked maiden was singing and dancing around the room, whilst she put all to rights. He burst into the cottage and set himself with his back against the door. Watermelon grabbed the shift she had made from his curtains, held out her hands beseechingly, and begged the gardener to let her stay and work for him if he kept her presence a secret. Hardly able to believe his good fortune, he readily agreed. Pressing some seeds into his hands, she begged him to plant them behind the cottage. There they became the only patch of watermelons in the whole country.

Time passed, and the king, who felt he had little to live for, became ill and could not or would not recover. Soon it was rumoured that he was dying and none could cure him. The gardener was saddened by what he had heard and Watermelon asked what was troubling him. When she heard the news, she went behind the cottage under cover of darkness, and cut the ripest watermelon. She then insisted that the gardener take a slice and put it in the king's mouth with his own hand. At first light he went to the palace where all the servants were in disarray and confusion reigned. It was therefore easy for the gardener to make his way to the king's chamber, where, needless to say, Ugly was not to be found comforting her husband in his last moments.

As soon as that piece of watermelon was placed between the king's lips, he began to dream – of a graceful pear tree, of a little white bird with the sweetest of songs, of a face lovely as the full moon. His eyes opened and he sat up. Seizing the slice of watermelon, he shouted at the gardener to tell him where he had found it. Because a promise is a promise, even if you are a gardener, he refused to tell him. By now the king was running through the palace, servants and courtiers rushing after him.

Now that they had all reached the audience chamber, Ugly had heard the commotion and blundered into the hall, looking none too pleased at her husband's recovery. There he was, shaking the silent gardener and threatening to have him executed if he didn't say where he had found that fruit. Ugly glared at the gardener, remembering the tree, the bird, the maiden. She was just offering to execute the gardener herself when the great doors opened and the sweet scent of pears wafted into the hall. Then birdsong was heard, each note a pearly dewdrop hanging in the scented air. Watermelon stepped through the throng, silvery-pale limbs misted over with a thin cotton shift, her face lovelier than the full moon.

The king turned to Ugly: 'Which would you prefer, the sword or the horse?' Thwarted, enraged, and for the first time, frightened, she wasn't sure what to say.

'The horse, the horse, give me a horse!'

'That is the last wrong answer you will ever give me.'

The king ordered his war horse to be saddled and for Ugly to be tied to the beast's tail. Then the chief of his bodyguards rode the horse throughout the kingdom until there was not a scrap of flesh left on Ugly's bones.

'Now, at last, we shall have a proper wedding. But look at you, Watermelon, you can't get married in that. I must get you a wedding dress.'

'No, my beloved! Remember what happened last time you said you would fetch me a wedding dress? I will get my own.'

And perhaps she was the only royal bride ever to be married in a tablecloth.

THE SHADOW OF SHAME

KOREA

A stranger walked wearily into the village. He was dusty and dirty from his long journey and all he wanted to do was rest. Before him rose a magnificent chestnut tree, its outspread branches casting a most inviting shade. Gratefully, he slipped his back along the trunk until he was sitting against it. Stretching his legs, he let his head loll back and he fell into a doze. However, he was soon roused by angry shouting.

Before him stood a man, his face dark with rage. At first the stranger found it hard to understand what was being shouted at him, so he observed carefully: from his clothing, a wealthy man; from his stomach, very well fed; from his tone, furious. Eventually the stranger realised that the rich man owned the tree and didn't want him taking advantage of its shadow. How dare this vagabond just help himself to another man's shade? Who did he think he was? At last, he had to stop shouting in order to catch his breath. By then the villagers, attracted by the noise, were crowding round to see what would happen next. They were used to the rich man's bullying outbursts but were wondering how this stranger would respond.

In the sudden quiet, haltingly, but courteously, the stranger asked if he could buy the tree's shadow from its owner. The rich man thought that was certainly something worth hearing. What fools these foreigners are! Not only did he have the right to prevent his shade from being used, he could now make money from it. He hadn't become rich for no reason, and he wasn't going to let any opportunity pass him by that would make him even richer. He named a ridiculously high price. The crowd gasped. The stranger smiled. Standing, he rummaged through his pockets. He emptied them and counted all the money he had. To the very last coin, it came to exactly the outrageous amount mentioned. The stranger gave it all to the rich man, and bowed his thanks. The tree owner stomped off to his large home, which was nearby. As the traveller settled down again for a snooze, the villagers, muttering among themselves, went back to their tasks.

The sun continued its journey and the tree's shadow lengthened. By the time the traveller awoke, it had reached the rich man's garden. Much refreshed, he passed through the gate and took up his position in the shade. The day was still sultry and he appreciated its coolness as he looked around the vast garden. Despite the owner's wealth, it was terribly neglected. His observations were interrupted by the house owner screaming at him from the veranda. The whole village could hear his imprecations. Gradually a crowd gathered once more. When the stranger could make himself heard, he politely pointed out that he was merely using what was now his. After all, hadn't he just bought the tree's shadow, in front of witnesses? The crowd began to titter and the rich man retreated into his house, slamming the door. None of the villagers could remember such an entertaining occasion.

As sunset drew near, the shadow lengthened, spilling over the veranda into the house itself. The stranger followed it. Even coming from inside, the rich man's howls of protest could be heard clearly. Perhaps more drama could be enjoyed. Yet again the people collected to watch, and this time they had the courage to intervene. Their titters had turned to open laughter and they were no longer afraid of the richest man in the village. Laughter turned to jeers and cries of how he was only getting what he deserved. The rich man was so embarrassed that he hurriedly packed a bag and left. Where he went, nobody knew, and nobody cared, unless it was to relish the joy at seeing the back of him.

Night had fallen and the newcomer decided that it might not be a good idea to leave such a large house, with so many valuables, empty and unprotected. He spent the night there, a grateful traveller with nowhere else to go, but on hand if needed. In the morning light he was dismayed to see that this once sumptuous residence was as dilapidated inside as the garden was neglected outside. The truth was that its owner was as miserly as he was rich and hadn't wanted to spend any money on repairs. Gradually the new occupant started to make good, first making the structure weatherproof, then mending and repairing throughout. He spent his days alternating between putting both the house and the garden to rights. Whenever he was working outside, the curious villagers would peer over the now mended fence to see what he was up to. The man had a different way of doing things, skills that had not yet been seen in those parts.

Sometimes he would look up from his work and chat to the passers-by. Soon they were coming into the garden to take a closer look at his methods, whether it was weeding or watering. When autumn came, there was even more to be done. By then he had a steady stream of neighbours dropping in. It was time for the autumn planting and he not only showed but shared different kinds of seeds that he had brought in his pack. The garden was so large that he suggested that his neighbours might like to take over a plot to cultivate. Many were glad of the extra land and of the new vegetables and flowers that appeared as the wheel of the year turned, until summer had come again.

It was then that the rich man decided it was time to return home – surely everyone would have forgotten his humiliation by now. To his relief, it all seemed rather quiet and empty, until he neared his house at the far side of the village. Then he could hear many voices, laughter and even singing. If his hadn't been the last house, he might almost have walked past, as it was so altered. And what of the garden? That vast neglected tangle now looked more like a park. There were children playing on swings and floating bark boats on a new pond. Trees that had been barren from neglect were now heavy with fruit. Everywhere were beds full of flowers and vegetables at which the whole village seemed to be working.

Everyone stopped when they saw the owner had returned. The newcomer's voice broke the silence: 'There you are! I was wondering what had become of you, and now you have come home at last!'

The rich man gaped, stared, didn't know what to say at first. Then he heard a voice he couldn't recognise as his own, saying what wonderful changes had been made – how grateful he was for everyone's efforts – how they had transformed the house and the garden to a beautiful place, and how could he ever repay them? He looked at the man who once had been a stranger, and asked him to live there and work for him. But the traveller replied that he really couldn't stay, he was only passing through after all, and needed to be on his way. He took some seeds from the garden and put them with his meagre possessions into his pack. Then he bowed to everybody and left. People say that he is still travelling, and may even pass this way sometime soon.

THE MAGIC POMEGRANATE SEED

YEMEN

Where the dreams die, there the people perish.

Virgil

There was once a poor widow who could never earn enough to feed her children. All day she worked in the hot sun, carrying water. No matter how many hours she laboured, there was never quite enough to show for it at the end of the day, and every night she would hear them crying with hunger as they tried to sleep. The sound of it wore away at her heart like water dripping onto a stone, until one night she made a promise to herself that she would never hear that sound again.

The next day, instead of going back to work, she went into town looking for employment that would pay higher wages. However, there was none to be found, and feeling desperate, she joined the beggars in the marketplace. It was a rich town and there were many beggars. She held out her hand with the other unfortunates, but nobody gave her anything. Night was coming and still she had nothing for her children. The stallholders were closing up and, in her panic, the woman did something that she had never done before: she stole. She stole a loaf of bread. Never having done such a thing, she didn't have the skill to get away with it, and was caught instantly. The soldiers were sent for and she knew she would be thrown into prison, never to see her children again.

Sure enough, two soldiers arrived, tied her hands behind her back and started to drag her through the town towards the sultan's palace and the dungeons beneath. Frantically twisting her bound hands, she managed to get one of them into the pocket of her ragged dress, knowing as she did so that it would be empty. And so it was, except for something small and hard that she could feel underneath her fingernail. It was a pomegranate seed. But it was not just a pomegranate seed, it was also a seed of hope, and with it came an idea. As she was being hustled through the town, the woman started to call out, 'I have a secret and if I die, my secret will die with me!'

The townspeople who had been jeering and pointing at her now stared curiously. Louder and louder she shouted, 'I have a secret and if I die my secret will die with me!'

By now people were coming out onto their balconies. Others hurried to see what the commotion was about. The soldiers exchanged uneasy looks.

'I have a secret and if I die my secret will die with me!'

The soldiers decided that they should bring her before the sultan rather than take her straight to prison. When they arrived at the palace, she was dragged, still shouting, across the audience chamber and pushed to the floor in front of the royal throne. The sultan ordered her to share the secret she had been boasting about. The prisoner explained that she had a magic pomegranate seed and that if she planted it, a huge pomegranate tree would grow overnight. This didn't impress the sultan. He had hundreds of orchards in which grew thousands of pomegranate trees. Why would he be interested in another? However, on thinking about it, there was the possibility that if such a tree grew from a seed overnight, his enemies would get to hear of it and conclude that magical powers were at his command. Perhaps, if they believed this, they would be less likely to cause trouble.

The sultan gave the order that the woman was to plant the seed, but also warned her that if she was deceiving him, not only would she be put to death, but she would be tortured first. The entire court followed her into the courtyard, where she scraped a little hole in the ground. They saw the seed on the palm of her hand before it slipped into the hole and was covered. She tore a scrap off her robe and tucked it into the ground to mark the place. By now it was getting dark and everyone retired to the palace for the night.

Strange to say, but true: everyone in the palace that night dreamed the same dream. In it they saw that a huge pomegranate tree had grown in the middle of the palace courtyard. The singing of the birds in its branches could be heard throughout the land. Breezes bore the perfume from its blossoms to neighbouring countries. Its spreading branches provided enough shade for all and its boughs were so heavy with fruit that there was plenty for everybody to share.

At dawn, everyone in the palace awoke at the same moment and they all hurried down to the courtyard to see the magical tree.

There was nothing there. The courtyard was empty except for a forlorn scrap of cloth barely visible in the early light. The sultan was furious. He threw the prisoner down in the dust and roared that he would carry out his warning now that she had tried to make a fool of him. There she was, kneeling in the dust, quietly poking in the ground to uncover the pomegranate seed.

'Your Majesty, I understand what has happened. As you know, I am a thief. It should not have been me who planted the seed. If an honest person had planted it the magic would have worked. I have proved unworthy. Please, Majesty, ask someone more deserving than I, to do the deed.'

The sultan snapped his fingers and summoned his chancellor of the exchequer. With some hesitation he knelt by the prisoner, but although he had taken the seed from her, he did not plant it.

'Well get on with it man,' roared the sultan, 'What are you waiting for?'

'Majesty, it has just come to me that, er, possibly, working late at night you understand, by the light of a single guttering oil lamp, to save your household expenses, you understand, er, Majesty, that maybe, just possibly, quite mistakenly, due to the flickering shadow, I might have put some figures in one column that would have been better placed in another ...'

'Get out of my sight!' shouted the sultan, 'And send for the chief of police, get him to plant the seed!'

Strange to say, but true – the chief of police who was usually to be found everywhere at all times, was, on this occasion, nowhere to be found at all.

'Majesty, my mother always used to say that if she wanted a job done properly, she would have to do it herself. Why don't you plant the seed?'

With an impatient sigh, the sultan knelt beside his prisoner and placed the seed in the hole. But the hand that had started to scrape the soil back to cover it grew slower and slower and stopped. Something that looked like a bright, gleaming seed plopped into the hole, followed by another and another. The sultan was crying!

'I have just remembered that when I was a little boy, my mother used to let me play with her favourite jewels before I went bed. How beautifully they sparkled in my hands! My favourite was an emerald necklace. One night I didn't replace it in the box and hid it under my clothes. When she asked if I had taken it I lied, and said that I hadn't. Next day she dismissed her favourite maid. She was my favourite too, always so kind. Whenever one of my tempers gave me a headache, she knew how to hold my head and stroke my bad mood and my headache away with her special touch. I never saw her again and I never found out what became of her.'

'Yes, I know,' said the woman as she stroked the sultan's head in the special way that only she knew, with a touch that the sultan had not felt for many years.

'So you see, I too am a thief, and I am not worthy to plant the magic seed either. But I also see that you really do have a secret, and that secret is also known by the name of wisdom. So, dearest of ladies, will you please return to the palace which you should never have left, and share your secret with us all by becoming my advisor?'

Her children were sent for, and their mother managed to keep her promise to herself as she never heard them cry with hunger again, and neither did any others.

THE CHAMPION POETS

Four companions were drinking rice wine at their local inn. How pleasant it was to be in familiar company. How delicious the wine was, although they had drunk so much they had long ceased being able to taste it. How beautiful was the full moon even though it seemed to waver somewhat in and out of focus. It was inevitable that one of them proposed composing a poem together.

'My idea, so I'll start!'

This met with no resistance from his eager companions. The poet looked around for a suitable subject and noticed that a toad had appeared from a drainpipe. Inspiration struck: 'Tiny toady by his drainpipe is sitting ...'

Such brilliance was hard to follow. Fortunately for the awestruck second poet, the toad let out a large burp: 'Tiny toady by his drainpipe is burping ...'

Another hard line to follow, but the third poet was rescued by the toad blinking repeatedly: 'Tiny toady by his drainpipe is blinking ...'

What more was there to be said? The fourth poet felt his mouth grow dry with the solemnity of the task, when the toad retreated back into the drainpipe.

'Tiny toady to his drainpipe is returning.'

There it was, a perfect passion of poetry. The four friends recited their composition at the tops of their voices:

Tiny toady by his drainpipe is sitting
Tiny toady by his drainpipe is burping
Tiny toady by his drainpipe is blinking
Tiny toady to his drainpipe is returning!

Suddenly the first poet threw himself on the floor and clutched his head, weeping and groaning. When asked what the matter was, he explained that they had incurred the wrath of the gods by creating poetry so divine. The gods would waste no time in punishing them for their literary pride and they would be struck down by lightning at any moment. Howling with fear, the companions accordingly summoned the innkeeper and instructed her to send for four coffins.

Never had such drunkards sobered up so rapidly, and all because of their imminent demise by divine retribution. The innkeeper did not protest at her instructions but nevertheless asked the reason for their imminent demise. Impassively she listened to the divine poetry, recited by the four poets as if with one voice. Without further delay, she went off to arrange for the coffins. She soon returned with five, and her customers were by now sober enough to notice the extra one, which they were reluctant to pay for, so they asked why she had brought it.

'Such poetry as this will not only be the death of you, it will also be the death of me,' she replied.

MOHAMMED AND ANOTHER MOUNTAIN

KURDISTAN

The Prophet Mohammed, peace be upon him, had been God's faithful servant for years, following the holy teachings and spreading the holy message in his preaching. One day, while alone in the mountains, he prayed that Allah reveal himself to his humble servant. Mohammed said that he would be happy with just one glimpse of the Creator he had served so loyally. So mighty was the voice that came in response, that the prophet could not tell in the midst of his shaking whether the words were booming inside him or echoing around the mountains, but there was no mistaking their meaning.

Allah told him that so great was his power that even a glimpse would blind him. He commanded Mohammed to lie face down and cover his eyes. Then came an immeasurably powerful flash, which nearly blinded Mohammed even in that position. Before he dared open his eyes, he could smell burning. When he felt brave enough to sit up and look, he saw that the mountain had been burned black through and through.

Then the mountain started to complain to Allah: 'Why have you done this to me? Before this a clear stream ran down my side and plants grew near it. I was a haven for birds and beasts to find water, shelter and food in this wilderness. Now I am black and barren.'

Allah explained to the mountain that people would treasure the black rocks that had now transformed it. They would come from far and near to collect those rocks with their black dust and grind it into kohl, with which they would line their eyes. They would be grateful to the mountain for giving them a substance that improved their vision, and gave health and beauty to their eyes. All this came to pass, and, to this day, thanks to Allah the Merciful, people still collect the minerals from that mountain to make kohl.

HODJA AND THE SPARROW

TURKEY

Everybody loves a fool who is wise and everybody loves a wise man who is a fool. Hodja was both of these, and his sermons attracted crowds wherever he went. But there are always those who are jealous of success, no matter how well deserved. One of these bitter souls was determined to prove Hodja wrong in public. He trapped a sparrow, and held it in his cupped hands until it was time for questions at the end of his talk. He couldn't put his hand up because the bird would have escaped, but even among all those people, Hodja noticed that he had something to ask and gestured for him to speak.

'Oh! wise Hodja, can you tell me whether the bird hidden in my hands is dead or alive?'

The jealous cynic knew that if Hodja said that the bird was alive, he could crush it to death in a moment and show everyone the corpse. He also knew that if Hodja said that it was dead, he could release it and everybody would see it flying away. Hodja's reply filled the expectant hush: 'Well, my friend, doesn't that rather depend on you?'

THE POWERFUL PRAWN

On the bank of the great Irrawaddy River stood a man sharpening his hunting weapons. As his feet churned the mud, he disturbed a prawn. Annoyed at this great clumsy two-legged creature, the prawn stabbed him with one of his feelers. The sharpness and suddenness of the pain were intolerable and the man lashed out at the nearest thing, which happened to be a breadfruit tree. As he was holding an axe at the time, it caused a gash in the tree's trunk.

The outraged tree dropped one of its huge breadfruit on the man to teach him a lesson, but its fall was intercepted by a branch and deflected. The fruit fell on a passing cockerel instead, all but crushing him. Not strong enough to get his own back on the tree, the cockerel turned to the next best thing, which was the ants' nest that was aerating the tree's roots. He scratched it up, sarcastically telling the ants to repair the damage, as they liked nothing better than to work anyway.

The long-suffering ants were used to the envy of others who were all lazier than they were, but they were also angry that their nest had been exposed. To make it worse, just then, a snake came slithering along and they well knew how snakes like to take over ants' nests if they can find a way in. Fired up with indignation at their treatment from the cockerel, they swarmed all over the snake, biting it mercilessly.

For the snake, who had spent a life of being shunned or driven off, this was the last straw, so she lunged at a passing boar, narrowly missing giving him a bite above his rear trotter. The boar demanded to know why she had done that; she was in no danger of being stepped on and he was far too large to swallow. In reply the snake hissed that she was not obliged to give a reason and perhaps the boar should use his imagination to come up with an answer.

Badly frightened by his narrow brush with a poisonous death, and humiliated that the snake had called out a weakness that his wife frequently remarked upon, Boar took out his discomfiture on a nearby plantain tree, by uprooting it.

It so happened that a bat roosted in that tree and was furious at having her abode flattened. She fluttered off in the unaccustomed daylight, looking for somewhere else to make her home. There, looming large and dark, appeared a cave. The bat blundered in but was dismayed to discover that the cave kept lurching about. This is because she had mistaken an elephant's ear for a cave. Sleep deprived and furious, the bat bit the elephant on the inside of his ear.

The elephant trumpeted with pain and charged down the slope towards one of the forest dwellings. On the way he passed near a mortar, on which he took out his anger by giving it a mighty kick. That mortar, made from a single slab of stone and used to pound enough rice for an entire village, could only have been moved by four adults but with one blow it was sent rolling down the slope. Gathering speed, it arrived at the bottom, demolishing a house on the way.

Out of its ruins rushed a tiny old lady whose powers of persuasion were matched only by her fierceness. She demanded that the mortar give her the money to rebuild her house.

The mortar refused to pay, saying that the elephant had been responsible for the incident. Furthermore, it was considering suing the woman for the scratches that her house had inflicted on its smooth surfaces. The old woman rushed up the hill and confronted the elephant, who was still looking for the bat so that he could trample her. Having been directed to the bat with her complaint, the woman was told that, far from being accused, the bat should be pitied and all the creatures of the forest should be rallying around offering her help. The old woman continued her journey from bat to plantain tree, to boar, to snake, to ants, to cockerel, to the breadfruit tree, listening to the tirade of complaints and blame as she went. There on the trunk she recognised the slash mark of her son's axe. Hadn't she forged that blade for it herself? Her son would start to rebuild her house immediately. After all, she had taught him all the skills he knew, and when had he dared to disobey his mother? He could start by replanting that plantain tree before it perished.

She trotted along the river bank searching for him, followed by all the animals, and even the mortar, that had been involved in the fracas. There he was nursing his pierced heel when she demanded to know why he had caused such disruption in the forest. Hanging his head, he murmured that he had been wounded. When she demanded to know by what, he hung his head even lower and was barely able to whisper that it had been by a prawn. His mother made the most of his embarrassment by shouting out to the entire forest that her brave son, the hunter, had been brought low by a prawn!

When all the other animals and even the mortar had finished laughing, it was decided that the prawn should be brought to justice. Elephant drained the puddle where it was hiding, and boar suggested it should be punished with death by drowning. The question was whether it would prefer drowning in cold or hot water, the snake hissed sarcastically. The prawn chose to be drowned with cold water, the elephant blew it into the river and everyone was satisfied.

However, some do not agree that this was the end of the story, and say that a toad, who had appeared to see what all the excitement was about, had suggested that the prawn should be made into soup. He volunteered to watch the pot boiling while everyone else attended to the repairs that were so urgently needed around the forest. As soon as they were all busy elsewhere, the toad ate the prawn. Later, when all returned to eat the soup, they agreed that it didn't taste of prawn at all, and the toad was forced to admit that it was he who had eaten it. In their anger at the toad, in whom they had placed their trust, everyone pinched or pecked him and even the mortar rolled on his feet. That is why from that day to this day, Toad is covered in bumps and blemishes, and that is why his feet are flat.

THE GOOD WISH

Every day Ali went to the bazaar to buy the handful of rice with which to feed himself, his wife and his old mother. That day he was feeling particularly sorry for himself as he saw all the delicious foods, ornaments, furniture, carpets and clothes that he would never be able to afford. Suddenly he heard a voice in his ear, 'Ali! It's your lucky day! Make a wish, anything you like, it will come true!'

At first Ali thought he had a mosquito in his ear, but the voice returned, assuring him that it wasn't a mosquito. Next Ali thought that he was going mad, but the voice reassured him that he wasn't. Then Ali started to panic in case the voice was real, because he didn't know what to wish for. All he could remember were those stories his grandmother had told him in which people in his position had made foolish wishes and had to live with the consequences. At last he asked the little voice whether, if it wouldn't be using up his wish, he could have more time to think about it? The voice agreed and told him to come back to the bazaar the next day.

As it was late, Ali returned home to his angry wife, who had been waiting all day for the rice he had forgotten to buy. He tried to mollify her by telling her about his extraordinary experience, and at that his old mother spoke up.

'Ali, isn't it obvious what you should wish for? I am going blind, surely you should wish for my sight to be restored so that I can end my days with independence and dignity.'

Ali thought that would be an excellent wish until his wife said, 'Ali, don't listen to her. Your mother has had her life, but what about us? We have been married for twelve years and still have not been blessed with a child. You should wish for us to have a baby.'

Ali thought that too was an excellent wish until it occurred to him that they were too poor to support a child.

'My dear, what would be the point of bringing another life into this world when we can't even feed ourselves properly? Why wish for another mouth to feed only to watch it starve?'

All night long, the family argued. What was the point of wealth when it couldn't buy you health, couldn't buy you a child? What was the point of health if you were pining for a baby?

And so it went on. When Ali returned to the bazaar he still had no idea what to wish for. Then he heard the little voice again: 'Ali! It's still your lucky day! Make a wish. Anything you like, it will come true. What's your wish?'

From that day to this, Ali doesn't know how it was that his mouth opened and he heard his voice saying, 'I wish that when I go home, I will see my mother watching my wife rocking our baby in a golden cradle.'

And that is exactly what happened, and why shouldn't it?

DON'T COMPLAIN ABOUT THE RAIN

Gecko was resenting the Fireflies because they were dazzling and distracting him when he was trying to catch Mosquitos, so he complained to Tiger, the chief of the beasts. Being the chief, Tiger thought he should do something about it and went to the Fireflies to tell them that they were causing a nuisance. The Fireflies explained that they were only passing on a warning that had been hammered out by Woodpecker, so that it would reach all the animals whether by sound or sight. Tiger asked what the warning was about and the Fireflies told him that the path was dangerously slippery.

Tiger went to see the path for himself and could see that parts of it were covered in dung. Only one animal could be responsible for such huge piles, and that was Buffalo. Tiger remonstrated with Buffalo and was told that Dung Beetle had asked her to defecate on the path because the large holes needed filling in, as they were also a hazard. It took some close looking to find Dung Beetle, who was rolling the dung so smoothly that the path had become slippery with his manoeuvres. On being approached, Dung Beetle explained that it was Rain that made all the holes on the path, and he was only trying to make repairs.

Looking up, Tiger could see a large raincloud hovering above a nearby hill, which Tiger climbed to get as close to it as possible. From his vantage point, he roared at Rain about all the damage it was causing. Rain's response was to let down a gentle shower in which Tiger heard the whispered words, 'Look all around you. Look how I make everything green and fertile. Without me you would not eat, without me there would be no shelter.'

Tiger returned to Gecko and told him of his journey.

'Just think, Gecko, if it weren't for Rain, you would have no puddles for the Mosquitos to breed in, and what would you do then?'

Since then, Gecko never complains about the rain, but you can hear him calling out a greeting just before Rain starts to fall.

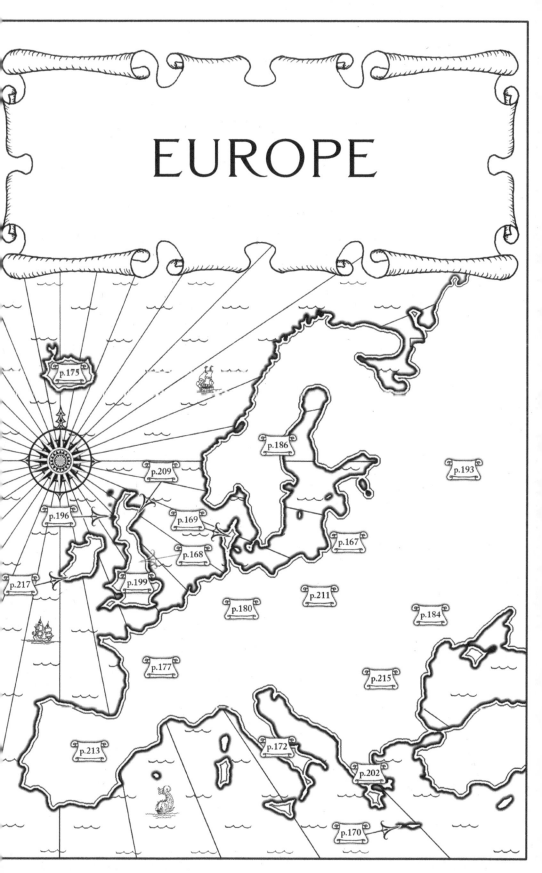

EUROPE

p.175

p.186

p.193

p.209

p.196

p.169

p.167

p.168

p.217

p.199

p.180

p.211

p.184

p.177

p.215

p.213

p.172

p.202

p.170

One day, a close friend of Albert Einstein's asked which books her son should read in order to become a brilliant scientist. To her surprise, Einstein replied, 'fairy tales and more fairy tales!' The mother remonstrated that this was a serious question, whereupon the affable Einstein insisted that, as far as he was concerned, a creative imagination was the most essential component of a scientific intellect. From the earliest years, fairy tales were therefore the best way to stimulate this characteristic.

Folklore around Albert Einstein, German theoretical physicist, and his love of folk tales.

SUN AND MOON GIVE BIRTH TO EARTH

It may surprise European readers that in this tale, Sun is female and Moon is male. This was often the case until Greek Classical mythology, later Latinised and spread by the Romans, brought their different and widely shared gender perspective based on their own celestial pantheon.

Two wonderous beings, Sun and Moon, lived in the sky. As they had no equal in power and beauty, all the other celestial beings waited for them to fall in love. Eventually this happened, and their union was blessed with an exquisite daughter, Earth. At first all went well with this celestial family, but then Sun and Moon began to compete for the love of their daughter. Their own relationship gave way to jealousy and anger, and there was no peace in the heavens. Even though Sun and Moon now lived in separate parts of the sky, they continued to argue about which one of them should care for Earth.

The other celestial beings knew that this state of affairs could not continue and that the matter had to be decided once and for all. They suggested that Sun and Moon run a race through the heavens, and whoever won would take care of Earth. There was great excitement when this was agreed to, and the course was set across the breadth of the sky according to the positions of the many stars eager to help.

Sun decided to cheat by asking her friend, Wind, to blow behind her to give her extra speed. Moon, ever distrustful, suspected that this would happen and had his own plan to counteract any cheating. He asked his friend, Clouds, to be at the ready. All the heavenly bodies were there for the race, cheering on the contestants as they raced along the plotted course from star to star. Soon Moon noticed Sun drawing ahead as Wind blew behind her and called for his friends to help. Clouds began to cover some of the stars that were part of the course. This confused Sun, and being uncertain about which way to go, she ran a longer route. Losing the advantage of speed that Wind had given her, she and Moon arrived at the finish together.

It was therefore decided that Sun and Moon should share Earth's care equally. That is why, from that time to this time, Sun and Moon are only equally present together when they hand over Earth's care one to the other. We call these occasions the equinoxes. When Sun cares more for Earth, we call this summer. When Moon cares more for Earth, we call this winter. Some say that when this first happened, it was the birth of Time itself.

HARE HERE ON EARTH

ROMA (GYPSY)

Reproduced with kind permission of The History Press from Animal Folk Tales of Britain and Ireland *by Sharon Jacksties.*

Long ago, when Time was new, all things were alive and all creatures spoke to each other. Sun and Moon, those most glorious of beings, showed their celestial love by creating a daughter. Hare leaped and bounded across the heavens, zigzagging her way between one parent and the other. Every time one of her paws touched the sky, a star appeared. Time smiled to see how her increase was measured across the sky in countless silver tracks.

Sun and Moon smiled to see how strong and fast their daughter had become, how tireless and nimble. Hare had reached her full strength. One day – or was it night? – she looked down and noticed Earth for the first time. Earth felt her gaze and looked upwards at the delicate paths of silver that followed this magical creature as she danced about. The moment when Earth noticed Hare was the moment they fell in love.

Hare bounded off to tell her parents the wonderful news that she had found a lover, and one, moreover, who requited her feelings. Sun and Moon asked who she was considering uniting herself with, and Hare proudly told them that it was Earth. Her parents were appalled. How could their celestial daughter decide to have anything to do with a creature so base, so dense, who was incapable of producing any light? They told her that they would never have anything to do with her choice, and that if she persisted they would not bless this shameful liaison.

But Hare was in love and hurt that her parents' love for her did not exceed their misplaced pride. She decided to leave the sky forever and live with her lover. From that day – or was it night? – to this, she has stayed on Earth. She became the totem animal of love and fertility, and was venerated as the Goddess Oestra. She gave her name to our spring festival of

Easter, and the female hormone oestrogen. During the spring equinox her children dance upright to give Sun and Moon an equal chance to see their grandchildren.

SUN BOAT, SUN CHARIOT

SCANDINAVIA AND DENMARK

Throughout Scandinavia and Denmark, archaeological remains show depictions of this story picked out in stone or engraved into metal. A widespread myth in 'Nordic' culture, its images are often to be found engraved on metal razors. Apart from the practical aspect of these artefacts presenting a flat surface on which to engrave, metal was a precious commodity in ancient cultures, and the implement's purpose is connected to the theme of death and rebirth as cut body hair continually renews itself. This narrative imagery is echoed in funerary rituals that infer a belief in rebirth, one that is so minutely explored in a form of story that developed later: the genre of pantheonic myth.

When the sun has disappeared into the sea, we call it night time. It slips into a boat that awaits it on the horizon in the west. Then the mighty ocean serpent seizes the boat and overturns it, dragging the sun down into the depths. Rolling it in its coils beneath the waves, the serpent swims through the watery Underworld towards the east. At the end of its journey there is a fish already waiting. The fish takes the sun from the serpent and rolls it onto its back and into a boat. It nudges the craft along to where a horse-drawn chariot hovers at the edge of the horizon. With a mighty leap, the fish rises from the sea, tipping the boat so that the sun rolls from the vessel into the chariot. Before the fish can land back in the water, a bird has swooped low out of the sky and seized it. We call the sun's first flash of light on the gull's wing the dawn. But the sun is now in its chariot and being drawn up into the sky by the horse. Their journey gives us the morning. Ever higher the sun chariot rises until it can go no further. Then the horse kicks free of its traces, the chariot is overturned, and the sun begins to fall back towards the ocean. We call this the afternoon. Sometimes the sun is wounded as it is jostled from the chariot. We see this in its deepening colours, bruised or bleeding, before it falls towards the sea. There, in the west, it again slips into the boat, which will be caught in the jaws of the great serpent so the journey can start anew.

When people die, their body is placed on a boat and all is set alight. Blazing like the sun, the boat is pushed out onto the water, where it will sink into the watery Underworld. Perhaps serpent, fish, bird and horse will repeat the same journey with the soul of the dead. Perhaps, in this way, something of the dead returns to the living.

DIVINE RETRIBUTION
OR NATURAL FORCES?

CRETE

This Ancient Greek myth refers to a pantheon of divinities reacting to and influencing the deeds of mortals – particularly after acts of 'hubris' where human arrogance offends divine power or judgement. The mediator between the divine and human world is, as is so often the case, an epic hero. In this instance it is the Athenian prince Theseus, whose back story affords him two fathers, one mortal and one divine. Furthermore, this story incorporates legendary elements as a reaction to actual historical events. The first of these is the catastrophic earthquake and volcanic eruption that destroyed Cretan civilisation, causing a massive crater that destroyed neighbouring islands, and even changed the climate temporarily (as in human rather than geological time). That cataclysm, in turn, is one of the origins of the Atlantis myth. Just as layers of lava flow and volcanic ash can still be seen on Crete today, so can layers of interpretation provide deeper understandings of how historical facts and religious beliefs have become overlaid within this mythic structure. An example includes the destruction of the ancient Minoan culture by the Greeks, as represented here by the Athenian hero. Another is the bringing low of former all-powerful deities, the Titans, by the more recent classical Greek pantheon that holds sway within this story. Yet another is the archaeological evidence of human sacrifice being practised on Crete, particularly during the period leading up to the volcanic explosion. I often use the labyrinth that is constructed within this narrative as a visual metaphor for mythic story structures, with their twists and turns and difficulties in finding entrances and exits. Here I have found my way in, but readers unfamiliar with this story may have to find their way out by summoning its hero from other writings.

Pasiphae, queen of Crete, was used to getting what she wanted. Daughter of the ancient Titan Sun God and of a Titan sea nymph, she was also a powerful sorceress, and if magic couldn't provide what she wanted, ingenuity could. Her husband, Minos, was the most powerful king in the region, his Minoan navigators and vessels the most redoubtable in the whole of the Mediterranean sea. The envy of other peoples and city states, had not the Minoans been the first to introduce writing to the region, and that in service to their trading empire? Time then to make another sacrifice to Poseidon, God of the Sea, without which watery realm such wealth and power would never have been possible.

For the sacrifice, Minos acquired the most magnificent pure white bull, an animal worthy of the most powerful divinity in his seafaring world. How his skin gleamed like sea foam, how his horns sickled like the new moon dipping into the watery horizon, how his bellowing sounded like the breakers in a storm. There was just one difficulty, which was that Minos decided to keep the bull for himself. However, no mortal can deceive the gods – Poseidon was incensed at this display of hubris and visited a punishment on Minos, but worked it through his wife. Pasiphae was suddenly stricken with lust for the beast, and there was only one way in which to relieve her torment. Her sorcery could work on humans but was not effective on animals – ingenuity would have to succeed where magic failed.

In service to Minos was the most skilled of inventors. Daedalus had already been credited with inventing such vital tools as drawing compasses and even the masts that graced the king's merchant fleet. Pasiphae ordered him to build a structure resembling a cow into which she could insert herself and hide. When the bull mounted the cow, by this means her own lust would be satisfied. All went according to plan, especially Poseidon's. This unnatural act resulted in her conceiving a monstrous child with the body of a human and the head of a bull. This abominable creature was named the Minotaur, meaning Minos's Bull, a further reminder of his royal father's transgression. Such a monster could not be tolerated in the royal court where he reminded everyone of his parents' shame, moreover he lived on raw human flesh and was too dangerous and uncontrollable to be near people.

Daedalus was again commissioned, and this time it was to construct a prison for this monstrous prince. Feeding him was another difficulty, which was solved by the penalty exacted from the king of Athens for the killing of Minos's only legitimate son. This was to provide live young nobles for the Minotaur to devour. So Daedalus created a labyrinthine prison beneath the royal palace. Into this were released the captive Athenian youths, who were never able to find their way out before they fell victim to the monster's ravening appetite. Hidden he may have been, but his furious bellowing could be heard beneath the palace floors. The ground trembled and masonry and columns tumbled. As the monster's rages increased in strength, so did the tremors. A catastrophe was building. When Theseus, who had been sent with the quota of other Athenian youths, succeeded in destroying the Minotaur, this heroic act was also the harbinger of the end of the Minoan civilisation. Just as the young Athenian set light to the Minoan fleet to prevent vengeful pursuit, so do fires rampage unchecked during earthquakes.

DIDO AND AENEAS

ANCIENT ROME

Although the main body of this story takes place far from Rome, without a single Roman character, it was extremely popular with the Romans, who claimed it as their national epic. The Romans were trying to distance themselves from their cultural predecessors, the Greeks, establishing themselves as a distinct culture and power for which a separate mythological legacy was needed. This tale, part pantheonic myth, part epic and part legend, served their purposes in providing antecedents distinct from Greek ancestry. I was lucky enough to meet one of the people present at the discovery of one of Britain's most important Roman archaeological remains – that of the Dido and Aeneas mosaic. This was found at Low Ham in Somerset in 1938. During a local storytelling project, I became acquainted with someone who lived on the farm where this Roman bathhouse floor was found, during the farmer's attempt to bury a dead sheep. It was particularly satisfying to hear her family story, told as oral history, contributing as it does to the different story genres represented in this book. Almost perfectly preserved, the subject of the artwork must have been a significant choice for the villa's original occupants, representing as it did the origins of an empire to those who were living at its furthest and most recent reach.

Cesser d'aimer ou d'eter aimable, c'est un mort insupportable.
Cesser de vivre ce n'est rien.

Ceasing to love or to be loveable is an unbearable death.
Ceasing to live is nothing.

Voltaire

Troy had fallen to the Greeks. The Trojan warrior hero Aeneas had seen in a vision the ghost of his slain commander, who had ordered him to flee. Nevertheless, he rushed back into the burning city to rescue his wife, not knowing that she was already dead. Her ghost also appeared to him, and told him to escape in order to fulfil the destiny ordained by his divine mother, which was to found a city in the west.

As it was on Earth, so it was on Mount Olympus, seat of the divine pantheon. There the gods and goddesses feuded, took sides, battled out their disputes and more often than not used people as human puppets to get their divine way. The Trojans and the Greeks, superpowers of their day, had fallen victim to the animosity of two of the most powerful goddesses. Juno, known for her jealous nature, had never forgiven Venus, goddess of love, for having been judged the most beautiful among the goddesses. The mortal judge of the beauty contest had been a Trojan and thus incurring Juno's animosity, had sealed the fate of all Trojans as far as she was concerned. Venus, however, delighted at this accolade, sought to protect Troy, and indeed, one of her sons, Aeneas, was the now defeated Trojan hero.

It was this pride and power jostling among the gods and goddesses that saved Aeneas's life. As he fled from his burning city by boat, Juno conjured up a storm to sink it. However, this annoyed Neptune, god of the ocean, who, feeling that she had trespassed into his domain, calmed the sea to teach her a lesson, allowing Aeneas to be washed safely ashore. Now a refugee on the coast of North Africa, he was welcomed as a guest by a queen who had also been a refugee, victim of a dynastic coup. Queen Dido had not only survived her flight, but through her own ingenuity had succeeded in founding the mighty city of Carthage. The ancient laws of hospitality, the empathy that Queen Dido would have felt for another noble who had lost everything, were honed and manipulated by the other goddess in the picture. Venus ensured that Dido and Aeneas fell in love, thus prolonging her son's protection in a strange land.

Dido and Aeneas's passion was so idyllic that any observer might have believed that they were the first to invent love itself. Furthermore, Aeneas had given Dido his sword, to pledge that he was now a hero of love not war. However, after a while, Aeneas began to be haunted by dreams in which he was visited by the spirits of his old commander and his wife. Both were reminding him that the reason his life had been spared at the fall of Troy was so that he could fulfil a higher destiny – that of founding a new city. These dreams became more troubling when his mother Venus appeared with the same message. Aeneas decided that the will of a goddess took precedence over his commitment to a mere mortal.

None of this explanation could appease Dido. Despite being the founder and ruler of a great city herself, she was now ruled by her heart. When Aeneas's departing ship touched the horizon, she ordered a funeral pyre to be built beneath her palace walls. As the flames grew higher, she cursed her departing lover, prophesying that there would be a great war between his people and hers, a curse that Juno would have delighted in hearing. Dido then stabbed herself with Aeneas's sword and plummeted, already mortally wounded, to be consumed by the flames.

Aeneas journeyed westward according to his mother's divine will, reaching a land that we now call Italy. There he founded a dynasty that was to include his great-great grandsons, the twins Romulus and Remus, who were conceived by another act of divine intervention, their father being Mars, god of war.

Many readers will know that it was Romulus who built Rome, named after its founder, and one of the greatest cities in antiquity. With the god of war in Romulus's pedigree, small wonder that the Roman empire became one of the most extensive and powerful of the ancient world. Dido's prophecy too came to pass, with the Punic Wars that lasted for almost forty years before Carthage was crushed by the Romans, thus enabling them to extend their empire to the furthest reaches of the Eastern Mediterranean.

GUDRUN'S DREAMS

This is an excerpt from an episode in an Icelandic saga, the term for this form of story being used beyond its country of origin to describe narratives with convoluted and lengthy plots. The Icelandic sagas were often based on family feuds that drove the action over generations with protagonists who would have been familiar as historical or ancestral characters for their early listeners. Gudrun's story is so well known because she was an exceptional woman for her time, who did much for women's education. Perhaps her legacy contributed to the fact that in the nineteenth century, Iceland had the highest literacy rate in Europe, including among women. This was due to the practice of spending long winter nights with each family member taking it in turns to read the Bible, and, of course, the participant's culture and climate had also cradled this ability to listen to a story for many hours.

Gudrun knew that she was poised upon the threshold of her future. She had known this even before her father told her that she was to be married to a man in whom she had no interest – a man who was beneath her. Just now she was lying in her bed, musing about a sequence of portentous dreams. Although they were so clear, so memorable, so imbued with significance, she was unable to extract their meaning. That day she had been ordered to intercept a kinsman's journey with a message from her father. A distant cousin and a chieftain, her kinsman also had the gift of second sight.

Gudrun and Gest Oddleifson did not have the opportunity to speak often, but on these rare occasions they enjoyed each other's company – he entertained by her precocious intelligence and she appreciative that he spoke to her as an equal, despite her youth and sex. Delivering her father's message was also an opportunity to ask Gest to interpret her dreams, which he invited her to describe when she had broached the subject.

During the first dream she was standing by a fast-flowing stream, wearing a close-fitting cap that would not fit properly. She kept tugging at it and was about to drag it off when others present told her not to remove it. Nevertheless, she tore it off her head, flung it into the water and watched it wash away for ever.

During the second dream, she noticed that she was wearing a silver arm band that encircled her arm perfectly. However, it somehow slipped off into the water and disappeared without a trace, at which she felt an overwhelming and unaccountable sense of loss.

During the third dream, she noticed that she was wearing a gold ring and thought that this should more than recompense her for the silver armband, gold being more valuable. But somehow, she could not value it as highly, and at this thought she stumbled and put out that hand to save herself. In doing so, she knocked the ring against a rock and broke it in two. As she examined the pieces, there was blood on them and the metal seemed seeded with flaws. Nevertheless, she reproached herself for not taking better care of it.

During the fourth dream, she found herself to be wearing a helm of gold in which precious jewels were set. It was so heavy that she was unable to hold her head straight, but despite this awkwardness she didn't want to remove it. Nevertheless, of its own accord, it fell from her and into the sea.

Gest's grave expression deepened as he listened. At last, he told his kinswoman that all these dreams referred to the four husbands she would have. The first would make her feel constrained. She would want to be rid of him, and would find a way to divorce him and be free from him forever. The second would be higher born, hence the precious metal, but although happy with him she would lose him in an untimely way as he would die by drowning. The third husband would not be as valued by her as the previous one, and despite converting to the new religion, he would be slain in a dispute for which she was not responsible. The fourth husband would be the noblest of them all in every way. Whereas up until then she would have been the one to take a lead in her marriages, on this occasion she would be led by him. However, he would be lost at sea.

Such was Gest's clarity of vision that his interpretations came to pass. Perhaps Gudrun, as she told her kinsman how hard all this was for her to hear, also noted that she started off in the humblest of headgear, a coif such as the meanest slave would wear, but ended up, however briefly, with one of gold and jewels.

WHO IS BLAMELESS?

There are so many stories about the epic and legendary hero King Arthur that storytellers often refer to these as the 'Arthurian Cycle'. They are found in all the countries of the United Kingdom and in France and Germany. I am indebted to John Matthews, author, lecturer and storyteller, not only for the breadth and depth of his scholarship, but for his very encouraging comments as a visiting tutor, about my work with Arthurian material. Many readers will know that one of the medieval Arthurian themes was that of chivalry and the high moral standard that it demanded. Here is a lesser-known story in the cycle, perhaps so, because it satirises these courtly ideals.

It was always King Arthur's custom, wherever the court was assembled, to insist on seeing or hearing of a wonder before the evening banquet was served. Many a course had gone cold or been burned, many a cook had grumbled at this tradition, and tonight was to be no exception. The Knights of the Round Table and the other knights of the court had not yet taken their seats as all were still waiting for their ladies to join them. Into this throng came a stranger who knelt before King Arthur and asked for a boon,* which was readily granted.

All the ladies of the court were to be invited to try on a magical cloak, one that would only fit a lady who had never deceived her husband or lover. Whoever the cloak fitted would keep it as a gift. To a man, all thought that this would be easily accomplished as none there could think ill of their own lady. However, they didn't wonder how so many women could be given the same cloak, or did they believe that only theirs was beyond reproach?

A message was sent requesting the ladies to make all haste with their toilette, which they duly ignored as was their custom. At last, all were assembled, and the stranger produced a purse of crimson silk. How could a cloak fit into such a small receptacle? The marvel had already begun. He drew it out, and as he shook out its filmy folds, ethereal music filled the room, ceasing only when the delicate fabric ceased to stir. As the courtiers stared at the cloth, each saw a different scene embroidered by hands defter than those of any human: as if in a dream, some saw hunting scenes,

---

* A favour or gift that if granted must be given no matter how difficult.

some saw peaceful lakes, some orchards full of blossom, some snow-capped mountains and others, distant, turreted castles.

As first among the ladies, King Arthur invited his wife, Queen Guinevere, to try the cloak, and she accepted eagerly. However, she was mystified when she couldn't seem to make it fit. First it was too short on one side and when she adjusted it, too short on the other. She was so busy trying to make it hang correctly that, at first, she didn't notice how the atmosphere had changed. Rather than being celebratory, it felt tense. King Arthur hastily beckoned the stranger to give it to another lady to try. But, turn and turn about, it didn't fit any of them. Too short, too long, lopsided, the magical cloak showed that each and every lady had been unfaithful to husband or lover.

The stranger tried to alleviate the now sombre mood by telling King Arthur that the result had been the same in all of the other courts he had visited, but this did nothing to mollify the king. He ordered a search of the castle to make sure that all the gentlewomen had been present, and he was right to do so. One lady had not joined them because she was unwell: Guinier, Sir Caradoc's wife, who now hurried to the great hall at her king's command. Her husband called out to her not to try on the cloak as he wanted to spare her the risk of being humiliated. She replied that she would happily try it as long as Caradoc's love for her was strong enough to triumph over anything that the cloak might reveal. At that Sir Caradoc raised his right arm, which was twisted like a snake, and declared, 'By this twisted arm of mine, I take this oath and swear before all of you who know the tangled tale of how my arm came to be so shaped, that however this cloak falls on the Lady Guinier, whether foul or fair, to me she shall be blameless!'

The whispers then flew around the court, as each knight and lady made sure that their neighbour knew the twisted story to which Caradoc referred. Did they know that a magician had fallen in love with Caradoc's mother and had disguised himself into the semblance of her husband on their wedding night? If so, who did Caradoc's father believe he was spending his wedding night with? Well, hadn't the wicked magician enchanted a pig, a greyhound and a horse to resemble the bride! So nobody knew that Caradoc was really the sorcerer's son, conceived under a magical deception. In that case how did anyone find out? When Caradoc was a young knight, a stranger had appeared at the court with a game called Behead Thy Neighbour. Whoever struck off the stranger's head would have to be the victim a year and a day hence, so no risk to the player! Young and impulsive, Caradoc seized his sword and with one blow sliced off the gamester's head. Much was everyone's consternation when the stranger picked up his severed head, replaced it, and rode away saying that he would be back for the return match in a year and a day! True to his word, back he came. Caradoc had to lay his head on a table to be decapitated. The stranger's axe fell but chopped into the wood instead of his neck. Then the stranger revealed that he couldn't kill Caradoc because he was the lad's natural father. The gamester was also the magician!

At this point King Arthur clapped his hands and declared that they had both seen and heard marvels enough, and ordered that the banquet be served. By this time, some of it was cold, some of it was burnt and the cook was furious. Whatever the state of the food, little of it was eaten due to the disconsolate mood of the company and due to many wanting to continue Caradoc's story without spitting at their neighbours with their mouths full.

The tale, with its many twists and turns, continued in this vein: Caradoc wanted to kill the magician but refrained because he was his natural father. He also confronted his parents with the truth. His mother's husband punished the magician by forcing him to have sex with a pig, a greyhound and a horse. Caradoc punished his mother by confining her in a tower, even though she had no idea that she had slept with anyone other than her husband. This punishment, however, recoiled onto Caradoc as the magician could make himself invisible and gained entry to the tower whenever he felt like it. In her prison, Caradoc's mother agreed to indulge in what she had been wrongfully punished for. Caradoc had discovered this because enchanted music had been heard to come from the tower, and he had gone to investigate. Deciding to punish her son for the injustice of her incarceration, his mother persuaded her magician lover to hide an enchanted snake in a cupboard. When she asked Caradoc to fetch her comb from inside it, the snake fastened itself on his arm and dripped poison into it …

Just before the story of how Carantoc got rid of the snake could fly around the room, there was a sudden mighty bang as King Arthur thumped the table.

'Enough!' He cried. 'Let the Lady Guinier try the cloak.'

Again, that cascade of enchanted music as the cloak slipped out of the crimson purse. But nothing could be as sweet as the sigh of relief that swept the room when all could see how perfectly the cloak fitted. Of all the ladies that night who were skilled with a needle, none thought it would be worth their while to make a garment that would test the fidelity of their menfolk – for why ask what you already know?

THE ILL-FATED PRINCESS

FROM THE *NIBELUNGENLIED* EPIC
(SONG OF THE NIBELUNGS), GERMANY

By the mighty river Rhine rose the castles of the Burgundian royal house. Its three princes had but one sister. On the threshold of womanhood, Kriemhild was disturbed by a dream. She told her mother that in it she had seen a falcon torn apart by two eagles. Her mother, who had the second sight, prophesied that Kriemhild's husband, represented by the falcon, would be murdered by two men who were close to him in rank, all the characters in her dream being birds of prey. On hearing this, the princess vowed that she would never marry. But what destiny awaited princesses? They were valuable commodities to be bargained with to seal alliances, and had no say in whether or whom they would marry.

Kriemhild's brother, Gunther, was in love with a famous and untameable princess who vowed she would only marry one who could beat her in armed combat. Either this unique warrior queen was too powerful to be gainsaid, or her relatives did not oppose her scheme as an even more powerful husband would provide an invaluable alliance. However, it was another prince, Siegfried, who was in love with Kriemhild, who enabled this conquest to happen. Disguised as Gunther, but using his own enchanted sword along with other magical powers, Siegfried won the bride for the prince he hoped would become his brother-in-law.

However, not even this successful feat was enough for Gunther to consent to Siegfried marrying his sister. His wedding night with the warrior princess had been a fiasco: realising that he was not the man she thought he was, the warrior bride had trussed him up with the marital bedsheets, and he had spent the night hanging upside down from the rafters! It was our hero Siegfried who yet again had to come to the rescue: wearing his magical cloak of invisibility, he fought the warrior bride on the second night of her honeymoon, and at last she was beaten again by Siegfried, but because her assailant remained invisible, she yet again believed him to be her husband.

Siegfried took her girdle and ring, in which much of her strength lay. When at last he was allowed to marry Kriemhild, he gave these to her with no explanation of how he had got them. Perhaps if he had mentioned how he had won them, they would not have helped to seal her fate. Certainly, her brother Gunther had wondered whether Siegfried had taken his wife's virginity when he had conquered her. Perhaps he had, or perhaps Gunther suspected it because that was what he would have done if their roles had been reversed. Perhaps, also, Gunther finally allowed Siegfried to marry Kriemhild, because he hoped, one day, to lay hands on the legendary treasure hoard that Siegfried had taken from the dragon he had slain.

At last the two couples were to meet, with neither of the women knowing the full story about the other. Kriemhild's sister-in-law didn't know Prince Siegfried's full identity and therefore believed herself to be above rather than equal in rank to Kriemhild. This caused an awkward altercation about precedence, during which the insulted Kriemhild showed her the girdle and ring that she had been given and accused her sister-in-law of being Siegfried's mistress. Now that there was a rift between the two couples, there was someone ready to exploit it. Hagen, one of Gunther's mightiest warriors, who was also thought to be his half-brother, determined to turn the situation to his advantage in order to get rid of his perceived rival, Siegfried.

Hagen began a campaign of poisonous deceit, in which he managed to persuade Kriemhild's brother to become compliant. He started false rumours of an impending war, knowing that Siegfried would help his friend with the fighting. Under the pretext of protecting him, he was told by the unsuspecting Kriemhild about the only vulnerable place on her husband's body. It was only there, on a small spot on his shoulder, that a weapon could harm him. Not long after, as Siegfried knelt to drink from a stream, Hagen's spear ended his life. He might have got away with that cowardly assassination had not Kriemhild noticed that Siegfried's wound started to bleed again in Hagen's presence. This was known to happen when the corpse was in the presence of its murderer. As she saw fresh blood seeping from her husband's wound, Kriemhild remembered her mother's prophecy – her husband's death had been brought about by two of her brothers.

Before the wound had ceased to bleed, she was planning her revenge.

Returning to her own court, she lost no time in preparations, and the first thing to do was to amass her own army. It was the Nibelung treasure that enabled her to do this, as she could pay soldiers to be in her service. However, it would not have been possible to do so in secret and Hagen soon got to hear of it. Up to his devious ways again, he managed to steal the treasure, which he sank into the Rhine. Whether he meant to retrieve it one day or whether he just wanted to prevent Kriemhild from having it, it was gone, perhaps forever.

But the mighty river Rhine bears more than mere mortals in their flimsy boats. Beneath its waters, in its caves and whirlpools, live creatures not subject to the human race. The Nixies, those fearsome elemental water spirits who have the power to wreck ships and drag people to their deaths, thought that the treasure had been a gift to them and so, in gratitude, when the time came, they tried to warn Hagen of the danger he was in.

Meanwhile, the theft of Kriemhild's treasure further fuelled the slow-burning fires of revenge. With nothing left to lose, and perhaps it would serve her purpose, she agreed to marry a warlord in the east, King Etzel who, in Britain, was to become known as Attila the Hun.

When their son was born, she invited her treacherous brother and his henchman Hagen to the child's christening. So skilled in deceit was Hagen that he suspected a trap and advised his half-brother, Gunther, not to go. However, he was mocked for 'being frightened of a mere woman'. Clearly enough time had passed for Gunther to have forgotten his wedding night!

Just as all the blood in our veins is connected throughout our entire body, so too are the waters that run in all the rivers throughout the body of the land. As Gunther, with his courtly retinue and men at arms, crossed the Danube, the Nixies, in gratitude for the treasure that they believed had been gifted to them, warned them to return. They prophesied that not one of their party – courtier, priest or soldier – would survive the journey save for the poorest among them, a wandering monk. That was easy to deal with. The monk was brought to Hagen, who strangled him and threw him overboard to drown. But it is not so easy to thwart a prophesy – the unfortunate was saved by the Nixies and brought safely to shore. Thus far their prediction still held, despite the trickster's attempt to circumvent it.

When at last Gunther's court arrived at their host's, King Etzen gave them a warm welcome, as honoured guests. However, Kriemhild soon accused Hagen of murdering her husband and stealing their treasure. Brandishing Siegfried's sword, which he had stolen from the funeral pyre, Hagen didn't try to deny the accusations, and even sneered that she had only brought these calamities upon herself. Amidst this tension, Gunther's soldiers and the Huns were squaring up to each other. It wasn't long before a fight broke out, which was the opportunity that Hagen had been waiting for. With one blow, he severed the baby's head. With that, his retinue seized the feasting hall while Etzel's men laid siege to it from the outside.

Knowing who was the true villain, Kriemhild offered to spare her brothers' lives if they surrendered Hagen. They refused to do this and she gave the order that the hall should be burned down and no prisoners taken except for Hagen and Gunther. When these two were brought to her she ordered Gunther's execution. Hagen was made to watch his beloved king and half-brother's head being struck off just as Kriemhild had seen the horrific beheading of her son. He was given a last chance to reveal the hiding place of the Nibelung treasure but, of course, he refused. Enraged, Kriemhild seized a sword and, with one blow, sliced off his head. Some say that it was the very sword that Hagen had stolen from Siegfried – how fitting that Siegfried's own weapon avenged his murder.

Surprisingly, one of King Etzen's inner circle was aghast at Kriemhild's impropriety in breaking the laws of hospitality in this way. But had Hagen not set the precedent by murdering his host's innocent baby son? The nobleman may also have been furious that she had disposed of the men who were, according to the rules of war, actually his prisoners. Worst of all, he deemed that it was not fitting for a woman to behave in such a savage way. In the face of all the tragic acts of the day, he judged hers to be the worst on the basis of her sex alone. Outraged that such an act could be perpetrated by a mere woman, he cut her trunk in two with one swipe of his sword. Still consumed by rage and a berserker's imperviousness to pain, Kriemhild declared that she didn't even feel the blow and hadn't been harmed. Her assailant then rolled a ring towards her and dared her to pick it up. As she bent forward to do so, her body separated and she died before it had crumpled to the floor.

If, from the Other World, her mother had been watching this tragedy unfold, she might have revisited her interpretation of her daughter's dream. Kriemhild, too, was the falcon torn apart by two treacherous royal brothers.

THE JEWEL PRINCE

HASIDIC TRADITION, UKRAINE

From the telling of Rabbi Nachman. The Hasidic phase of development within Jewish religious practice and culture gave rise to many mystical teachings and stories in which the layers of symbology are intrinsic to the narratives.

There was once a king and queen who longed for a child, but had not been blessed. Furthermore, there was a custom at that time that if they did not have an heir, the realm would pass to a stranger. The royal couple consulted physicians from far and wide, but none could help. Orders were given for all subjects to pray for the queen to have a child, including the Jewish community living at the edges of the kingdom.

The Jews then searched among their own community for a tzaddik, a person so righteous and holy that they are close to God, and thereby not only have the 'ear of God', but are gifted with special powers. When a tzaddik was at last found, he replied that he knew nothing about this affair, but rumours of his existence reached the court and he was summoned to appear before the king. During his audience, the king reminded the tzaddik that the fate of his people was in the king's hands and the tzaddik merely replied that a child would be born to them. Soon after, the queen gave birth to a girl.

The princess was of exceptional cleverness and beauty. By the time she was aged 4 she could play a number of musical instruments and speak many languages. Her parents delighted in her but overhanging them was the thought that because they didn't have a male child, the problem of the succession still had not been solved. The king again gave orders for his Jewish subjects to pray that this time the queen give birth to a son. The Jews immediately tried to find the tzaddik but he had since died. In due course they found another, who also had to present himself to the king. He too was reminded that the fate of his people was in the king's hands. The tzaddik then asked the king whether he was prepared to follow his instructions, and the king was so desperate for a son that he agreed.

Every kind of precious stone in the land was to be brought to the tzaddik. Every person in the realm brought their gems and the king emptied his treasury. When this was done, the tzaddik took one of each kind of gemstone, each with its particular quality, and ground them all into a paste.

He mixed this into a cup of wine, and the king and queen each drank half. When the queen became pregnant, the tzaddik told them that their son would be made entirely of jewels.

When the baby was born, the princess was relieved that there was no evidence of this prophecy, but she was still jealous of her brother not just because she was no longer an only child, but because he was heir to the realm's future. The prince grew as she had done, exceptionally talented and beautiful. One day he was carving some wood and cut his finger. Binding the wound with a bandage, the princess saw that beneath his skin, he was, indeed, made of jewels.

She immediately took to her bed, saying that she was ill. As she was only pretending, no physician could cure her. Sorcerers were therefore the next to be summoned. The king got so desperate that he decreed that if the next sorcerer did not cure his daughter he would be beheaded. After that there was only one who made the attempt, which was what the princess had been waiting for. She used the situation to extract from him a spell that would cause her brother to develop a fast and fatal form of leprosy. She also ascertained that no other sorcerer would be able to undo the spell, if it was confined to an amulet and cast into water. Having learned the spell, the princess whispered it into the locket she had worn since babyhood and snapped it shut. She then bound it with strands of her own hair and hid it in her secret bathing spot – a pool beneath the roots of a tree.

Delighted at their daughter's recovery, the royal couple now feared for their son. The prince became incurably ill and his suffering was terrible to see. Again, the tzaddik was summoned. As it happened, he had never stopped praying for the prince, but he had also complained in the 'ear of God' that the prince had not been made of jewels according to the prophecy. Now, however, he was aware of the sorcery that had been practised on the dying child. Looking at the princess, he told the king that only the one who had cast the spell could destroy it.

Was it from fear or was it from remorse that the princess hastened to the pool? She swam deeper and deeper, closer and closer to drowning, as she dived under the tree's roots searching for the charm. The breath had left her body by the time she found it. When she surfaced, her fingers were already undoing the charmed amulet and the water washing its evil spell away. At the palace, the prince had risen from his bed. His leprous skin started to peel away. There he stood, resplendent with every dazzling colour of every jewel in the land.

TWELVE SWAN BROTHERS

The sleigh bells tinkled clear as chiming icicles, followed by a great whoosh of spraying snow from the runners, as the horses drew up outside the house. The woman sat and looked about her at the crisp clean snow on this perfect winter's day with the low-slung sun casting purple shadows to where her boys were playing. The sky had never been such an intense blue, the snow almost too bright to look at where the sunlight sparkled. The shouts of her sons playing soared into the blue air and all was shining and clear in that perfect world as she watched her twelve bold, beautiful boys. How fortunate she was, how wonderful the scene as those young men frolicked in the snow.

Twelve sons but no daughter. How she wished for a daughter to make everything even more perfect. Why couldn't she have a daughter? She longed for a daughter. As this thought possessed her, she started to pace up and down, faster and faster. Passing a clump of thistles, she struck the snow off them, pricking her finger on a thorn. The pain brought her up sharply and she watched three drops of blood splash onto the snow.

'My daughter will have skin as white as snow, her lips will be as red as blood and her eyes as dark as the deepest shadow. Why shouldn't I have such a daughter? Is it too much to ask, to have just one daughter among so many sons? What wouldn't I give to have just the one little girl? I would give my sons for a daughter, I would give all my sons!'

Had she given voice to her thoughts? Had she spoken them out loud? Perhaps it was a trick of the light – too much dazzle on the snow – or too much glooming shadow, the purple now a blooming bruise as the reddening sun dipped lower. Her sons had fallen silent. Slowly they turned to look towards her, not spinning round nimbly, but paddling on great webbed feet. They tried to call to her, but their necks were stretching, longer and longer, and when they opened their mouths only hissing sounds squeezed out of orange beaks. They held out their arms beseechingly, but these were now wings, feathered white as the snow. Necks stretched low, wings beating, feet churning, they rushed towards their mother, each one struggling into the air before they reached her. They circled her once and flew away, their wings gilded at first, then turning blood crimson as the sun set. Proving that this was a nightmare and not a dream, twelve sets of clothes lay crumpled on the snow. She picked them up and burned them. Nine months later, her baby daughter, Karolina, was born.

As she grew older, Karolina would help her mother around the house. Every winter, a special meal would be prepared and the girl would help to lay the table. Each year it was the same, twelve extra places would be laid, each one with a silver christening spoon. One winter, when Karolina was 12, she was laying out these places as usual when she suddenly asked, 'Mother, how is it that every year we lay these twelve extra places, but nobody ever comes to fill them?'

At that her mother started to weep, and when she could speak, she told her daughter of her foolish, foolish wish and of how somewhere in the world, Karolina had twelve swan brothers.

'Then I will go and look for them, and I will not stop searching until I have found them.'

With that, she scooped the silver christening spoons from the table into her apron pocket. Without another word she left the house to search the wild wide world for her brothers.

She walked past farms, through villages and towns. She crossed fields and rivers, forests and mountains, begging or working for food. Wherever she slept, she would wrap herself in her apron with her hand in its pocket so that she could hold the christening spoons. Everywhere she asked whether anyone had seen a flock of twelve swans.

'Do we count how many birds are in a flock? There are so many swans,' would come the reply.

Months passed, years passed. At last, she came to a lake set in a forest wilderness. The lake was round and its water was black. If you had been able to fly over it, it would have seemed like a great, gleaming, darkly shining eye. Karolina couldn't cross it, but she could walk around it. There on the shingly shore she saw a little wooden house. It felt empty in that deserted place. She tried the door and it swung open. The first thing she saw when she stepped inside was a table laid with twelve wooden plates and twelve wooden cups. Upstairs there were twelve beds. Her hand closed over the christening spoons that, until then, had never left her apron pocket. Gently, lovingly, she laid a spoon on each of the plates.

Then a sound came towards the house, like a gust of wind in which could be heard a great creaking and pulsing. Nearer it came and louder it grew and the girl became frightened. She looked for somewhere to hide and noticed a cupboard under the stairs into which she crept. From where she was, she could peer through a crack in the wood, and was just in time to see the front door opening. In waddled twelve swans. Through the window behind them Karolina could see the last gleam of the setting sun and then the room was full of a swirl of white feathers. Like a blizzard they whirled around, so thick that nothing could be seen through them until they settled and disappeared like melting snow. It was then that the girl found herself looking at twelve young men, her brothers.

But they had noticed the spoons, and the eldest who could remember the most about their childhood, knew instantly what they were.

'These come from our mother's house. Has she found us, or were they brought by the one whose birthing was our cursing?'

Their sister could not bear to hear those words and burst from her hiding place, 'Oh! My brothers! I have searched the wild wide world for you and now that I have found you, I will not rest until I have undone the curse that has befallen you.'

It was then that the brothers told her that they were under an enchantment that turned them into swans during the day and back into human form during the night. In the summertime, with only a short twilight and no full darkness, their lives were almost intolerable. Had she not found them in wintertime, she may not have seen their transformation. If that was not bad enough, their curse would deepen, and in another three years they would not be able to transform back into men at all. There was only one way in which the spell could be broken, but that would never happen because it was too hard to do. The eldest brother explained that if anyone was able to sew each of them a shirt made only from thistles, without allowing a single sound to escape them until all the shirts were finished, only then would their curse be broken.

'I have not searched so far and so long for no purpose. I will break this curse that our mother's foolish wish has brought about.'

And those were the last words the swan brothers heard their sister speak. At first light she was out in the woods, gathering thistles and bundling them into her apron. Scratched and bleeding she would bite her lips to prevent herself from crying out. When she had enough thistles, she would soak them in a pool until they had softened, and then pound them into a pulp with a branch. As it dried, she was able to tease and roll the softened fibres into a rough thread. These she wove into a lumpy cloth, and, using a thinner thread for sewing, thorns for needles, and thistle heads for buttons, she started to stitch the first shirt.

Before long, she had gathered all the thistles that grew nearby and needed to walk further and further into the forest, her brothers taking it in turns to fly above the trees so that they could guide her back. One day, as she was desperately plucking nettles, she heard a distant hunting horn. Her swan companion knew the danger it posed for him so he circled further off, beyond the reach of arrows, but not so far that he couldn't see what happened next.

The sound of the hunt drew closer. The hounds had caught a strange scent and the notes of the horn changed, rallying all in pursuit. Karolina realised that she had become the quarry and that she needed to hide. There stood a hollow tree and she managed to squeeze inside it just as the king's hunt burst into the clearing. Of course, the hounds immediately followed her scent and were baying and circling around her hiding place. Again, the horn sounded, 'To earth! To earth!' The king gave the order to smoke out whatever was hiding in the tree. Wet leaves were laid around the trunk and Karolina could hear the crackle of flames, which was soon followed by the choking smoke that forced her out into the open.

'Well, and what have we here, I wonder?' asked the king.

He was looking at the most bedraggled wretch he had ever seen, even more ragged and filthy than the beggars at his gate. And what was that curious bundle she was clutching to her? Could those really be hands? Covered with scabs and scaly skin they looked more like claws than anything human. The king asked her who she was and what she was doing there. But the only reply was a wary look from eyes lake-deep and dark, and washed with sorrow. Believing at last that the girl was dumb, he said, 'Well, we can't leave you here all by yourself in the wilderness to be eaten by wolves. You'll come back with us until I can decide what's to be done with you.'

Orders had been given and servants made to lift her onto one of the horses, but when they tried to take her bundle from her to make it easier, it was as though they were suddenly dealing with a wild animal that snarled silently, bit and scratched.

'Let her hang on to that rubbish if it means so much to her,' laughed the king, 'Can't you manage to get a mere girl on a horse? Here, hand her up to me.'

As Karolina refused to let go of her precious work, the king rode with her seated on his pommel, his arms around her as he held the reins. High above and unnoticed flew a solitary swan.

By the time they reached the palace he had rather taken to this strange, half-wild creature. When they dismounted, she looked at him with such wise eyes, and as she held his gaze and saw that he could tell that she was no dumb beast or dimwit, a shy smile cracked her scabbed lips. For his part, the king was wise enough to see that her damaged hands and her silence were the signs of some great and sorrowful secret.

He gave orders that she was to have the run of the palace, to come and go as she pleased, and that the ladies of the court were to be kind to her and see to it that she had everything she needed. Always eager to find favour with the king, the ladies vied to do what was best. When she had finished eating like the famished body that she was, she was taken off for a bath. Still clutching her bundle, Karolina allowed this to happen. As the filthy garments were peeled off her and the tangles teased from her hair, those in attendance were transfixed when they saw the girl's beauty. Beyond those clawed hands and roughened lips, her skin was as smooth and unblemished as winter's first fall of snow. Karolina lay back in the warm water, her silent tears adding salt to sweet as she felt the first comfort in years.

Every day she disappeared into the woods that surrounded the palace, every evening she returned with new scratches and scabs on her hands. Whenever she encountered any of the court ladies in the palace she curt-sied deferentially, eyes respectfully downcast, and was a silent little ghost as she ate her evening meal amongst them. She did not know how good food and shelter had put a glow in her cheeks, glossed her hair, filled out her figure from a starving waif into the loveliest of young women. But they noticed, and most of all, the king noticed, and worst of all, the ladies of the court noticed that the king had noticed.

How different she was from the other primping and simpering women who didn't have a single intelligent thing to say for themselves. The king preferred Karolina's steady silence to their flirtatious nonsense. At last, he had to admit that he was in love, and if his bride couldn't say yes, she couldn't say no either. Was that a nod or a modestly lowered head when the moment came for her to take her vows? The king was happy, the ladies of the court were furious, the new bride was soon pregnant and her delighted husband gave her a golden necklace, which she never took off.

The time came when she was to give birth, attended by the ladies of the court. This was when they had plotted to take their revenge. After an entirely silent labour, Karolina removed the necklace and looped it twice around her baby's neck before falling into an exhausted sleep. Then the ladies pounced. They took the baby away and threw it into the river. They killed a puppy and removed its skin. Smearing the young mother with blood, they covered the bedclothes with gore and tiny bones before shrieking hysterically for the king.

'Your Majesty! Your Majesty! The queen has murdered and eaten her own child!'

There was the evidence, but the king could not believe that his sweet, gentle wife could do such a thing. Weeping silently, she shook her head as he asked her. As he looked into those pain-filled eyes, he remembered riding with his arms protectively around her when they first met. He would protect her still.

Life at the palace went on much as it had done before. Karolina spent every spare moment searching for thistles and working on the shirts while the ladies of the court bided their time. The happy king gave her a golden bracelet when they realised that she was pregnant again and as soon as the ladies saw it on her wrist they knew they didn't have long to wait. After another silent labour the new mother placed the bracelet on the child's ankle and fell into a deep sleep. All passed as before, with the ladies of the court screaming for the king after they had thrown the baby into the river and smeared its mother with the fresh remains of a puppy.

Although he still took his wife's part, the king felt the spreading shadow of doubt darken his mind. Did he imagine it or did his silent wife hold his gaze less often? Did she have something to hide or was it that she could not bear to see love mingled with mistrust? Things were not as easy between them and it seemed as though this totally silent woman was even quieter than before. Nevertheless, a third baby was on the way, but this time the king did not give his wife a gift.

'Watch her well,' was all he said to the ladies when she went into labour, and, of course, they did. When her third baby was born, all she had was her wedding ring, which she placed around the baby's big toe. The ladies of the court, now well practiced in their evil ways, also threw the third baby into the river and again covered the helpless mother with puppy gore. The king did not notice the gloating tones with which he was summoned, but now he was hearing what all the courtiers and many of the townspeople had been saying in secret: 'Majesty, your queen is a witch. How many of your heirs must she murder before you have her burned at the stake as she deserves?'

Doubt consumed him utterly and beckoned suspicion into his heart. He shook Karolina by the shoulders and pleaded, 'You who have always been silent, if you would save your life, then for God's sake, for my sake, speak now. As your husband I have tried to protect you but now, with what everyone is saying about you, well, just look at you, and, and, what have you done with the wedding ring I gave you?'

The only reply was a look from those dark eyes whose tears did not hide the depths of her secret. So the order was given and the fire on which she was to be burned as a witch was built in the centre of the town square, so that everybody could see what punishment awaited witchcraft. The king did not want to attend the burning, but his advisors insisted that his presence would set the right example and show everyone that he could be counted on to mete out justice above favour.

The square was thronging, the stake stood stark above the vast stack of firewood and there was Karolina being hustled towards it, her hands still clutching at her curious bundle. But they needed to be pulled behind her back and forced around the stake where her wrists would be tied together. Until now unresisting, she fought like a wild cat. The king, seeing from his balcony, what was happening below, was also looking back through time's tunnel, to a distant day when a bedraggled waif had fought to protect that same grubby bag. How her wounded hands, warped into claws, had moved him to pity. He remembered, too, how he had to put his arms around her to prevent her from falling from his horse, and, now, in his despair he cried out, 'Let her hands alone! Is it not enough that she burns for you?'

So, stumbling, she was dragged over the faggots and propped up against the stake as the fires were lit. How quickly, how hungrily those flames reached towards her as though fed not by wood alone but also with the oil of malice. The smoke rose, the fire crackled, but above smoke and flame there came another sound. A great gusting, a creaking and a pulsing as though the sky itself was breathing, and swooping low over the crowd there flew twelve swans. The largest held a small naked child in his beak. Flying over the balcony, the swan opened his beak and the king only just managed to catch the child as it was dropped from the sky, a golden necklace sparkling around its neck. A second swan came past and dropped a naked toddler, which the king caught by the golden bracelet around its ankle. A third swan flew over and the king caught his newborn baby in his hands, his wife's wedding ring still clinging to its big toe.

At that sight the townspeople and the soldiers started pulling away the burning faggots and beating them out. Above them all circled twelve swans. Reaching as high as their wingbeats a voice called out, 'My brothers! Oh my brothers!'

Karolina flung up her bundle into the air and there came a wind that caught it, carried it higher, and unfurled it until twelve thistle shirts were swirled up towards the swans. Twelve long necks thrust into them and the cloth folded over their bodies as each plummeted to earth. Rolling and skittering as they landed, they regained their human forms as soon as their feet touched the ground, to remain human daytime or night time, human then and for the rest of their lives, but not entirely so for the youngest brother. Because of the burning, there had been no time to finish his shirt and it was missing a sleeve. Until the end of his days he had one human arm, but the other remained a swan's wing.

THE SNAKE AND THE KING'S DREAM

The king was burdened by troubles and feared many enemies. He slept at the top of a tall tower believing that there he would be better protected. One night he had a vivid dream in which he saw his own bedchamber as though he were lying in bed and staring up at the ceiling. From its rafters dangled the corpse of a fox. Even in death the creature was grinning. With a cry of horror, the king awoke, knowing that this was no ordinary dream and that he must discover what it meant.

Although he consulted all his advisors, nobody could offer a suitable interpretation. Perhaps they feared to give him the wrong answer, perhaps they did not know it, or perhaps they feared to tell him the truth. Still haunted by the dream, the king ordered that every adult in the land be questioned until his dream had been interpreted correctly. He was now so desperate that he also let it be known that anyone with a believable reply would be rewarded with a sack of gold. However, just as before, nobody could provide a satisfactory answer. By now his soldiers were looking in the furthest corners of the realm for anyone who had not yet been asked.

At last they reached the most distant farm. There the farmer, who lived alone, was told that he must report to the palace to be questioned about the king's dream. The farmer was bewildered; he who had never travelled further than his few visits to the nearest village did not know how he would ever be able to advise a king. The soldiers pointed the way towards the palace, which lay through the mountains, and the farmer set off.

On a path in that rocky wilderness, a huge snake suddenly reared up before him. The farmer, too frightened to try to pass it or to flee back the way he had come, stood there transfixed. The snake then began to speak: 'I know why you are here, Man, and what you must do. When you hear of the king's dream with that dead fox hanging from the ceiling, you must say that the fox is a sign of the most cunning treachery close at hand. You must tell the king that he should trust nobody, especially those advisors closest to him.'

The farmer was so grateful to the snake that far from being fearful, he now promised to show his thanks by sharing his reward on his return. Even as the snake was slithering away, the farmer was still promising him half a sack of gold. When he reached the palace, he told the king the meaning of the dream. Delighted, the king had all his advisors imprisoned and gave the farmer his reward.

As he was returning home with the sack of gold, he remembered his promise to the snake but decided that now that he had been successful, he no longer needed to keep it. The farmer decided to take a different path through the mountains and reached home safely. The first thing he did was to hide all the gold up his chimney, and life went on as it had done before.

It wasn't long before the king had another portentous dream. This time, as he lay in bed staring at the ceiling, he saw a rusty sword dangling from the rafters, its point towards his throat. As he watched, the fibres of the rope began to snap one by one, and, as they did so, the rust gave way to gleaming steel. Just as the last thread was giving way, he awoke with a shout of horror.

None of his advisors could tell him the meaning of his dream and he wondered whether these stupid replacements were any improvement on those who had been untrustworthy. Then he remembered the farmer who had given him such a fitting answer before. Enquiries were made, and some soldiers who were about to patrol in that region were tasked to order the man back to the palace. The farmer, who had believed himself to be out of harm's way, did not know whether to yearn for the snake or dread its appearance. But suddenly, there she was as before, rearing up before him.

'The meaning of the king's dream is this: having foiled his enemies within, he has been too lax about those at his borders. Neighbouring powers have secretly been preparing to make war on him. He should strike first to gain the advantage in battle.'

The farmer was so relieved to hear this wisdom that he apologised to the snake for not keeping his promise and renewed his pledge to share any further reward. The king was so delighted to hear the interpretation that he rewarded the farmer with two sacks of gold.

As orders were given to attack, the farmer made his way back home through the mountains. Again, he thought that there was no need to keep his promises to the snake, and in any case, the sacks were extremely heavy and a shortcut would be in order. When he reached his farm, he buried the gold in his yard.

The king's forces triumphed, his neighbour's armies were subdued and life went on, for a while, as it had before. Then he had another vivid dream. This time, hanging from the rafters and bleating lustily was a fat sheep with a luxuriantly glossy fleece.

The king wasted no time in asking the right person to interpret this significant image. The exhausted messenger arrived at the distant farm and the farmer was instantly dispatched to the palace. How he feared to meet the snake whom he had twice betrayed. How he feared not meeting her and arriving at the palace without an answer. Choosing a path at random, nevertheless, there was the snake once more rearing up before him.

'The meaning of the king's dream is this: he has triumphed at home and abroad. Now there is a period of peace and plenty throughout the land. This is the time to be generous and forgiving and to invite former enemies back into the fold.'

Shamefaced, the farmer again promised the snake half of any reward he would be given, and hastened towards the palace. On learning the meaning of this latest dream, the delighted king rewarded the farmer with three sacks of gold. As they were too much to manage by himself, the farmer bought a donkey to transport them back through the mountains. Allowing the beast to pick its own way through the rugged ground, he did not pay attention to which path it chose. Although, on this occasion, he had nothing to carry, his tread and his heart were heavy. Suddenly there was the snake again.

This time the farmer rejoiced to see her: 'Dear snake, I am so glad to see you. I have been regretting breaking my promises and now I have the chance to make amends. I should have given you half a sack of gold for the first dream, one for the second, and one and a half sacks for the third. Please take these three sacks from me and I will have kept my word at last.'

However, the snake replied: 'How little you men understand. The first dream came at a time of great treachery and deception. You too were subject to that time and so you betrayed your promise to me. The second dream came at a time of impending war. During conflict each holds on to what they have, hiding resources for their time of need, so you buried your wealth rather than keeping your promise. The third dream comes at a time of peace when people feel that they can afford to be generous. This is when they ask for forgiveness and heal old wounds, so you offer to make amends by giving me all of what you promised.

'I am not a foolish man like yourself, I am a snake. What need have I of your gold? Can I eat it? Will it keep me warm in winter? Will it make a soft nest for my young? Keep your gold and use it wisely.'

And perhaps the farmer did.

THE FAERY FLAG OF DUNVEGAN

ISLE OF SKYE, SCOTLAND

Malcolm, chief of the MacLeods, was walking by Dunvegan Loch, which lay below his castle. Deep in thought about the constant state of warfare between his clan and that of the McDonalds, it took him some time to hear the singing, so ethereal, so otherworldly that it could only come from Fairyland itself. There, beneath the fairy bridge was one of the fairy folk, curious about this world of mortals. Before long they were married, and soon a son and heir was born to them.

The fairy folk may visit this world, but they never linger. The fairy bride felt the calling of her own people and slipped away back over the fairy bridge to her own world. A nurse was hired for the child and a great feast was prepared to celebrate his birth. As he was sleeping peacefully, his nurse could not resist leaving him to catch a glimpse of the festivities. However, no sooner had she gone than that messenger from the Otherworld, the owl, flew hooting past the window. Maybe it was his fairy blood that woke him, but the baby began to cry. The nurse did not hear him above the sound of the music, but his mother did. Since she had returned to the fairy world, she could no longer touch him, but nevertheless she could bring him a comforting gift. This was a green silk cloth, sprinkled with exquisite elf spots embroidered with a finesse beyond the skill of mortal hands. As it floated over him, he sensed his mother's presence, and went back to sleep.

MacLeod had noticed the nurse on the gallery, and signalled for her to bring his heir so that the guests could swear fealty to him.* Having first feared that she would be reprimanded for leaving her charge, she soon marvelled at the magical cloth that now covered him. She caught him up and brought him down to the guests who were to become his retainers. As she held him aloft, the green fairy silk swirling, a sound of distant unearthly singing filled the hall. At that sound, all fell silent in amazement.

Louder and louder it grew until everyone could make out the words sung by those fairy voices as they prophesied that the cloth was to be known as the Faery Flag of Dunvegan. Three times it would come to their aid and only then if it was waved in a situation of overwhelming need. However, if the power of the flag was not respected and waved for any trivial reason, three dooms would fall on the clan MacLeod. These would be the untimely death of the chief's heir soon after; the loss of the Three Maidens to their clan Campbell enemies, these being a strategic group of rocks near Dunvegan; and for the MacLeod lands and menfolk to diminish until there would not be enough of them to row a war galley across their own loch – this last to happen when a vixen had given birth in a tower of Dunvegan castle.

Malcolm MacLeod, grateful for and respectful of his wife's gift, immediately gave orders for a chest to be made in which to keep the flag. He would be the one who kept the only key, and it would always accompany the MacLeods into battle.

Generations of MacLeods came and went, but the flag and its prophecies were never forgotten. Then came the dreadful day in 1578 when the MacDonald clan burned an entire congregation in Trumpan church, with only one survivor – a little girl small enough to climb through one of the windows, who escaped to raise the alarm.** Weakened by this atrocity, and vastly outnumbered by the MacDonalds, a retreat was about to become a

* Take an oath of loyalty.
** This incident is frequently spoken of even today in the oral history of my partner's family.

rout, followed by a massacre. The Faery Flag of Dunvegan was taken from its casket and waved aloft. As it unfurled, the enemy mistakenly believed that reinforcements had joined the MacLeods, and the MacDonalds fell back. With renewed hope, the MacLeods pursued and beat them off. The Faery Flag had fulfilled one of the prophecies at last.

The next time it was used was when all the cattle were inflicted with the cattle plague murrain. So many beasts had died that the people risked starvation. Once again, the casket was unlocked and the Faery Flag of Dunvegan was unfurled over a field of many dead and dying beasts. No more became infected and even the incurably sick recovered. The Faery Flag was returned to its safekeeping and many wondered what the third and last calamity might be when it would save the MacLeods for the last time.

More generations came and went until in 1799 a new employee entered the chief's service. Buchanan was a sceptic and sought to disprove what he considered to be a ridiculous legend and nest of superstition. When the chief was away, he took the casket to an English blacksmith to force it open, the chief, of course, having the key about his person as custom demanded. As an incomer, the blacksmith would be ignorant of, nor show loyalty to a local legend. A native of Skye would never have been party to such an act. When the lock had been broken, Buchanan waved the Faery Flag of Dunvegan. Surely there could have been no worse reason for perpetrating what was such a disrespectful act.

Soon after, on 3 March 1800, the HMS *Charlotte* blew up, killing nearly 700 men, including the chief of the MacLeod's heir. Later, a Lieutenant MacLean was staying in Dunvegan castle. He had been accommodated in one of the towers because he had brought his tame fox with him. The animal was a vixen and she gave birth to a litter during their stay. At this time, the MacLeods' fortunes dwindled and much of the land, including The Three maidens, was sold off. The chief's family diminished too, leaving only three close male relatives, an insufficient crew to row a galley on their loch.

Visitors can see the Faery Flag at Dunvegan Castle, fragmented and faded beyond sight of its fairy green. Who knows whether, after Buchanan's contemptuous treatment, it would save clan MacLeod for a third time.

THE WOMAN WHO HAD TWO

ENGLAND

Rewritten here with kind permission from storyteller June Peters. Widely assumed to be a traditional story, its form fooled most of the storytellers I know. However, it was created by June herself. She was inspired to create it by listening to a radio broadcast in which an Arab woman was talking about a particular genre of stories that would normally only be shared among women. If I have also responded to the spirit of invention, I wonder whether June will approve.

There was once a man who was reluctant to get married because no woman was good enough for him. His ageing mother was getting anxious as she wanted to see him married and in safe hands before she died. At last, he had to admit that the only woman who would be good enough for him was one who had 'two' – and he spared his mother's sensitivities by merely gesturing downwards towards that part of the anatomy to which he was referring. Needless to say, women answering this description were hard to come by, so his mother advised him to advertise.

We do not know whether he was surprised to get a reply to his advertisement, or whether he was surprised not to get a stampede, but as there was only one, he reluctantly arranged a rendezvous before his mother did. The woman was personable in every way and any bachelor would have been keen to have her as his fiancée. However, there was still the delicate matter of her having 'two'. There was no other way to find out, except by asking her outright.

'Of course,' she replied, 'You made it quite clear that that is what you require and I only replied because I fulfil that particular stipulation.'

The man squirmed with pleasure. But then there was another problem. How could he believe her? He mentioned this concern and suggested that just a tiny peep would allay any doubts.

The woman looked quite shocked, and then she started to laugh: 'Oh I see what you are up to! You are just testing me to see if I have loose morals and will show myself to a complete stranger. The very idea! Well, you can rest assured that I'm not one of those girls who just lets everything hang out on a first date.'

And with that he had to be content. They were married soon after and he spent most of the wedding celebrations wishing that the ground would swallow up their guests so that he could get on with the wedding night.

At last the couple were alone, and his bride insisted that they went to bed in the dark as, having always been a virtuous maiden, she was shy. He respected her wishes and for several weeks that was how they made love. Eventually he could bear it no longer and asked to see her 'second' or 'spare'.

At this she hurled herself on the bed sobbing violently: 'Have I not been a loving wife to you? Have you not experienced married bliss with me in so many ways? Have I ever turned from you or pretended to have a headache? What will our marriage be like if this early on you are already dissatisfied?'

She was almost inconsolable and he learned not to make that mistake again. However, he continued to have wistful thoughts about 'the number two', which alternated with feelings of pride at being the only man in England who had a wife with a spare. Time passed and they got on pretty well together until he needed to go on a business trip that would take some days. It wasn't appropriate for her to accompany him as he would be travelling with colleagues, so it was, as he thought, entirely in order for him to ask if he could take her 'number two' with him.

At that she went very quiet and, expecting that this was just the lull before the storm, he looked at her apprehensively. Surprise mingled with joy when she said, 'Yes of course, I will pack it for you. But you must promise me one thing. You know how shy I am, promise that you will only take it out of its box in the dark.'

That seemed a small price to pay as he had become used to making love in the dark anyway. That night his wife made sure that he drank too much wine at dinner. When he was snoring, she went to the garden and removed the netting from the raspberry bushes. Carefully she strung it up between some trees, then she re-joined her husband, but only for a while. When the sky was paling to a pearly grey she slipped into the garden with a softly lined box. Caught in the net, just as she had hoped, was a sparrow. She gently disentangled the little creature and slipped him into the box where he would be safe. This she packed with her husband's luggage, reminding him of his promise as she kissed him goodbye.

All afternoon, he sat through interminable Zoom seminars and PowerPoint presentations, wishing that the ground would swallow up his colleagues so that he could get to bed. At last the moment came. He rushed to his room and drew the box from his suitcase.

He remembered his promise about not shedding any light on his wife's 'spare'. But what if he kept the lights out and opened the curtains? He hoped to see more in the half-light from the window. In any case, the room was stuffy and the window needed opening. However, it was still too gloomy to see much.

Trembling, he undressed and carefully opened the box. Under his hand he could feel something warm, soft and pulsing – at last! He opened the lid fully and felt an expectant throbbing and then it was suddenly gone. He groped around the bedclothes while the sparrow fluttered to the floor. As the man rummaged amongst the covers, the little bird made for that patch of light that was slightly less gloomy than the rest of the room.

The man was none the wiser that the sparrow had flown through the open window. By now he was distraught; what had become of 'number two'? Desperation made him turn on the lights. His wife's spare was nowhere to be found. How would he face her when she asked for it back after his trip?

When he returned home he appeared, to his wife's eyes, satisfactorily crestfallen. She made no mention of her 'number two' for a while, leaving him to steep in the juices of apprehension. At last, when they were on their way to bed, she asked for the return of her 'number two'. Her husband had to admit that he had lost it. Having had plenty of time to rehearse her reaction to the situation that she had engineered, her response was a tour de force of feminine outrage.

It may be concluded that no reference was ever made to 'number two' ever again, but that would be wrong. From time to time – and it could be almost anywhere – at a dinner party, at the supermarket checkout, before curtain up in the theatre – his wife would start to shiver and moan, utter inarticulate cries and sometimes even roll her eyes.

When this had first happened, the man was full of concern. When she managed to gasp out, 'Oh! My goodness, someone must have found my "spare!"' it did nothing to allay his consternation.

RICH MOTHER, POOR MOTHER

Europe is the only continent which experiences the four seasons throughout its land mass. These have been a huge influence in the development of cultures and their traditional narratives. Other continents share these distinct seasons in part, and this story is found in neighbouring countries as Europe extends towards the Caucasus. Perhaps this version, with its central striking and improbable image, originated further East and found its way to Europe, where it remains a favourite with oral storytellers. When I first heard this story, I was rather sceptical about the candelabra burning in a tent. Apart from the magical elements in folk tales, other physical details are often very accurate and true to life. The magical feature of the blue flames passed the credibility test, but a tent with a candelabra seemed too impractical and far-fetched! However, a visit to an exhibition of Islamic art revealed a display of an enormous tent from Dagestan. Complete with its own tent furniture, it included a twelve-branched candelabra, whereupon all scepticism was crushed.

Two widows were neighbours, and each had six children. One was very wealthy, the other very poor. The poor woman worked for her rich neighbour from dawn until dusk. Her final task of the day was to knead the dough and leave it to rise overnight before she returned to bake it for the rich family's breakfast. No matter how hard she worked, her only payment at the end of the day was the dough that was left clinging to her fingers. With this she managed to make a tiny loaf for her own children, who always went to bed hungry.

Strange to say, but true, the poor children were always laughing and playing happily together even though they had no toys, and were dressed in rags through which poked their skinny elbows and knees. Next door, however, the rich children were always miserable, even though they had never known hunger. Although they had enough toys to break and more than enough clothes to trample, they never stopped complaining and squabbling among themselves.

One evening their mother was in her bedroom at the top of the house, where she often retired with a headache from their noise and indigestion at their constant quarrelling. At first, she didn't know what that sound was that she found even more annoying than theirs until she realised that it was coming from next door. It was easy to see into her neighbour's yard from her vantage point, and she realised that what was distressing her was the sound of the poor children's joyful laughter as they played together. How was it that they were always happy and hers were always miserable? Didn't she ply her own with delicacies, new toys and clothes? Why were her neighbour's half-starved children always cheerful? As far as she was concerned, there was no sense or justice to this, so she set to pondering how things had been set against her.

At last, she decided that her predicament was due to misfortune. She suspected that her neighbour must be stealing her good luck from her every time she went home after work, and was passing it on to her own children. But how was she doing it? The next evening as the poor mother was about to leave, her employer stopped her and demanded that she empty her pockets in case her good luck was somehow hidden in them. Needless to say, the pockets were empty.

The following evening the rich mother insisted on looking under her servant's apron, down the neckline of her dress and shaking out her skirts. Still nothing. Then she realised that the only thing that left her house every day with her servant was the dough on her fingers. The good luck must be hidden in that, and the poor mother was made to scrape every scrap of dough from her fingers before she left. Then came the worst blow of all. The rich woman told the poor mother never to darken her doorstep again and that she was to find work elsewhere.

It was the first time she had come home empty-handed and the first time she heard her children cry themselves to sleep with hunger. Even in their sleep, they were whimpering and their mother couldn't bear to hear that sound any longer, so she stepped outside the house. Desperate with worry she paced the empty streets, her own stomach churning, not with hunger, but with anxiety in the knowledge that she was not going to be able to provide for her children.

Without realising it, her footsteps had taken her to the edge of the village, after which the ground began to climb into the hills. Looking beyond the houses into the night, the poor mother was surprised to see a bright blue ball of light glowing among the hills. Nothing could account for it, and, despite her troubles, she was drawn to discover what it was. Higher and higher she climbed, the ball of light getting bigger and brighter as she approached. At last, she could see that it was emanating from a circular candelabra with twelve branches, at the ends of which were burning steady blue flames. It was these that, from a distance, had appeared as a great globe of blue light. Now she was close enough to see that the candelabra was suspended inside a huge tent, the front of which had been fastened back, revealing also a blue fire encircled by twelve seated figures.

There was no retreating from this strange sight, and curiosity drove her on until, as she neared the tent's threshold, she heard, 'Come in my dear. Come in out of the dark and cold and take a seat by our fire.'

As though in a dream, she did as she had been invited, the figures shuffling up to give her room. She looked about and saw men and women of all ages, youths and maidens, boys and girls. The same voice spoke again: 'You have travelled far, my dear. While you are resting yourself may we ask you some questions?'

'Certainly Sir. And if I can answer them I shall do so as best I can.'

'Indeed, your best, whatever it may be, will suffice.'

At that a sturdy matron lumbered to her feet, skirts swirling, untidy grey whisps escaping from her bun. In a voice that roared like the autumn gales trying to hold off the icy clutches of winter, she demanded, 'Mistress! What do you think of the month of November?'

'November? Such a blessed month. The toiling in fields and orchards is over for a while, with only the olive harvest to look forward to. When that is safely in, we can all keep warm inside together. It is then that we take stock of the stores that will see us through the winter. We give thanks for what our labours have earned and we relish our time together in the evenings around the fire. That is when we remember the old songs and stories, sharing them so that they shall not be forgotten from one generation to the next.'

'A good answer,' howled the matron, loudly enough to rattle an entire forest of bare-branched trees.

A youth then leaped to his feet, lithe as a young stag. The lilting of birdsong could be heard in his voice and his breath carried the sweetness of wild flowers.

'Lady! What do you think of the month of May?'

'May?' Another blessed month. Each morning the little birds waken us to the promise of increase and plenty. The gentle sun allows us to take our ease outside in the lush meadows, or work in the fields without strain. The evening light has lengthened, showing the setting fruit in the orchards, and the grass grows high for the cattle and sheep to make rich milk for their young.'

'Thank you, Lady,' his smile shone like the sun emerging after the last of the spring showers.

An ancient white-bearded man creaked to his feet. In a voice as thin and piercing as an icicle he asked, 'Daughter, what think you of the month of January?'

'January? Yet another blessed month. Beasts and people alike need a period of rest, and does Mother Earth herself not show us how? She is wrapped in a blanket of darkness for much of the time, allowing us to sleep for longer with the earlier nights and later mornings. Wild animals lie low in the woodland, some even sleeping beneath the earth that is her very body. The icy breath of the winter wind breathes "shelter and rest" to all living things, and that is how we build our strength for the labours of the coming seasons.'

'A full answer, Daughter!' cackled the old man, with a sound of frosty twigs snapping in his joints as he creaked back to his place.

'Sister,' called out a round-limbed young woman in a voice as full and warm as a southern sea breeze, 'Tell us what you think of the month of July.'

'July? Again, another blessed month. One when we need never fear the cold. We can swim in sea or lake without so much as a shiver and it is a pleasure, not a chore, to do our washing in the cool streams. We rejoice to see the bounteous sun ripening our crops, and look forward to making a good harvest.'

'A generous answer, Sister,' laughed the young woman, and in her pleasure could be heard the rustling of fields of ripening corn.

When all the questions had been asked, and all the answers given, the oldest of the assembly creaked upright once more.

'Indeed, Daughter, you have answered as best you can and in so doing have given us the best of yourself, for which we thank you. Morning will soon be upon us, and your children await. Please take this gift with you.'

So saying, the old man placed in her hands a damp, weighty ball wrapped in a blue cloth. Taking her gift in both hands, she stepped outside, but when she turned to thank him, the tent, the candelabra, and all the people had disappeared. Wondering if her troubles had led her to sleepwalk, she stumbled back down the hillside. But her hands were still clutching that blue cloth – so it can't all have been a dream. In the growing greyness of morning, she sat on a rock and unwrapped her gift. Beneath the cloth was a large lump of sticky dough. At least her children would have some bread for breakfast.

Early sunlight filled the village as she reached it. There in the square, the women were clustered around the communal oven where they brought their dough to turn into the bread and pastries that would last them throughout the day. The poor mother was never seen among them as she always had to be at work for her rich neighbour at first light. With murmurs of welcome and surprise, they parted for her so she too could put her dough in the oven with theirs, knowing that she was too poor to be able to offer her share of the fuel. Eager to return to her children, she shaped it hurriedly and slipped it in with the others.

Within moments a delicious smell hovered above the oven, far surpassing the comforting, homely waft of baking bread. This was not the same everyday scent of nourishing goodness that wrapped the village every morning. It was as though every harvest from every wheat crop that had ever been was being cradled in that oven. Beneath that heaven-sent earthly scent, lingered the trace of all the flowers of spring and summer. Beyond it drifted the flavour of woodsmoke and the frost-nipped smell of fallen leaves, and then a hint of the fresh nip of snowflakes on the tongue. Every season seemed held in that dough before finding their way to the outside air, eddying on the rising heat from the oven.

As they breathed in those smells, the women's eyes closed and they rocked gently where they stood, reliving their memories of every month and season until water filled their hungry mouths and squeezed its way between closed lids. No need to check if the loaf was ready – at once there was a stirring in the group and the poor mother took it from the oven.

But how had it grown so large? The poor mother had hardly been able to get it out! There it lay with its golden crust gleaming like it had been stroked by the sun itself. Nobody had ever seen such perfect bread. Never had a group of women been so silent around the oven – a favourite place for gossip. Then she noticed that all the women's gazes were fixed longingly on the wonderful loaf. It was far larger than anything she had brought home before; perhaps she could spare enough to let everyone have a taste.

As she had no knife with her, she reached out to tear off the crust, but she didn't need to, as at that moment, several knives appeared. Taking the nearest, she cut a slice and that richest of smells intensified. Handing the piece to the nearest woman, she didn't see at first why all the others had let out such a gasp. Turning again to the loaf, she saw that the missing piece had grown back. No matter how quickly she sliced, or how many pieces she cut, the bread always grew back until the loaf was whole once more. When everybody had taken their share, she took it home to feed the children.

They had never eaten so well. Their happy shouts of laughter continued unabated, and next door so did the endless grumbles and complaints. The rich mother couldn't understand it. Looking from her high window she saw her neighbour in the yard, slicing bread for her children in the middle of the day. How was that possible? Those children were never fed lunch and where had she got that enormous loaf from? She had to find out. She tore down the stairs, flung herself out of the house and wrenched open her neighbour's gate. Everyone stared in astonishment as she had never paid them a visit before. She demanded to know how her neighbour had come by such a loaf, and, quietly, the poor mother told her the whole story.

Determined to receive such a good luck gift herself, she was cursing each daylight hour as she waited impatiently for night to fall. At last it was dusk, and she hurried through the village in the direction her neighbour had indicated. Now that it was night, she could clearly see the glowing blue globe. She scrambled up the hillside towards it until she was at the threshold of the tent. There hung the candelabra with its twelve branches of blue flame, there sat the twelve figures around the blue burning fire. Without waiting for an invitation, she rushed in and thrust herself between two of the seated people. Her entrance was met with silence and twelve pairs of eyes stared at her expressionlessly.

'Well, aren't you going to ask me my questions?' she demanded.

An ancient white-bearded man rose slowly to his feet, leaning on a neighbour's shoulder to do so.

'Madam, if you are sure you want to answer, I must counsel you to answer as well as you can.'

'Of course I want to answer, otherwise why would I have come all this way? Let's get it over with.'

A rosy-cheeked boy bounded to his feet and, bouncing on his toes, asked, 'Madam, what can you tell us of the month of March?'

'March? What a cursed month! Raining one moment, watery sunshine the next, puddles and mud everywhere, impossible to know what to wear. Gusty winds blowing this way and that, a most untrustworthy month, and if that isn't bad enough those shrieking birds wake people up too early and give no peace all day long.'

The boy folded back into his place, all the bounce crushed out of him.

Red hair streaked with grey, apple-cheeked and round-bellied, a matron crossed her rosy arms above straddling legs.

'Madam, what think you of the month of October?' she asked in a rich deep voice.

'October? Another cursed month! That cold wind blowing all those messy leaves and rubbish about, and all that piercing cold rain. The days are too short for comfort, there is no evening light and the nights are too long.'

The matron's cheeks darkened and she stared long and silently at the visitor before sitting once more.

Then a man stood up. He was in the prime of life, his skin nut brown from the sun, the down on his strong arms bleached golden. His voice blazed out, 'Madam, what can you say about the month of August?'

'August? A most cursed month! The air is too scorching to breathe and everything is covered in dust. The ruts are set hard like stone and to journey anywhere is to be jolted at every turn of the wheels or to be overturned. Even the trees are limp with the heat and the rumbling of distant thunder brings no relief, and if it does rain, the storms are too violent to be refreshing.'

The man stared at her implacably with his tawny-gold eyes, and sat down silently.

Lastly, a little girl crept towards her. She twisted her hands nervously as though to hide that one of her little fingers was missing. Head drooping like a snowdrop with shyness, in a voice like pattering rain she whispered, 'Madam what do you think of the month of February?'

'February! Yet another cursed month! Slipping on ice or squelching through mud. Bitter winds, snow turning to rain and back again, promising spring yet still spitting out winter, a most treacherous month.'

The child whipped her hand with the missing finger behind her back and crept back to her place. All were silent, staring into the blue flames. Before their visitor could burst out once more, the old man with the white beard spoke.

'We have something to give you, but again I must counsel you to only open it when you are alone.'

A clay jar, like those used to store olive oil, was placed in her hands. She couldn't wait to get home to open it. If she had turned back to say a 'thank you', she would have seen that the tent, the blue burning flames and all the people had disappeared. What could be in the jar? Surely some treasure that others should not see in case they tried to steal it from her. Why else would she have been told to open it when alone?

She hurried past the women gathered around the communal oven without greeting them. When she reached her house, she ran up the stairs to her room and kicked the door shut behind her. Setting the jar down near the windows, she opened them for better light. Then she prised open the lid. The snakes were particularly aroused and bad tempered after the journey that had so shaken and jostled them. They lost no time in biting her before slipping out of the open window, down the vine-covered wall, and away to do no more harm, as the rich mother slipped to the floor and died.

What would become of her children now that they were orphans? 'Plenty of room for more,' thought the poor mother next door. So she took them in to raise them with her own. Within a month they had learned how to play and were smiling and laughing with each other and their new friends. Some villagers said that they could barely tell which children were which, and everyone knew that it didn't matter.

STONE SOUP

TRAVELLER COMMUNITY, SCOTLAND

I first heard this story from Duncan Williamson, who was a living archive of stories and songs and reputed to have the largest traditional oral repertoire of anyone in Europe. It is not surprising that versions of this story can be found all over the Continent.

A grandfather and his young granddaughter had been on the road a long time. They were hungry and tired and had been unlucky in finding any shelter or food. They reached a prosperous-looking village, but although they had knocked on every door, all the villagers had refused to give them anything. The grandfather told the little girl that it was time to make stone soup and sent her to find sticks with which to make a fire. Then he took a cooking pot from his pack and told her to fill it from the stream. When all this had been done, he set the pot on the fire for the water to boil. Knowing that all this time the suspicious villagers would have been peering at them from behind their curtains, he took a round white stone from his pocket with a great flourish. Holding it up to catch the light and the gaze of the villagers, he then placed it in the pot and sat down to wait.

As expected, the villagers could not contain their curiosity, and as soon as one came to see what he was cooking, the others followed. They knew that none of them had given the strangers any food and they all stared bemusedly at the stone in the boiling water. One of them ventured to ask what the old man was cooking, and 'Stone Soup' was the reply. For a while the only sound was the bubbling water as the stone rolled around in it, until at last, another asked whether the soup was ready yet. With great ceremony, the old man took a horn spoon from his pocket and dipped it into the pot. After blowing on the stone soup, he tasted it and remarked that it was nearly ready, it just lacked a little something. 'What was it?' he wondered aloud, 'Could it be some onion?' At that one of the onlookers said that she had pulled some onions only that morning and hurried off to fetch them.

Time and time again, this procedure was repeated: the soup was always nearly ready, but needed just that little extra ingredient, which villager after villager hurried to supply. Before long the stone soup also consisted of onions, herbs, potatoes, carrots, rabbit, parsnips and swedes. It was the most delicious soup anyone had ever smelled. Grandfather produced two bowls and another spoon from his pack, and served his granddaughter and himself. When they had eaten their fill there still seemed to be plenty left in the pot and he invited everybody to try some. They trotted off to fetch spoons and bowls, and soon all were seated around the pot eating the most delicious soup they had ever tasted. At last, the pot was empty, the old man retrieved the stone, wiped it clean on the grass and was just about to put it in his pocket when one of the villagers asked to buy it.

'Oh no!' Came the reply, 'This is a magic stone and it is not for sale.'

The stone disappeared back inside his coat and the two strangers left the village.

'Now I know how to make stone soup, and I will never forget it,' said the little girl, and she never did.

THE SHOEMAKER AND THE WATER NYMPH

POLAND

This comes from a region of north-eastern Poland called, poetically, 'the Land of a Thousand Lakes', where in reality there are thousands more.

A huge head shines brightly
In a golden crown with diamonds,
The king, ruler of the lakes.

Ryszard Orszulak

Jasiek* was a shoemaker who worked hard but never managed to escape poverty. In those days, shoemakers would travel with their bag of tools and repair shoes in distant farms and villages. It seemed to Jasiek that he was wearing out as much of his own shoe leather as he was repairing. His route often took him along the banks of a river, and he was in the habit of resting near a great willow tree. There, where he knew nobody could hear him, he would sing all the songs he knew in his sweet, full voice that rang out across the water. He was not to know that beneath it lived a nimfa wodna, a water nymph, who heard and cherished every note:

Deszczyk pada, slonce swieci,
Baba Jaga maslokleci

Rain is falling, sun is shining,
Baba Yaga is churning butter

One day in early spring, when rain was falling at the same time as the sun was shining between the cloud – as people say during such mixed weather, 'the witches are making butter' – he paused by the willow tree. Today he wasn't singing, but thinking deep thoughts about what he could do to improve his fortune. He decided to ask his friend, who was a fisherman, to give him some extra work, to which his friend readily agreed.

On Jasiek's first day of fishing, the two men felt a huge weight in the net. Only Jasiek's first day and what had they caught? The King of the Thousand Lakes himself! How he thrashed about and fought not to be hauled up into

---

* Pronounced 'Yasheck', diminutive of Jack.

the boat. He begged for his freedom and proposed a bargain: if they released him, he would give one of them his daughter to marry. The fisherman was already married and as for Jasiek, he knew he was too poor to woo an ordinary girl, so he was delighted at the suggestion. In gratitude for his release, the King of the Thousand Lakes ensured that the net was full of fish for the rest of the day, but best of all was his beautiful daughter, none other than the water nymph, Lyna,* who had so delighted in Jasiek's singing. Already half in love with him, she was eager to leave her watery home and explore life on land with a man she thought of as quite a catch.

If only life were that simple. How would she manage with her fish's tail, and how could a shoemaker marry a woman with no feet? Furthermore, if she went to live on land, she could never regain her water nymph form, and would not be able to return to the river. The first difficulty was resolved by the King of the Thousand Lakes using his magic to change her fish's tail into human feet as her dowry. The bridegroom then made the loveliest white kid shoes ever seen, in which his bride followed him up the aisle.

Shoemaker and nymph lived happily together, rain or shine, or when the 'witches were making butter'. However, there came a time when Jasiek fell gravely ill and his life could only be saved by a particular plant that grew at the bottom of the river. Only Lyna would be able to dive that deep to retrieve it, but she was not permitted to return to the river and still keep her form. Nevertheless, Lyna decided that saving her husband was more important and so she dived into the river and plucked the life-saving plant as quickly as she could. As soon as it was on the bank, she felt herself changing. Gone were the human feet, never to be replaced by a fish's tail. Instead, she felt her limbs getting longer and longer and watched her skin becoming indistinguishable from the ripples in the water, until her form became one with the long silver ribbon of the river.

As for Jasiek, he recovered, and in time was even able to marry again. He prospered, and knew that this was because, somehow, the river was sending him good luck as it flowed past his home. Jasiek never forgot his water nymph bride, and whenever he could he would return to the ancient willow tree and sing out across the water every song he knew, with the wind in the leaves whispering an echo. As he sang, the river would silence her ripples as she flowed past him, all the better to listen. You can find that willow tree yourself if you walk along the banks of the River Lyna, in the region that is called the Land of a Thousand Lakes.

* Pronounced 'Winner'.

But Lyna will no longer be herself,
She will become the river, grey water.
This is her father's harsh sentence,
She feels how cold her legs have already become,
Icy cold fills her body,
The hot heart stopped beating.
Lyna winds with a silver ribbon,
And a willow tree looms over her.

Translated from Polish by Karolina Mackiewicz.

HALF A CHICKEN

SPAIN

I'm half a chicken, I'm half a chicken
I don't feel chicken to be only half a chicken!
I'm half a chicken and quite decided
It is so cool to be totally one sided!

There was once a hen who was very successful at raising her broods. She was most often to be seen with many fluffy yellow chicks scuttling around her, too many to count. One day a chick peeped out to tell her that one of their brothers was only half a chicken. Peering down, she could see that this was true: only one wing, one leg, half a head, half a beak and one eye. From that moment everyone called him 'Half a Chicken', and he was more than proud because he was so special.

Even before he had all his feathers, Half a Chicken was determined to visit the king's palace, where he was convinced the king would have a golden cage waiting for him because he was so special. He set off for the town, singing his special song. Before long he was about to pass a pool when it called out to him, 'Half a Chicken! Half a Chicken! just one moment if you please. My cool water is being choked by this scummy weed. Please use your half beak to pull the weed away so that I may survive.'

'Do you think that I have time to delay my journey while even now the king himself is polishing my golden cage? I should think not indeed!' And Half a Chicken continued on his way.

He soon passed a small heap of glowing embers by the roadside. The fire called out to him, 'Half a Chicken! Half a Chicken! just one moment if you please. My embers are about to go out. Please, with your half beak, pick up some twigs to coax them into flames so that I may survive.'

'Do you think that I have time to delay my journey while even now the king himself has instructed his servants to lay down a golden carpet for me? I should think not indeed!'

He could already see the towers of the palace in the distance, when he passed a tree with tangled branches from which came a whistling noise. This sound called out to him, 'Half a Chicken! Half a Chicken! just one moment if you please. I have been caught in this thicket of branches. Please use your half beak to pull them back so that I may fly as freely as the wind should.'

'Do you think that I have time to delay my journey while even now the king himself is looking anxiously from his window for me? I should think not indeed!'

Half a Chicken arrived at the palace and hopped up to the entrance. He was rather surprised when soldiers barred his way and said, 'No chickens through here. Chickens go round the back.'

As he didn't like the look of their spears, he hopped round to the back entrance. Beside it, leaning against the wall was the king's chef, wondering what to cook for the king's lunch. The chicken that suddenly appeared was the answer. The chef swept him up and threw him into the pot of water that had just been put on the fire.

Fearing that he was about to drown, Half a Chicken called out to the water to help him.

'Why should I help you when you wouldn't help me?' came the reply.

Now the water was getting rather hot and Half a Chicken called out to the fire to help him.

'Why should I help you when you wouldn't help me?' came the reply.

At that moment, the chef looked into the pot to see how the chicken was cooking. Half a Chicken was rolling around just as the water was about to bubble. For the first time the chef noticed that Half a Chicken wasn't a whole chicken. Deciding that he couldn't serve the king only half a chicken, the chef picked him out of the pot by his wing and threw him out of the window.

Just then the wind came hurtling by having managed to extricate itself from the tangle of branches. The wind caught Half a Chicken and hurled him high into the sky. Buffeted this way and that, feeling sick and dizzy, Half a Chicken called out to the wind to help him.

'Why should I help you when you wouldn't help me?' came the reply.

Higher and higher went Half a Chicken, when suddenly the wind stopped blowing. Down, down he plummeted until his fall was stopped by a rather sharp spike on which he had landed in a most sensitive place, one where the sun would never shine. Half a Chicken was now on the lightning conductor of the highest building in the city. Even higher than the king's palace, the cathedral towered above all. How proud he was now that he could look down upon the king himself! How special he felt!

Wind would often return to play with his new friend, blowing Half a Chicken first in one direction and then another. People were so happy to see him up there because he would point the way in which the wind was heading. Half a Chicken's fame spread throughout the country and to neighbouring lands. Everybody wanted their churches to have a weather vane. That is why, from that day to this day, most of our churches are topped by half a chicken.

THE STONE SPIRIT

ROMANIA

Vilva Pietrelor, 'Stone Spirit', is an elemental being, a survivor from animistic beliefs still to be found in folklore and traditional tales. Here she is encountered during Midsummer's Eve when these elemental beings and otherworldly creatures gather in the forests to dance. This traditional belief, marking the summer solstice, is to be found all over Europe, from the forests of Scandinavia and the Balkans in the north-west all the way to those in the south-east. Living near a fairy hill in England, I can attest that this tradition was respected within living memory as nobody dared to go there on Midsummer's Eve, when the fairies were dancing.

It was the summer solstice and the spirits of the elements and all the other fairies had gathered at the court of the Queen of the Fairies to prepare for their Midsummer's Eve celebration. Their circular dance would draw down the power of the sun, ensuring the health and survival of the forest throughout the dark and cold of winter. On this occasion, the stone elemental approached the Queen of the Fairies and mentioned something that had been concerning her. She had noticed that, in contrast to her own great strength, the creatures of the forest, including the humans, all gave birth to very fragile young. Because they were so vulnerable, many young lives were lost, and those that survived took a long time to grow, and so were exposed to many dangers.

When they had finished their dancing ritual, in that magical time between the fading of the shortest night and the dawning of the longest day, Stone Spirit promised to help all the mothers with young, for at that time of year the forest was teeming with new life. She summoned all the animals, including human mothers, and told them that if they threw their babies over their dwellings – be they caves, or nests or holes in the ground or trees, or even houses, that when their babies were in the air, she would imbue them with some of her immense stony strength. All who heard her words rushed home to do this.

As the young of every species landed on the ground on the far side of their dwellings, they instantly became more robust. The baby birds soon fledged and were flying on their own, the bear cubs were tumbling down slopes and swarming up trees, you could hardly tell the squirrel youngsters apart from their parents – they were so agile. Only the woman hesitated. Full of trepidation, she could hardly bear to throw her vulnerable baby into the air. Sensing her anxiety, it had begun to whimper. Stone Spirit exhorted her to do the deed and the woman steeled herself to hurl the child away from her. Just at that moment, she felt the tiny fingers clinging to her own, and was not able to bring herself to let go of her child.

Stone Spirit gave her a stony glare and told her that as she had refused her gift, so would women from that time until all time be bound to carry their children for a whole year. Of all creatures, human children would take the longest to grow into their independence, and remain vulnerable for longer than any other.

THE FIRST MIRROR

IRELAND

Paddy rarely went into town and almost never went by himself. On this occasion he was alone and visited the store, which happened to have some new stock. His attention was caught by something round and shiny. As he picked it up, he nearly dropped it with shock. How did they manage to get that portrait of his dear departed father in there? The likeness was truly wonderful! He quickly paid for it and took it home. Paddy didn't show what he called his 'Twinky Winky' to his wife, because she and his father hadn't got on, so he looked at the portrait at the bottom of the garden where she couldn't see him.

After a while Mary grew suspicious and spied on her husband. She saw him take something out of his pocket and watched his expression soften with love as he stared at whatever it was that he was holding in his hand. Suspicion justified, she waited until he was asleep, crept downstairs and lit a candle. She took the object out of his pocket to see what had been so fascinating that he had needed to hide it from her. Now she knew; there was a portrait of the woman he had been deceiving her with. And what a hideous article she was to be sure! How could he prefer that creature with three warts at the end of her nose and that straggly grey hair, to her? The next morning she was off to the priest to complain that her husband was having an extramarital dalliance.

Having known Paddy for many years, the priest was rather surprised to hear this, but Mary was insistent that she had proof. At that, the priest agreed to come to the house and see it for himself. Mary made some excuse to get Paddy out of the room where his jacket was hanging, to give the priest the opportunity to pick his pocket.

He nearly dropped the Twinky Winky with horror. He had never seen such a lifelike picture of the Devil before! There were those deep-set smouldering eyes, the hooked nose and cruel mouth, the pale skin and the hair drawn back in a widow's peak. How the devil had the Devil crept into that thing? It must be cursed.

Without more ado, the priest rushed outside with it and ground it beneath his heel. For good measure he sprinkled it with holy water. The first mirror in Ireland did not last long, and some say that it is a pity that it was soon followed by others

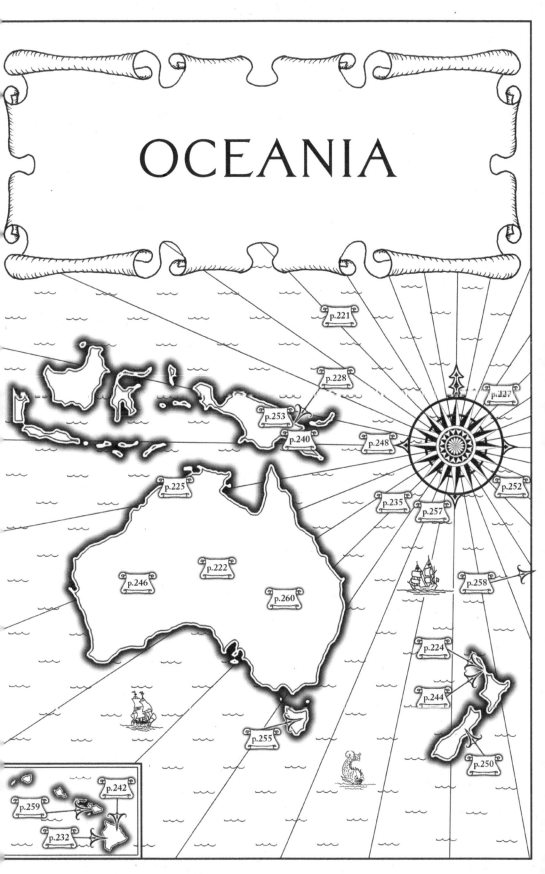

OCEANIA

p.221

p.228

p.117

p.253

p.240

p.248

p.252

p.225

p.235

p.257

p.222

p.246

p.258

p.260

p.224

p.244

p.255

p.250

p.242

p.259

p.232

'In the word there is life, in the word there is death.'

Hawaiian proverb

MAKING THE WORLD IN A SHELL

In the beginning there was only endless water and a being who hung poised above it. This was Aerop-Enap, whose name means Ancient Spider. Dipping her legs in the water, she discovered a giant clam shell. Drumming her feet upon it, it seemed hollow and she determined to get inside. Using a spell of power, she just managed to squeeze in and found herself in total darkness with no room to stand or sit.

At last, by groping about, she felt another creature, a small and helpless snail. To imbue the snail with strength, Ancient Spider placed it in one of her armpits and slept for three nights to allow her power to seep into it. After this she continued to search and found an even bigger snail, which she also empowered, using the same method. She then asked the smaller snail to try to prise apart the two halves of the clam shell to create more room. It managed this with a great effort, and Ancient Spider turned it into the moon. The larger snail was then turned into the sun.

Now that there was light, she could see that there was also a huge worm in the shell with a great writhing strength. She asked him to prise open the shell even further and aided his efforts with another incantation. So hard did he work that sweat streamed off him and collected in the lower part of the shell. By now the clam had separated into two, the upper part becoming the sky, and the lower part becoming the earth.

The worm's salty sweat became the ocean, but his efforts had exhausted him to the point of death. Aerop-Enap took up his corpse and spun a mighty web around it. Then she placed it in the heavens so that all who saw it could honour him by remembering his great deed. Some people now call that pale, luminous web the Milky Way.

RAINBOW SERPENT FINDS COMPANIONS

AUSTRALIA

Rainbow Serpent is revered as an ancestor and a divinity throughout Australia. This being is never referred to as 'it' and always referred to as 'she' or 'he' according to region and tribe. I have tried to respect this despite it seeming clumsy at times in the English language.

In the Dreamtime, which was before our time, the earth was flat and featureless and without colour. How people longed for colours to fill their eyes and swell their spirit. They knew that colours existed because, sometimes, after rain, they raised their eyes to the sky and saw a rainbow. The rainbow was the body of the Rainbow Serpent, and each one of his/her scales was a water droplet drinking in the sun's warmth and reflecting back the gratitude the giant creature felt, with shimmering rainbow colours. Rainbow Serpent was the most beautiful sight that people had ever seen, but they were yet to know the power. Although the most beautiful thing in all of creation, s/he was alone. Feeling this loneliness, Rainbow Serpent stretched out onto the Earth instead of arching above it. Then began a mighty journey, the search to find kindred, the search to find a tribe.

During Rainbow Serpent's travels, the features of all the land that had once been so flat were created by the serpent's immense body and powerful movements. Wherever s/he passed, colour was absorbed by rivers, lakes and puddles. How the people rejoiced to see it. From tribe to tribe Rainbow Serpent meandered, looking for the right ones to settle with. It was a long journey because none of the languages spoken by the people made any sense. At last the pulsing of distant music was heard, then song, and then Rainbow Serpent could feel the trembling of the Earth as the people danced. As Rainbow Serpent listened, sense and meaning emerged from the song. The people were terrified of this huge being until they realised that Rainbow Serpent had suddenly joined in with their singing and knew their language. Now that radiant vision of colour was welcomed as Rainbow Snake asked if s/he could live among them. Colour and company had found each other at last.

One night, when the being had curled up to sleep, it began to rain. Rainbow Serpent opened up a huge gaping mouth to let the sweet drops trickle down that long throat, wider and deeper than any tunnel, and soon felt two drops slide down into that enormous belly. But these started to bounce and run about in a most unwaterly way. It was only then that Rainbow Serpent realised that they hadn't been water drops at all – they were two young brothers from the host tribe. Mistaking the mouth for a cave, they had sought shelter from the rainstorm and been swallowed. What to do? Tell the people what had happened and incur their anger? Behave as though nothing had happened and have those who had disappeared tracked to this sleeping place?

Rainbow Serpent decided to leave silently in the middle of the night and moved far away to wrap coils around a distant and massive rock. But something of that size must leave signs of its passage. The same body that had carved gullies and riverbeds and forced up mountains had left a similar trail. At first light, when those young hunters had not returned, but the Rainbow Serpent had left, people understood that the disappearances were connected, and the tribe easily followed the new trail. By the time Rainbow Serpent had been found, still fast asleep, those powerful coils had squeezed the rock into even higher cliffs with each breath. Rocks and boulders were rolling down the cliff face and the tribe had to keep back because of the danger.

Nevertheless, three of the lost brother's friends climbed the tallest cliff and dropped down onto those beautiful scales that spread bursts of rainbow colours with every breath. Silently they slit open the belly to look for their missing friends. No corpses were to be found, but two birds flew out of its darkness. Deepest indigo and blue turning to vibrant green, their feathers rivalled the intense hues of the scaly skin that had covered them. Iridescent in the morning light, the birds flew high into the sky and away.

Rainbow Snake, now feeling the wound and angered at being treated in this stealthily disrespectful way, reared up over the people, blotting out the sun and covering them all in shadow. Terrified, most of them ran to escape or to hide. Those who leaped over boulders became kangaroos; those who tried to hide under the water became turtles or frogs; those who hid among the rocks became lizards; those who climbed trees became koala bears with their huge frightened eyes; those who were so paralysed with fear that they couldn't move at all became rooted to the spot as trees. And so it went on.

Many animals were created in this way, which in time became gifts to other people and other tribes. However, not all fled or hid, and some picked up their spears and threw them to inflict more wounds on the mighty threat that reared above them. With one lash of that huge tail, the brave tribespeople who fought back were hurled into the sky, where they turned into stars. So it was that when Rainbow Serpent returned home to the sky, these stars that had once welcomed this divine being into their tribe on Earth now remained as companions forever.

MATARIKI – THE LITTLE EYES
(THE PLEIADES)

AOTEAROA (NEW ZEALAND)

This is a lesser-known version of the origin story of this well-known constellation. Matariki's stories of seasonal change and renewal are told all over the world in other languages and cultures.

Rangi, god of the heavens, wore the stars in his cloak as an ornament. How he and the people on Earth loved to see their brilliance as he swirled his cloak across the sky to cover the Earth with night. His favourite star was the brightest and all waited for the moment when its brilliance would appear and fill their hearts with joy. Even the moon shone modestly in another part of the sky to avoid rivalling its light.

But there was one who did not welcome it: Tane, god of light and forests. He was jealous of its brilliance and resented humankind looking up to the heavens instead of always marvelling at the enormous trees he had provided on Earth. He decided to destroy that star and enlisted the aid of two others – Taumatakuku (Aldebaran) and Takurua (Sirius). However, his plot was overheard by a lake in whose waters the brightest star was reflected, and whose beauty was magnified by the wind's ripples that created even more refractions and facets of its light.

The lake wanted to warn the threatened star but didn't know how. The wind wanted to help but knew that his voice would not reach that high. He suggested that the lake tell Rangi the following morning, when the dawn was closest to the Earth. On hearing Tane's plan, the sky god was furious and sent down the great heat of the sun to cause water vapour from the lake to rise up into the sky so that, in this way, it could tell the star of its danger. The wind then cooled the vapour so that it could replenish the lake as rain.

Alerted, the star was able to escape just in time when Tane and his helpers chased it from its place in the sky. He fled to his friend, the lake, and hid himself in its waters. However, Takurua saw him there and sucked up the water so that he was exposed. Onward he raced, pursued by jealous Tane. Although he was tired, his brilliance gave him speed and Tane raged that he could not catch up to him. He seized Taumatakuku and hurled him at the fugitive, who broke into six pieces. Tane contemptuously discarded these back into the sky.

So bright were these fragments that when the people saw this new cluster, they called them 'the Little Eyes'. Rangi was so angry at what had become of his favourite jewel that he commanded that this new constellation be revered more than any of the smaller stars and that to see it would bring good luck. At this decree, even more people gazed into the heavens for a sight of 'Little Eyes'. From that night, to this night, when Matariki appears on the horizon at sunset, it is a time for feasting and celebrating the Māori new year and the end of winter.

RAINBOW SERPENT

MURINBATA TRIBE, NORTHERN TERRITORY, AUSTRALIA

Rainbow Serpent is revered as an ancestor and a divinity throughout Australia. This being is never referred to as 'it' and always referred to as 'she' or 'he' according to region and tribe. Rainbow Serpent has many names according to their different languages. This English name was first used by an anthropologist in the 1920s as a means of describing the characteristics of this being that all indigenous peoples held in common. Reverence for the Rainbow Serpent continues to this day, not only in rituals observed by aboriginals, but also in their contemporary artworks, which are believed to be the longest continuous visual arts practice in the world.

Rainbow Serpent lived in the dreamtime with the other ancestors and with them s/he made the world. Today features in the landscape show where Rainbow Serpent slithered, curled up to sleep, or crept underground. During that time, many gifts were given to humans, including the taboos that taught them right from wrong. So generous were the gifts from Rainbow Serpent that it was fitting that the people who did wrong would be punished. Rainbow Serpent gave sweet water in all its forms – rivers, pools, lakes, billabongs and rain. When not on the Earth, s/he appeared as the rainbow. Where the rainbow touched the ground, those water sources were replenished. When on Earth, Rainbow Serpent lay beneath the waters of pools and in rivers. In this way the gifts of survival, fertility and renewal were entrusted to the people who took care not to defile these sacred places with men's blood from ritual cutting or women's blood from menstruation. The relationships between families and spouses were also set, firm and clear as the crests of the mountains and deep as the river gorges. Diseases and floods were among the punishments for wrongdoing, and incest incurred severe penalties.

One time Rainbow Serpent had fathered a son and two daughters. The brother schemed to sexually abuse his sisters and managed to do this when the siblings were away from camp. The young women determined to have their revenge, and, making sure that he was following them across a river, their song of power summoned hornets that stung him and then raised a flood that washed him away. He managed to come ashore and saw his sisters' fire on a cliff and dared to approach them again. They threw down a rope to haul him up and cut it as he reached the top. Despite breaking all his bones, he was able to mend them with his own song of power, and resolved to kill his father.

This incestuous rapist and murderer secretly made a spear, which he hid in the family's camp. Then he lit fires on the hilltops as an invitation to guests from all around for a celebration. During the festivities he danced in a sexually alluring way, and when the festivities were at their height, he hurled the spear at his father. At that everyone turned into birds and fruit bats and flew away. Although s/he crying with sorrow, nobody stayed to help Rainbow Serpent. He crawled from place to place trying to find somewhere that would stop him bleeding, and wherever he rested in his agony, precious water appeared. The sacred landscape still holds the memory of his wounded journey as he left his possessions one by one, on his wounded journey to the sea. You can still see their shapes left among the rocks.

At last he reached the shore, and as he crept into the water he gathered up all the fire of the world and shaped it into a headdress. Too late, the people realised that he meant to drown all fire as he sank deeper and deeper into the ocean. When someone managed to snatch a branch, it sizzled out.

It was Kestrel who taught the people how to make fire return by rubbing sticks together. From that time to this time, they have never forgotten this skill, lest Rainbow Snake ever becomes so angry again.

DISOBEYING NAKAA, LORD OF PLENTY

KIRIBATI (FORMERLY THE GILBERT ISLANDS), MICRONESIA

First Women and First Men did not live with each other; they had everything they needed in their separate places, which encircled two magical trees of plenty. The Lord of Plenty, Nakaa, who was also the guardian of this part of creation, had given Women their own tree, which fruited with a nut to satisfy their hunger and which was always renewed.

Men had their own such tree and were forbidden to take the nuts from Women's tree. They also had a fish trap of plenty, which was never empty.

One day, Nakaa needed to attend to matters in another part of creation. As soon as he was gone, Men took nuts from Women's tree.

Knowing that they were not allowed to do this, they hoped that this would go unnoticed, but Nakaa immediately smelt a different scent on the Men that they could only have received from being very close to Women. Furthermore, their hair was now flecked with grey. Age had come to them, and Death would follow age.

No longer their protector, Nakaa took away the Men's nut tree and their fish trap and left that part of creation to go to the place where this world and the spirit world, Land of the Ancestors, meet. There he sat and started to weave a great fishing net whose untied threads and filaments floated like mist between this world and the next. Those who died needed to pass that barrier if they were to move on to join their ancestors. Good people found a way through the mesh, but bad people remained entangled forever. From that time to this time, we all die, but it is only Women, who did not steal from another's Tree of Plenty, who are able to bring forth life.

DIVINE PIG, MONSTER AND BENEFACTOR

PAPUA NEW GUINEA, MELANESIA

Here I have blended two tales, one a creation myth, another a wonder or 'fairy' tale that bears similarities to those commonly found throughout the world. Perhaps influenced by the monster's greedy nature, I wanted to include both. Perhaps influenced by the benefactor's qualities, I wanted to emphasise its status in the religious, domestic and economic lives of all the country's diverse peoples. Here we meet Pig in several manifestations – as a supreme and malign agent of destruction, a magical helper, and a source of food and wealth.

When the world was new, life was difficult for the people. Because Sky and Earth were so close together, there was little room to plant crops. If any were planted, they were soon destroyed by the monstrous Pig God, Mugus. Devouring these crops was also a means of tracking down humans, who were his favourite prey. Being blind, he hunted by smell, his vast nostrils detecting the unmistakable scent of the broken earth in the sweet potato fields. The people's lives depended on cultivating these crops, but they also knew that they brought death in the shape of this ravening divinity with its insatiable appetite for human flesh.

Even the other gods and goddesses were terrified of Mugus and, not being dependent on earthly food, had made their homes elsewhere. By now, there were very few people left. The survivors had huddled together in fear at Mugu's relentless progress. When they could hear the grinding of his jaws in the next valley, they all fled – all except for an old woman, long past the age of being able to move quickly. Instead, she took refuge in a cave which led into the depth of the Earth. There she hid until all the tumult and destruction had passed.

When she emerged into the open, the slanting rays of the sunrise picked out a tuber of the only plant that had survived this latest round of destruction. There lay a taro, where giant trotters had scraped it halfway out of the ground on the monster's rampage to find more appealing flesh. Its leaves were now withered and hard. Old Woman scraped away more of the surrounding earth, then, next to this depression, she scraped another hole. Not having had time to collect any tools in her haste, she used the hardened edge of the taro leaf to cut herself, holding her wound in turn above each hole so that her life's blood ran into them, rich and red. Then she covered the holes with trampled leaves and slept. Was she surprised or was she expecting the occupants of those two holes when she awoke? Identical twin boys, the only exception being that one was right-handed, the other left-handed, were there to greet her. In unison they cried out their blessings:

Old Woman, Creator Woman, Spirit of the Earth Woman, she who has made us out of her own blood. How powerful must she be? How powerful will we also be, created from her life's blood, two working together as one!

In only a few days they had grown into men, and Old Earth Woman taught them the art of fighting, so that, united, they could conquer the monster god Mugus, while there was still any life left on Earth. It was easy to find him, all they had to do was to follow his trail of destruction, littered with gnawed bones. Mugus was unaccustomed to being challenged, did not all flee before him? He had not expected to fight a double enemy. Confused by the double image the twins presented, his monstrous head swung to and fro, not knowing who to charge first or which of the twins was the mirror of the other. From which hands would weapons next be wielded from, in their left- and right-handed assaults? After a heroic battle, the brothers' power prevailed, and they straddled his vanquished body. Now it was their turn to feast. The smell of Mugu's roasting flesh travelled as far as the fear he had once spread. At that scent even the other divinities returned, pushing Sky far from the Earth so that this most delicious smell could float even further. They too joined in the celebration feast and when it was over, they departed into the distant places. Now the Earth was left to humans as their domain, where they could at last lead peaceful lives. Any further trouble would be of their own making.

People never forgot what had happened and this story was celebrated for countless generations with sacred rituals. Some believed that the end of the Earth would eventually come, when the giant pig would return to devour every living thing. This time, it would appear with only the front of its body so that its belly would not be a defined space, leaving room to devour the whole world. Some believed that Old Earth Woman went to live in another world, one that could only be reached by plummeting through pools or travelling the subterranean waters that course through the immense network of limestone caves. There in her new realm, beautiful, fertile and fruitful, she ruled as goddess of animal life, fertility and of people yet to be born. Some say that in bringing about the defeat of Mugus, she absorbed his power, and that when she is angered, her face takes on his aspect. It is then that she appears to wrongdoers with the terrifying features of a giant pig.

Two wives were married to the same husband and each was blessed with a gift from that other world when they each gave birth to their daughters. One of the women had dark skin, and her children, a daughter and a son, closely resembled her. Their dark-skinned appearance was considered to be the most desirable, and reassured others that any power they might have would not be bent to a malign purpose. However, the second wife had reddish skin and hair, which was known, but less common and sometimes associated with using their power for evil deeds. So it was within this family, when the lighter-skinned wife practised evil magic on the other woman, causing her death. After that, it was easy to entrap the motherless daughter, who, quite apart from looking after her baby brother, had to do her stepmother's and half-sister's chores as well.

One day, she was sent to gather food by a pool that brimmed up from the limestone tunnels which led to the other world beneath. Of course she had to take her baby brother with her, and she propped him up safely away from the water's edge so he couldn't roll in by accident. However, she was not expecting something to come out of the pool and seize him. With a speed that belied her years, a hideous old woman grabbed the baby and disappeared beneath the water. Without hesitating for a moment, his sister plunged after him to get him back.

What a strange and magical world she found, with exquisite plants and trees growing everywhere, all weighed down with edible fruits or precious objects. But despite all this beauty, there was something amiss. Coming from the only house, which must be where the old woman lived, came a sound that tore her heart. It was the hopeless crying that abandoned and neglected babies make, and the girl hastened towards it. Not knowing whether the old woman was in there or not, she stood outside for a while, uncertain about what to do next. Perhaps she could comfort them anyway, so she started to sing every soothing lullaby she knew. Singing gave her courage, and she went into the house where the old woman was sitting by the fire, only now she was smiling at her. However, that was not the most surprising thing because, once inside, she saw no children at all, but wild animals of all kinds and a profusion of piglets.

Still smiling, Old Earth Woman beckoned the girl to come and sit beside her. Reaching into the fire, she took out a piglet that had been roasting there and shared it with the girl. When they had finished eating, she gathered up every one of its bones, even the tiniest. With the power released in a single breath, she renewed its life, and as she clapped her hands, it scampered away. Then Old Woman fell asleep. The girl too was tired after her large meal and the adventures of the day, but if she managed to drift off, her dreams were tormented by thoughts of what might have happened to her baby brother. Between waking and sleeping was it a memory or a nightmare that brought back the sound of those crying babies?

In the morning, Old Earth Woman, still smiling, gave the girl a net bag in which were some sweet potatoes and the same piglet. Then she was sent on her way. The journey back through the pool was much harder. The sweet potatoes seemed to be getting heavier and heavier, dragging her back downwards. Just as she feared she would drown, she saw that the piglet had transformed into a mighty boar who could swim more strongly than any warrior, and he easily dragged her safely to the shore. At first the girl didn't take in everything that was happening because she was distracted by what was now in her net. Gleaming with all the colours of a moonlit dusk were enormous pearl shells, whereas the sweet potatoes had quite disappeared. Marvelling at these treasures she was almost missed the boar transforming into a young man as he clambered onto the land. Surely, he seemed familiar? At first the girl didn't recognise him, but slowly she realised he was her little brother, who had magically gained his adult form.

How happy the father was to see his children when he had given up hope of ever seeing them again. How proud he was to see that his son had been blessed with this magical leap to adulthood. His wife too was pleased to have her stepdaughter back to take over her work and that of her daughter. However, she wasn't glad for long – knowing that her husband wanted to replace her with another wife, she realised that with the pearl shells, he would now be able to pay her dowry. Be that as it may, she too could be given pearl shells of her own. She dragged her daughter to the pool and hurled her in, jumping in after her.

There was the magical land just as she had heard it described. Why waste any time singing to crying babies? She went straight into the house where Old Earth Woman beckoned her to a seat. Reaching into the fire she pulled out a piglet, which she shared with her visitor. However, this was not enough for the red-skinned woman, who, when she thought the old woman wasn't looking, helped herself to one of the piglet's legs to save for later. When it was time to leave, she was given the piglet, which had been restored to life, in her net. How heavy it became on her return journey, dragging her down so that she could not climb out of the water: she was drowned within sight of the bank. It was only then that the piglet climbed up, where it transformed back into the red-skinned daughter. However, because of her mother's transgression, she was missing a leg and even the wealthiest man would not have paid a single pearl shell for her dowry.

THE HEROINE'S JOURNEY

HAWAII, POLYNESIA

Hi'iaka, beloved youngest sister, gestated in the bosom of her fire goddess sister, Pele, had been sent on a quest. She was entrusted to fetch Lohi'au, her sister's lover, from a distant island. Knowing that this quest would be full of dangers, she asked to be allowed to take a companion. This request was granted, and Pele allowed their most loyal retainer to go. Although Pa'uopalapalai was only a servant in Pele's divine household, she had become, through her loyalty and spirituality, a being with more than mortal powers.

Soon after leaving their island, they came across another woman, Wahine'Oma'o, who was on her own journey to make offerings to goddess Pele. This was such a good omen that she was invited to join the others on their quest, when she had finished her devotions. As they too were in service to mighty Pele, she readily agreed, and they waited for her.

Now there were three companions on the quest, whose names meant many things. The first had several titles due to her many attributes and divine powers. On this journey she was known as 'Lightning Skirted Woman of Sunrise', because her skirt was woven with a celestial weapon of great striking power whose flashes never missed their mark. This was offset by her ability to bring joy and clarity to any situation. Her spiritual insight had been developed by her piety, and was to prove invaluable on this journey. The second companion's name meant 'Fern Skirt', due to her devotion to the goddess who brings forth those plants that are so distinctive to Hawaii, being among the first to grow on the fertile lava fields that Pele has created. The third companion's name meant 'Green Woman' and spoke of her reverence for nature and the goddesses that make the Hawaiian Islands such bountiful places.

The three travelled on together and passed through the lands of princess Papulehu, who welcomed them and ordered a feast to be prepared for her honoured guests. Although Papulehu was beautiful, generous and wealthy, Hi'iaka soon noticed that she was not devout, and neglected to say prayers and make offerings to the gods and goddesses. This lack of spirituality curtailed her inner vision and was to endanger her on her journey when she joined her three guests on their adventure. Papulehu also ignored a divine warning when Hi'iaka's serving of food disappeared without her touching it – divine presences are everywhere, and things seen with the outer eye may be seen differently if, through piety, one has developed the inner, spiritual eye …

During their journey, they came across some fishermen who worked for Papulehu's father, and she asked for some fish. Seeing these unaccompanied women, the fishermen tried to take advantage of them with their unwelcome sexual advances. They had no idea who they were dealing with. Letting them believe that they would bargain their favours for food, Hi'iaka first insisted that they be given plenty of fish. Then she transformed some rocks on the shore into their own likenesses, so true to form that they resembled the lovely women exactly. She and her companions laughingly made off with the fish, while the men discovered that they were trying to literally have sex with women of stone.

Not all their challenges were met so light-heartedly. Soon they had to pass through a forest guarded by an evil dragon lizard, with many shape-shifting demons at his command. With their spiritual inner eye, the three original companions could distinguish between the demons and the shapes they had adopted. Unfortunately for the princess, she was as unable to do this as the fishermen she had escaped from. As the mighty battle ensued, she rushed to a tree stump for some protection. Unable to discern that it was really the dragon lizard in disguise, she was devoured by him as the ancestor and divine spirits came to Hi'iaka's aid, and they were, at last, victorious.

Too numerous to tell here were the trials and dangers that beset these heroines as they pursued their quest, helping the needy at every opportunity. Who could imagine the horror of finding two formless heaps of flesh that had once been men? Weeping, they explained that a dragon demon had sucked out all their bones. But they could not have found anyone better to tell their story to, as Hi'iaka was also a goddess of healing. She stripped a plant with straight white stalks and replaced their bones with these. At that, in his rage at her having undone his evil deed, she was attacked by the dragon demon himself, and all his evil spirit army that guards the way to the Underworld. How numerous they were; she would never have prevailed were it not for her lightning skirt, flashing destruction in all directions and turning her adversaries into whirlwinds and locusts.

Towards the end of their journey, they encountered two other demons who guarded a narrow bridge, the only way across a deep gorge at the bottom of which foamed the Wailuka river. So powerful had these demons grown that the local people worshipped them as goddesses and, if they had not brought offerings for them, would be hurled into the river while midway across. With her inner all-seeing eye, Hi'iaka could see that this bridge was really a demon's tongue. Instead of presenting a gift, she ordered the demons to bring her refreshments as a token of hospitality. With this demand, battle was declared, the demons were routed and victorious Hi'iaka freed the region of this scourge. On she went to fulfil her sister Pele's request at last.

It was this epic journey and Hi'iaka's triumphs over adversity that made the island safe for any traveller that came afterwards.

MAUI TRICKSTER, HERO, HELPER

*With more than human powers, but nevertheless mortal, semi-divine Maui,
both trickster and hero, is found in stories throughout Polynesia. So widespread are these stories, of which there are many variations, that experts
may challenge the versions here if seen from the perspective of the heritage of
their own islands. While Maui could amply inhabit a book all to himself, I
am only attempting to give the reader an overall impression of this unique
character. We know about his birth, his death and many variants of his
exploits during his colourful life. If Oceania celebrates an epic hero, surely it
is Maui – complex, unpredictable and uniquely inventive.*

Taranga's four sons and one daughter were no longer children. Her eldest
boy was able to quell his quarrelsome brothers and her daughter was
already looking to choose herself a husband. Their mother could slip away
more often to the Underworld – that Otherworld where her consort was
chief. It was there that she conceived her youngest son.

Perhaps because his spark had begun in the Underworld, it could not
thrive in this one for long. The foetus struggled free from his mother, a
premature birth, an early death. Or perhaps it was because Maui was so
impulsive that he could not wait for his body to keep pace with his true
nature, and that was why he had appeared too soon on this Earth. There
stood Taranga on the seashore, singing all the rightful songs to prevent
this scrap of miscarried flesh from returning as an evil spirit to haunt the
lives of others. Her people knew that those who were born and perished
in this way returned to torment the living. There was just one last thing to
be done. His mother cut a hank of her hair and tied the lifeless shape into
it before casting it into the sea.

But Maui's tiny remains were not eaten by fishes. Others in the ocean
protected him, cradled him in the strong arms of kelp, buffered him against
the soft bodies of jellyfish, their trailing filaments warding off all harm.
Mighty Ocean, from which all living creatures of land and water had once
emerged, returned Maui's life to him. When at last Ocean knew that he
could survive on land, a great wave washed him up. There he lay with the
other flotsam, tangled in seaweed, while gulls squabbled among themselves
to be the first to get at him.

Their commotion attracted the attention of an elder, one who could claim the God of the Sky, Rangi, as an ancestor. In his wisdom, the old man instantly knew that here were no ordinary tide leavings. Just in time he chased the gulls away, picked up the baby, and knew him to be his own grandson. Maui grew under his grandfather's protection, learning from him how to become a man. Some say that he was still a boy, some that he was on the threshold of manhood when he set off to discover the other members of his family.

Hearing music and a thronging of people, he joined them at a celebration, and sat behind his brothers while the crowd danced. When Taranga collected her children at the end of the festivities, to her surprise she found an extra one in the group who was claiming to be hers. Maui insisted that he belonged to this family and described the circumstances of his death, rebirth and upbringing with such precision that she was convinced. How does a mother feel when a child known to be dead is restored to her alive? She lavished all her affection on him as though trying to make up for those lost years, and his brothers were jealous. Jealous but also full of admiration, even if they did not express it, for this precocious, fearless boy.

Maui had found his mother and siblings; now it was time to find his father. But where was he? He knew that his mother's disappearance before every sunrise had something to do with this mystery, but each morning when he awoke, she was already gone. He would make sure that he could see where she went. That night, silently, stealthily he blocked up all the cracks in their sleeping hut with mud so that the greying light could not penetrate the darkness inside. He also stole his mother's white belt to use later. Taranga slept on in the darkness. It was late when she finally woke, and sleepily she wondered why she had done so when it was still dark. It was only when she opened the door that she realised how much the day had progressed. In her panic she did not hide her tracks and Maui watched as she lifted a particular piece of turf, revealing a tunnel into which she disappeared.

Now his brothers could see another aspect of his power as Maui took the white belt, and tying it on, shape-shifted into the form of a bird with a white breast. Kereru Pigeon fluttered to where he had seen his mother disappear into the ground. Keen bird eyes could identify the very stalks of greenery she had touched. Kereru's beak caught them, his beautiful green neck jerked, the tuft lifted, and there was the tunnel that led to the Underworld, the Otherworld where his father lived. His brothers' hearts were filled with envy and their eyes shone with glee as they saw what their precocious baby brother could do.

The tunnel led to another land with strange trees and flowers. There he saw his father and mother together beneath the tree where he was perched. Were they about to create another child? Maui certainly wanted no rivals and shook the berries down from the branch where he was hidden. His distracted father looked up, but Maui was already fluttering down, regaining his human form as soon as his feet touched the soil of that strange place. At Taranga's insistence, his father accepted him as his son. This meant that the proper ritual would have to be performed. The chief of the Underworld started the recitation, but because he had been so taken by surprise, he omitted a portion of it, thus sealing Maui's mortality.

Now that he had been formally accepted into the family, it was as though Maui's brothers were at his command, and he needed them to help him to perform a great feat. Two magical fish hooks had been created – magical because they had been fashioned from the jaw bone of his own grandmother! Some say that this was a gift and came with an incantation of great summoning power. Some are not so sure that it was a gift at all and that Maui starved his own grandmother to death before extracting her jawbone from her corpse. Thus equipped, Maui and his brothers set off in his canoe.

Although strictly instructed not to question his actions, and to remain silent, his brothers disobeyed him and it took several attempts for Maui to succeed in his heroic task. As he sang his grandmother's sacred song, those fish hooks were cast into the sea, found their mark, and caught in a giant mass that reared up above the horizon. It was huge beyond understanding. The brothers were terrified of this monstrous fish and cut Maui's line. The next attempt was even more dangerous as, this time, they had to paddle even further out into the open ocean to stand a chance of catching the monster again. This time, when it appeared, his brothers' screams of fear drowned out the sound of their grandmother's incantation and it escaped again. At last, when they saw that Maui was not going to give up, they allowed him to finish the task, and the leviathan was caught.

Maui needed to leave them to offer thanks to the Old Man of the Sea who had surrendered part of his realm in this exploit. Perhaps influenced by the example of transgressive behaviour that he himself had set, his brothers defied Maui's instructions yet again when he told them not to touch the fish. As soon as he was gone, they set about hacking into it with their knives, all fear forgotten.

Maui's act of incomparable strength and bravery had turned that leviathan into new land. It was called Te Ika-a-Māui, which means 'Maui's Fish' in Māori. European settlers called it New Zealand's North Island. You can still see his brothers' slashes in the fish's body. They are the land's deep ravines and valleys. More than one bay lays claim to be the jawbone fish hooks. There are so many with smooth curves balanced by cruel promontories at each end.

Te Waipounamu, meaning 'Water where greenstone is found', is what Europeans call South Island, but Māoris know that this is what remains of Maui's canoe.

Maui did not know the meaning of the word 'enough'. Rebirthed from the Ocean, traveller to the Underworld, creator of two new islands, there was still plenty to do. Possessed of a magical weapon from one grandmother, he had also stolen fire from his other grandmother. She was the very spirit and body of the molten lava at the Earth's core and Maui had tricked her into casting her sparks into a tree, so now people would always be able to make fire for themselves by rubbing sticks together. All this had he accomplished, so what was left? It was time to tame the sun.

Gradually, Sun had taken to rolling its way closer to the Earth so that crops and creatures were being scorched by its heat. Not only that, it now travelled more quickly across the sky, making the days too short. So not only were the living incapacitated by the heat, there was not enough light. People had too little time to plant their crops and the few that they could get into the ground during the shortening days soon withered. Women did not have enough light to make their flax skirts with which to adorn their beauty. They did not have time to make the magnificent feathered cloaks that were such a symbol of honour and standing in the community. Something had to be done.

Maui still had his grandmother's jawbone, and did her name not mean 'As far as the Earth can reach'? At each dawn and sunset, Sun's journey passed within a hair's breadth of the Earth's edge, and this gave Maui an idea. Summoning his brothers once more from where they lay exhausted with heat, he ordered them to make ropes. He helped them to gather vast quantities of flax, and they started to plait the fibres together. So much was needed that their fingers became skilled enough to continue working in the dark. When the ropes were ready, Maui wove them into a net and they all carried its great weight to the place where the sun would rise. Trapped only for a moment, Sun burned his way through the fibres and rushed across the sky in the shortest day ever.

More magic was needed. Had not his mother's hair protected him from death itself? Taranga gave him the strands he needed and with these he wove a net in which he caught Sun and held him fast. Then he took the jawbone and beat Sun until he cried for mercy and promised that he would slow his journey through the sky. From that day to this day Sun moves slowly from dawn to sunset, maybe because he is keeping his promise, maybe because he is still limping from Maui's blows. Although the flax ropes were burned away, the skill of making them remained and were taught to the people, who passed on this art from generation to generation.

Maui could not accept that he was mortal and that, despite his divine deeds, he would die like other men. His family knew that his father had omitted the part of the ceremony that would have made him immortal, and now his son could not be persuaded against taking on Death herself. He would travel to the place where nothing grew, where Death in the form of a monstrous old woman lay sleeping. Every hero has followers, and, as he walked through the forest, more and more birds flocked around him, calling and twittering from tree to tree. Maui warned them that they would have to be silent when he reached Death so as not to wake her. Even asleep she would be the most dangerous enemy he had ever encountered.

There she lay, her ancient skin pitted and gouged like the rocks of the mountains. A glitter of ice gleamed from eyes slitted in sleep. Her snores were avalanches, her teeth shafts of obsidian. The birds were quiet, they knew that one day she would also be waiting for them.

Maui meant to undo the power of death by reversing what is the natural way of giving life. He was going to crawl up through Death's birth canal and emerge through her mouth. But as Death never gave birth, that part of her body was also full of obsidian teeth. It would be like crawling along a ladder of blades sharper than glass. To do this Maui would need to shape shift. He chose the form of a worm to be able to curve around those teeth in the dark. The birds watched silently. The man crept between the huge spread thighs. Already his head and shoulders had become worm-like as he slowly inserted himself into that place of darkness and danger. As he wriggled in deeper, his hips smoothed, rounded, stretched and just for a moment his legs flailed desperately before they too transformed. It was only for a moment, but it was long enough. His entourage of birds had never seen anything so comical. Unable to contain themselves, they shrieked and cackled with laughter. Death awoke and felt Maui inside her. She clasped her thighs together and crushed the life out of him. His body died, but his power lives on in all the stories we still tell about him.

THE EPIC OF SEIA, THE BEAUTIFUL

SAMOA, POLYNESIA

The great chief Tigilau convinced his counsellors to agree to a law that all male babies were to be killed, allowing only females to survive. This was because Tigilau had a dream in which it was prophesied that a boy would be born who would be even more beautiful than himself. Soon after, a couple gave birth to a male child and, true to his word, Tigilau killed him. The grieving parents moved far away to a distant part of the island, and lived there in seclusion. A second son, Seia, was born to them who was as beautiful as the full moon shimmering on water, and as strong as the midday sun.

Eventually news of this young man reached the chief and a summons was sent for Seia to appear and do some tasks for him. Although his weeping parents begged him not to go, knowing that the chief would try to kill him, Seia had no such fears and insisted on presenting himself. Not expecting him to reach his malae, the ceremonial centre of the village, so quickly, Chief Tigilau was still fast asleep. Seia had to call his name loudly several times, which also woke all the women of the village and they peered out of their homes to see who came with this voice they did not recognise. How beautiful this stranger was! The women exclaimed and pointed, called out excitedly to each other across the malae, and, of course, all this attention made Tigilau even angrier. It was exactly what he had dreaded all those years ago. Fortunately he had an impossible task lined up for Seia, and once he had failed at that he could be punished.

This was to demolish a toa, an ironwood tree that was too close to the chief's house. Not for nothing did its name mean 'warrior'. Many a stone axe had been shattered or blunted on its trunk, and still it stood. With a few kicks, Seia felled it, and the chief's increased rage was matched only by the women's admiration. Sighing with desire, they collapsed onto the grass, eyes shining, bosoms heaving, to see what would happen next.

Before long Seia was ordered to pick breadfruit from a nearby tree. Being a stranger, he was not to know that the tree was inhabited by an evil spirit, a cannibal who would emerge to pick up the fruit before the person who had shaken the branches could come down. If the cannibal picked up the fruit quickly, that meant that he would catch and eat the breadfruit thief. If he picked the breadfruit up slowly that meant that the thief would be spared on that occasion. Seia swarmed up that tree as quick as a skink. With one shake, all the breadfruit tumbled down. Everyone waited to see how the cannibal spirit would deal with this effrontery. Slowly, slowly as a turtle hauling herself up the beach to lay, the limbs of the monster emerged from the trunk. Laboriously he crawled to the first of the fruit, and it seemed as though the sun had moved in the sky before he had raised it.

'I don't have all day to wait for this!' screamed the enraged chief, and set another task.

This was to catch Tanihwa, a giant shark that frequented the waters on a nearby shore. Fatally savage, nobody knew how many people it had killed. With a turn of speed fuelled by its viciousness, Tanihwa was nevertheless not clever. Seia strolled down to the shore when the dawn was but a pearly promise in the sky. Behind him, at a respectful distance, followed a swooning party of women, maiden or married, and all weak at the knees. Searching the shoreline, he saw a rock that stretched like a finger into the sea. There he waited, knowing that the sunrise would cast his shadow on the water. As the sun rose, his silhouette hung, gently undulating on the surface, elongated by its low rays. At that, Tanihwa thought that a huge man was swimming and that this would be a larger than usual mouthful for him. He leaped out of the water, which was what Seia had been expecting. Thrusting his arm down the monster's throat, he choked him and beat him to death on the rock before dragging him onshore.

Still Tigilau would not give up, devising task after task including one that involved the seduction of the loveliest lady of the west. Whichever one, whether himself or Seia, managed to gain her love would be the winner. How Tigilau could think for one moment that any woman would not choose his rival must be the most surprising element of this entire tale, but it was he who set up this doomed contest and it was he who lost. Humiliated beyond any other recourse, he stabbed himself with his own spear as he threw himself into the sea to drown. How happy were Seia's parents that he had triumphed over the chief's plots and that they would not have to lose another son.

FIERY PASSION

All over the world natural phenomena have given rise to legends as people incorporate them into their mythology, thus assimilating them into, and simultaneously creating, their cultural perspectives.
   Sarah Zielinsi, writing for the Smithsonian Magazine, *includes fellow scientists' findings:*

Lava flowed continuously for 60 years in the 15th century, covering some 430 square kilometers of the island of Hawaii. 'If any flow were to be commemorated in oral tradition, this should be the one, because the destruction of such a large area of forest would have impacted Hawaiian life in many ways,' U.S. Geological Survey volcano scientist Donald A. Swanson wrote in the *Journal of Volcanology and Geothermal Research* in 2008. Hiʻiaka's furious digging may represent the formation of the volcano's modern caldera that occurred in the years after the lava flow.

Pele, divinity of volcanos and fire, was a passionate and jealous lover. If she was attracted to someone, she wanted him whether he had pledged his heart to another or not. If any dared to thwart her voracious desire, her vengeance was terrible.

Such a one was Ohia, deeply in love with beautiful, gentle Lehua. When he did not respond to Pele's advances, she furiously turned this handsome, vigorous young man into a withered tree. Knowing that Lehua would not want to live without her lover, other gods pitied her and transformed her into a flower blooming on those twisted branches. There she remains on the most common indigenous tree, unique to Hawaii's islands: the Ōhiʻa lehua. The first to take root on recent lava flows, the blossoms resemble the fiery sparks that shoot up from the craters at Pele's every outbreath.

Ohia was born with many brothers and sisters on Tahiti. Her mother was Goddess of the Earth and her father was God of the Heavens. Of all their children, she was the most uncontrollable, seducing a brother-in-law and losing her temper whenever she was crossed. At last, her parents banished her and she set off in a canoe paddled by one of her brothers, searching for the island that would become her home. Despite her fiery form needing protection from the element of water by her shark chieftain brother, Pele nevertheless could not resist a challenge. When she had found an island robust enough to contain her incandescent nature, she contrived a marriage with the God of Water. Perhaps he was too frightened to refuse, perhaps it was a case of the attraction of opposites, or a means to test her own strength. Inevitably, the union proved to be as brief as it was turbulent. She routed her husband, covering his watery retreat with her own rivers of lava as he ran towards the sea, his escape route being preserved to this day in that mighty lava flow.

Many are the eventful tales of Pele's arrival on Hawaii, where she made her home in Kilauea, a volcano whose fires continue to light the night skies with her power. They tell us of various siblings she arrived with, at times still fighting with them.

On her way to Hawaii, she fell in love with Lohi'au but knew that she could not remain with him there, his island being too small to contain her power for more than a short time. However, she was determined to be with him, and once settled on Hawaii she sent one of her sisters off to fetch him for her. Youngest of all the sisters, divinity of forests, dance, song, magic and healing, it was Hi'iaka that Pele had loved the most. She had protected this magical child as she grew inside an egg. Incubating it against her own hot body, she cradled it in her fiery arms now tempered to nurture, her destructive powers subdued. So it was this sister who was entrusted with the task of bringing Pele's lover. Hi'iaka only hesitated at the thought of leaving her beloved forest, but when Pele promised to look after it she left having been told to accomplish the whole journey within forty days.

Unbeknown to Pele, her loyal sister had to overcome unforeseen dangers, and, when Hi'iaka finally reached Lohi'au, it was to find that he had died from love sickness. After her epic journey, even more time was spent in using her magic and healing arts to restore him to life.

All these unexpected challenges caused delays, and, after forty days, Pele began to suspect the worst – that Hi'iaka had fallen in love with Lohi'au just as she had done – and that this delay was due to the dalliance of lovers.

Why, after all, would anyone behave differently from herself? Why would her own sister not do what she herself had done with another sister's lover? In revenge, she set Hi'iaka's beloved forest alight.

Whether Hi'iaka had been guilty of Pele's accusation, whether she decided she may as well do what she had already been punished for, or whether as an act of revenge for the destruction of her beloved forest, she made love to Lohi'au, making sure that Pele could see them. Pele killed him with an eruption from her volcano, and her sister dug frantically to find his body. You can still see the crater that is the hole she created in her search.

DAUGHTER OF THE OCEAN

AOTEAROA (NEW ZEALAND)

Hinauri, loyal wife, was in mourning because her mischievous brother, Maui, had turned her husband into a dog. There were many different stories being told as to why he had done this, but Maui wasn't telling, and his brother-in-law could only bark. People do not agree about what happened next. Some say that Hinauri threw herself into the sea to end her life, but the sea refused to drown her and she was washed up alive on a distant shore.

However, some say that such was her mana, her strength of spirit, that she determined to find a new life for herself. Throwing herself into the sea, she summoned a fish to ride on its back to another island. The fish was too small and soon tired, and when she slapped it the marks of her fingers striped it forever. From fish to fish she went, leaving her mark upon each one, spots where her fingertips had been, a flat body when she had stepped on it, and at last she found a shark strong enough to carry her to journey's end. Some say that she had travelled all the way from Hawaii to Aotearoa. During the final part of her journey, she was so overcome with thirst that she broke a coconut on the shark's back, where it has had a lump ever since.

At last she reached Motutapu, Sacred Island, where she was safe, at least for a while. Hinauri was a survivor and lived for a while along the shoreline and in the fringes of the forest. When the tide went out, she would fish in the rockpools, not having brought any tackle with her. She was not to know that these were the mirrors of Tinirau, god and guardian of all the sea creatures, who lived with his two wives on the other side of the island. Tinirau would come to these pools as that shore was in the lee of the wind, and their surfaces were not disturbed by the sea breezes. Now, when he tried to gaze at the beauty of his tattooing, their water was clouded by stirred-up sand. He determined to find out how this was happening, and hid behind a rock to watch. Before long he saw Hinauri, strong, beautiful, brave. When he heard her story, he named her 'Daughter of the Ocean' and he had already fallen in love with her.

He did not return home to his other two wives, knowing that they would not accept Hinauri, so the couple stayed on leeward side of the island. When he wanted to go back for food or supplies, so strong was Hinauri's power that these appeared at her command when she sang her chants imbued with her mana.

As expected, their marriage provoked the jealousy of the two wives he had abandoned, and they united in their efforts to get rid of the inter-loper. This came to a head when Tinirau saw them approaching along the beach. He warned Hinauri to be careful, but she was already prepared to defend herself if needed. First they tried to harm her by throwing a web of incantations around her, but her mana rendered these harmless and she attacked first one and then the other with her obsidian knife, slashing open their stomachs. As they died, Tinirau saw that they had swallowed all kinds of tools and fishing tackle that they had stolen and he had inexplicably lost. Even before Hinauri had arrived, theirs was a hunger that nothing could satisfy.

THE DANCER AND THE WHIRLWINDS

Wurrawilberoos were the brother whirlwinds that were a force to be reckoned with. When they swept down over the plains from their home in the mountains, they caused destruction in the people's camp and carried off anything that they wanted. Only the warriors' spears could pierce their swirling power.

Among the people lived a young woman who did little work because she brought so much joy with her dancing. The simplest movement was performed so gracefully that for her merely to pick up firewood was a series of exquisite gestures that became a dance. Always on the move, she was light and slender and seemed to be born of the air rather than the earth.

One day, she accompanied her mother, who had taken her digging stick to look for tubers. Further and further they went from the camp, with the daughter dancing rings and loops around her mother as was her custom. As she danced, she left patterns in the sand and these were noticed from afar by the Wurrawilberoos, the whirlwind brothers. How they admired those patterns – perhaps they wanted to adorn themselves with those designs when they painted their bodies. Then they noticed who was making them – how light she was, swirling and twirling about rather like themselves, but also unlike themselves, with her beauty and finesse.

Down rushed the brothers from the mountains, blinding the two women with the dust they whipped up. Each brother seized one of them and whirled back towards their mountain camp. Their captives heard them calling to each other with glee, saying that the daughter would be made to dance for them whilst they ate the mother who was heavier and had more flesh on her bones. Before they were halfway, one of the brothers complained that the mother was too heavy. To lessen his burden, the other took the stone axe from his brother's belt and tucked it into the daughter's, to spread the load. As soon as she could, she wiggled it out of her waist cord so that it fell on the ground and was lost.

When the Wurrawilberoos reached their home in the mountains, it was noticed that the axe was missing. It would be needed to butcher the older woman. This started an argument: the brother who had complained about the weight he was carrying accused the other that it was his fault for putting it in the young woman's waist cord, and told him to go and look for it, even though the light was fading. The accused brother didn't trust the other not to run off with the girl as soon as his back was turned. The argument became more heated until both agreed to look for the axe together.

As soon as she thought it safe, the daughter grabbed her mother's hand and they ran back towards their home, guided by the lights of the camp fires that had already been lit. The older woman grew too tired to run any more and told her daughter to run on and save herself. Of course, her child could not bear to do that and she carried her mother on her back, sinking further into the sand with each step. The Wurrawilberoos had detected their escape and were hurling themselves after the fugitives. Knowing that they would not reach safety in time, the daughter called for help and the warriors of the tribe rushed out into the night with their spears. All was a whirlwind of dust and darkness as the brave men stabbed into the wind with their weapons. In the confusion, the mother was left behind, but the daughter was swept away. How her mother mourned for her, how the tribe missed her dancing and the joy it brought to their hearts.

Years without counting passed, and the people never forgot the mother and her brave, beautiful daughter. Around the campfires, their story was often on their lips. One day a strange tall bird stalked into the camp. How lithe and elegant it was. Slowly, the bird began to dance with such ease and grace that joy filled the onlookers' hearts. Everyone said that the girl had come back to them in the form of this bird. They asked her where she had been all this time but, of course, she couldn't speak. However, they knew she understood them because she gestured towards the sky with her beak and the people knew that that was where the Wurrawilberoos had gone. She had been too heavy to carry for such a distance, so they had left her on the earth. Now that her abductors had gone, she was able to dance for herself, and she danced for joy at her freedom. Her dancing was now as light as a feather, and it caused her to grow wings and then the complete body of a bird. The people called her 'Brolga', which is also the name of an Australian crane. If you see Brolgas dancing, they will lighten your heart.

SNAKE DAUGHTER

SOLOMON ISLANDS, MELANESIA

Throughout this group of more than 900 islands, stories of snake divinities or spirits abound. Many derive from Agunua, the creator snake who manifests in many other serpentine forms. Like the Rainbow Serpent in Australia, this sacred snake can be both benign and destructive.

Who knows where mighty Agunua may next appear? Like the boa disguised as a branch, as the copperheads coloured like the very ground on which we tread, Agunua, creator and destroyer, may be within our touch without our knowing. Just as snakes lay many eggs, so does this powerful spirit appear in many forms; who is to say that the coral snake gliding across your path, banded with the colours of night and day, is not some part of that great spirit itself, too powerful for mortal eyes to see in its entirety?

Long ago there lived a woman who gave birth to a snake. The snake-child's grandmother, knowing that no good would come of this, hid this snake daughter from her son-in-law. How long can such a thing be kept secret? In time the couple had another child, resembling any other, and this one the father knew and loved. The firstborn, being a snake, was left to fend for herself in the forest, but when the parents left the younger child to work on their sago patches and to plant yams, the mother summoned her daughter to look after her younger sibling. At first the father thought that the child was being taken care of by his mother-in-law, but, often seeing her in the crop fields, he wondered who was looking after his child.

One day he went back early to their home and saw the baby being encircled by a large snake, who was singing:

Where are my hands to hold you?
I have none, so sleep little one
Where are my arms to support you?
I have none, so sleep little one
Where are my feet to steady you?
I have none, so sleep little one
Where are my legs to lean on?
I have none, so sleep little one, sleep.

Despite the tenderness of this song, the father was horrified at the sight and immediately chopped the creature into eight pieces, never suspecting that he was killing his own child while mistakenly trying to save another.

As soon as the eighth blow had struck, it started to rain violently and continued to rain for eight days. During this storm, the eight sections of the snake joined up and snake-daughter was whole again. Now able to crawl once more, she started on a vengeful journey, chasing and then eating whoever she found. Again she was attacked, again she was hacked into eight pieces, only this time her body was cooked and devoured by everyone, or almost everyone – only a mother and her child refused to participate in this strange feast. Perhaps it was the very woman who had birthed her. Silently they watched as all the snake-daughter's bones were thrown into the sea.

There beneath the waters, after eight tides had come and gone, those bones found each other once again and, reunited, slowly rose to the surface of the sea. Eight more downpours came to cover them, leaving them clothed with flesh and muscle. Whole once more, she began to thrash about in the waters. This created eight mighty sea surges that swept away the village, sparing only the woman and child who had not eaten her flesh or scattered her remains.

It is not fitting that a mother and child should be abandoned without help. The snake-daughter, named Walutahanga, meaning eight fathoms, ensured that these two would survive. She created a fresh water stream that flowed despite the sea-salt water that had invaded the land. New fruiting trees and crops appeared such as coconuts, sweet potatoes and yams. Then she slithered away to become guardian of a sacred place where people feared yet respected her.

WHALE RIDER

AOTEAROA (NEW ZEALAND)

Tinirau, god of all that lives in the sea, had several pet whales. The largest and favourite of these was Tutunui who would take Tinirau wherever he wanted to go on his back. When he felt that the water was about to get too shallow for him, he would give a little shake and Tinirau knew that he had to dismount. Sometimes he would swim to shore from there or sometimes he would summon a shark on which to complete his journey.

His new wife, Hinauri, had given birth to a son, and when the boy was of age, his father arranged for his initiation ceremony. Only the best would do for him, and Kae, the most high-ranking and powerful of priests, was engaged. Powerful not only because he was a priest, but because he was also a magician. Tremendous was the feast that accompanied the ceremony, but despite Tinirau's lavish generosity they ran out of food, so he went to the shore and summoned Tutunui. Kae was both impressed and jealous when he saw the command his host had over this magnificent creature, especially when Tinirau cut a large slice of blubber from him and gave it to the women to cook.

When the feast was over, Kae asked if he could borrow the whale to take him home. Tinirau was reluctant, but Kae was about to shame him for his lack of generosity in front of everyone – it was after all such a little thing to ask – so after his initial hesitation, he agreed. Kae set off on the whale's back and before long could see his own shore. Tutunui gave a shake to warn him that it was getting dangerous for him to go any closer, but Kae ignored it. Three times Kae ignored the warning, hoping that Tutunui would beach himself, which is what happened. Kae's family rushed down to the shore with whoops of delight and butchered Tutunui where he lay helpless.

Tinirau had begun to feel anxious that the whale had not returned. There was no response to his summons. On the distant horizon, a feather of black smoke stroked the sky, and on the sea breeze came a smell of roasting blubber that Tinirau recognised. He told his wife and sisters what had happened and asked them to go and avenge the death of Tutunui, knowing that their skills and subtle approach would enable them to get close to Kae without arousing his suspicions. Off went Hinirau and her sisters-in-law in their canoe, their strong, flashing arms a dance of death with each paddle stroke.

From island to island and beach to shoreline they went, visiting all the communities as entertainers. How they were praised for their wonderful dancing and songs of power. How their mana, their strength of spirit, brought beauty and respect to their audiences, how they made people laugh with their comic stories and risqué dances. Their reputation preceded them and they were welcomed wherever they landed. At last, they reached Kae's village and a feast was prepared to celebrate their arrival. People were flooding in from all around, and the women were concerned they might not recognise Kae among such a throng. Then they remembered that they would be able to recognise him from his distinctive front teeth as they were crooked and crossed over each other.

'As crooked as his deeds,' said Hinirau.

Now the women knew what they needed to do. The feast progressed, and as they performed, they searched with their eyes for Kae, but still could not make him out among the multitude. Time for the comic repertoire – at last they noticed the one man who was not laughing, sitting paddle-straight up against the central support in the wharenui. Surely this must be Kae, the only one in the meeting house who hadn't laughed all evening. Why was that? Did he suspect the purpose behind their visit? As host he couldn't leave, but the women needed to be sure. United as a wave, they undulated towards him, guests making way for them so they could advance as one through the wharenui. Their risqué dance became as comical as it was lewd; people were almost rolling about with mirth. At last, as the women bore down on Kae, flawless in gesture, and never missing an innuendo, Kae's composure cracked and even he, powerful priest and magician, laughed. It was only for a moment, but long enough for his enemies to glimpse those crooked teeth he had been trying to hide.

By now it was almost dawn, and still the women performed, changing to the sweetest singing, their voices rising and falling like the gentle swell of the sea. Who could not be lulled to sleep as their mana translated into song, their righteous spirit pursuing their intention. Everyone in the wharenui fell into an enchanted sleep, with the exception of one. There Kae still sat rigidly, his lips clamped, his eyes glittering coldly. Still singing, the women moved towards him, but now that they were close, Hinirau could see that his breathing was that of someone in a deep sleep. Furthermore, nobody could refrain from blinking for so long. With great daring, she nudged him with her foot and Kae rocked where he sat. Paua shells fell from his eyes. Their mother-of-pearl iridescence had been feigning open-eyed wakefulness. Feeling the spell of their voices, Kae had just managed to place them over his closing eyelids before he too succumbed.

Now it was easy to bind him where he sat and easy to carry him to their canoe. Across the ocean, their strong arms danced their paddles to a slower rhythm as they still sang to maintain the enchantment. Never pausing, they carried their prisoner into their own wharenui and bound him to the central support, and only then did they stop singing. Kae awoke and there was Tinirau poised above him with his greenstone axe at the ready. That was to be the last thing he ever saw. As he screamed in fear, Tinirau said, 'Coward, did Tutunui make such a sound when you murdered him?'

And that was the last thing Kae, the corrupt priest, ever heard.

THE GHOST IN THE IMAGE

BANKS ISLANDS, MELANESIA

There was once a woman who was given an image by a ghost. It was a depiction of a hooded and cloaked figure. Some say it was painted on bark, and that it was life-sized. Perhaps it was to reward her for being able to see it in the first place, perhaps it was payment for her to leave it alone or perhaps it was a means to extend its influence. In any case, so powerful was this image that she hid it from view, only allowing men to see it if they paid to do so.

In this way she became rich, but she also incurred her own death. Those who had paid to see this object of power killed the woman to seize it for themselves.

It was only then that this hooded and cloaked figure came into its own, manifesting as a ghost rather than as a mere representation of one. The ghost then taught the woman's killers to create a secret society. If others wanted to join it, they had to pay, and only men were allowed to become members. The initiates wore masks, hoods and cloaks made from foliage. Thus disguised, they were free to perpetrate any crime against people or property, carrying out acts of thievery, destruction and forbidden sexuality without being recognised. Indeed, those who witnessed or were victims of these believed that they were carried out by malevolent rather than ancestral ghosts and so these secret societies thrived.

RICH BROTHER, POOR BROTHER

PAPUA NEW GUINEA, MELANESIA

'For the people of Tangu this was no idle tale… it was one of the several versions of a myth offered to the visiting ethnologist Dr K Burridge in 1952, in conversations about the rites of the cargo cult they had performed the previous year with the object of obtaining the white man's goods or "cargo" for themselves …" The advent of outsiders to the Pacific Basin with their astonishing array, profusion and complexity of possessions caused some of the most rapid and dramatic cultural changes that anthropologists and ethnologists have been able to record. Below is an example of how this phenomenon has been incorporated into a myth prevalent throughout the region – that of the discovery and release of the sea – the ocean being the most essential resource to these master mariners, whose lives depended on fishing and trading between islands, some at vast distances.

Once there was a woman with a daughter who was alone in the world. There came a day when she needed to leave the child at home while she went further into the forest, so just as the woman had no husband to defend her, neither did the child have a parent for protection. A stranger found the girl and killed her. When the mother returned, she could not find her daughter, nor the body of her daughter, because the stranger had buried her so cunningly.

At last, her dreams showed her where the grave was hidden and she retrieved her daughter's remains. These she carried about with her until she could find somewhere suitable to re-bury her. Eventually she found a place in which two brothers were living. There she both buried her child and married one of the brothers. In time sons were born to her and it was not until then that she felt able to visit her daughter's grave.

---

* Poignant, Roslyn, *Oceanic Mythology*, Paul Hamlyn, 1967.

To her surprise she discovered water emerging from the ground, and, in the water, fish were swimming. She took the smallest of these and cooked it that night for the family. When she licked her fingers, her mouth puckered at the taste of salt. Her husband and children were also licking this new, salty taste from their lips. Next day, when the family awoke, her little boys had become fully grown men. Also, her husband had developed creating and fashioning skills that neither he, nor anyone they knew, had ever learned, or had ever been passed on from generation to generation. With these he made objects of great usefulness that had never been seen before, just as the very materials from which these objects were made had never been known in that place. Suddenly he was rich, as more and more of these marvellous things kept appearing such as tins of food, shoes, tents, weapons that reached the enemy faster than spears, boots that water could not pass, clothes that water could not penetrate, food with strange and delicious tastes … the list went on and on.

Naturally his brother also wanted these things for his own family and his sister-in-law told him where he could find the strange water with the miraculous fish. When he reached the girl's grave, he saw many fish swimming in it and, perhaps because he wanted to catch up with his brother who was already ahead of him in wealth, instead of taking a small fish like his sister-in-law, he took the largest.

At that the ground began to shake and tremble and a terrible grinding and roaring sound came from beneath the earth. The ground split apart as a roaring wall of water rose up and rushed away, followed by even more immeasurable torrents. The greedy brother had released the sea, and now the two families were separated by a channel of salt water that spread and spread, creating islands where once continuous land had been.

Eventually the brothers were able to contact each other once more by sending messages to each other inscribed on bark that floated between them on the tides. That is how they learned that one of them remained as poor if not poorer than he had been before. His skin remained dark and his food was what he could find or grow on the land. The other brother, however, discovered how to make more and more things such as boats that did not need oars or paddles, items that could create fire without using sticks, and ornaments of new materials such as glass. There were fabrics that did not fray or tear, different to the touch with strange patterns and colours that did not fade. The list went on and on … As all these things appeared, the rich brother's skin paled, and this new wealth welled up like the sea around him.

WHY TASMANIA IS AN ISLAND

TASMANIA

*While this is clearly a creation myth (according to certain European classifica-
tions of traditional stories), the interest for me is its overlap into legend, and
in its being one of the world's earliest recorded oral traditions, determined
by its combination of mythic events with contemporary scientific knowledge.
This is a story in which both mythic and geological time, place, and creation
story meet, making humanity's earliest known oral legend. The coincidence
of astronomical and geological phenomena gives a scientifically irrefutable
timeframe that has been preserved for twelve thousand years in traditional
oral literature among the Palawa first nation people in Tasmania. Despite
being considered to no longer exist due to genocidal practices by settlers,
European diseases and displacement, the Palawa and several first nation
languages have survived, albeit in depleted forms, and are reclaiming their
culture in dynamic and inventive ways.*

*Professor Gregory Lehman has emphasised the importance of academic
collaboration with indigenous scholars and that scientific validation of oral
traditions reinforces, rather than supersedes, the authority of indigenous
knowledge:*

Scientific investigation of colonial records that articulate traditional sys-
tems of knowledge preservation creates a wonderful multi-disciplinary
and cross-cultural way of making our history and our landscape more
meaningful in our lives … Physicists and astronomers sometimes struggle
to do this alone. This project has profoundly deepened our relationship
with history and science by taking Aboriginal traditions seriously …

*Professor Lehman, Pro Vice-Chancellor, University of Tasmania;
Aboriginal Leadership and Palawa cultural historian*

Our research suggests that Palawa oral traditions accurately recall the flooding of the land bridge between Tasmania and the mainland – showing that oral traditions can be passed down more than 400 successive generations while maintaining historical accuracy …

Professor Patrick Nunn, University of the Sunshine Coast;
geographer and co-author

Long time ago, Tasmania was not as it is today. Sometimes covered by the sea, sometimes by the path of icebergs, when it appeared it was just like a small sandbank that appears from time to time and is then lost beneath the tides. Sun and Moon were also appearing and disappearing, creating life on their journey before they sank beneath the ocean. Long time ago Sun and Moon were always in the sky together, but Sun was slower than Moon, so he gave her some of his light so that she could move faster. Sun's reflected light gave her extra speed, but when Sun risked not being able to keep up, he asked Moon to wait for him, and she did this by resting on the icebergs.

There came a day when Moon did not move. There she was, resting on the horizon before giving birth to their first child. What a strong, bright star he was! Moinee was placed in the sky and became known as the South Star. The following day his brother was born, shining with a softer light, and Dromerdene was placed in the sky in alignment with his brother and the land that was to become Tasmania.

Some fourteen thousand years later, calculated in linear time – which is not the only kind of time, and does not acknowledge mythical time – Moinee became known as Canopus, and Dromerdene became known as Sirius, the brightest stars near the South Celestial Pole.

When this had happened, Sun and Moon rose up from behind the sand bank and dropped all kinds of seeds so that it was able to grow vegetation. The icebergs pushed it closer to other land, shaping it on its journey. It became covered with forests and animals found their way onto this new land from the north. In that time, there were land bridges from mainland Australia to other southerly islands and to the place that we now call Tasmania. Then Sun and Moon created the first man from kangaroos. When people had multiplied, they made their way from the north until they reached Tasmania.

One day, some children found a strange object. Was it a tool? What could it do? With its long lanyard they tried tying and looping it, and finally one of them started to spin it. As it whirled, the strangest sound emerged from what was the first bullroarer, a sound to summon the wind, a sound to summon the spirits of who knew what? They ran back to their camp to show their mothers, but it was forbidden for women to behold such a magical object. Did not women have enough magic already, bringing forth life from their bodies? Because this taboo was broken, there would be consequences. The waters began to rise and swallow up the land bridges between the islands. The route that led northwards to Australia, which we now call the Bassian Land Bridge, was covered by the sea, and and Tasmania became an island, separated from Australia by the Bass Straight.

STEALING THE SKY MAIDEN

How the sky maidens loved to descend to Earth to bathe. Before they splashed and floated in the water, they would remove their wings to protect them. Even though the man/god Qat was powerful enough to create women out of wood or straw, he wanted one of the sky maidens for himself. Perhaps it was because he had been born from a stone that he yearned for the weightless qualities of air.

Secretly watching the sky maidens bathing, he seized his chance and stole a pair of wings, compelling their owner, Vinmara, to stay on Earth. One day, as a prisoner in her mother-in-law's home, she was chided harshly, and burst into tears. She wept so copiously that her tears washed away the earth that her wings had been hidden under. Vinmara snatched them up and was able to return to her home in the sky. Her abductor wound a banyan root around his arrows and shot them higher and higher into the sky so that he could climb up and fetch her back.

As he rushed through the Sky World looking for her, he saw one of the Sky People gardening with a hoe who he asked not to disturb his root until he had returned to Earth. Finding Vinmara, he grabbed her and dragged her back down it. However, the root snapped and he fell down to the ground. As he lay dying, the Sky Maiden flew back into the sky to live safely where she belonged.

EEL LOVER SPURNED

TAHITI, FRENCH POLYNESIA

*The moon goddess Hina was also the goddess of love, pleasure and poetry.
With her name meaning 'young woman', she is surely what most young
mortal women aspire to, particularly when it comes to their choices about
their love life. Small wonder that there are countless stories about this young
woman, mortal or divine, and that some of these stories contradict each other.
Let the reader decide which of these they prefer.*

All Tahiti was awaiting the marriage of Hina to the chieftain of Lake
Vaihiria, which, being the island's only lake, was a place of great power. To
her disgust, Hina discovered that her fiancé shape-shifted into the form of
a giant eel, and, moreover, that this was his preferred shape. She decided to
leave him, but he pursued her. Unaccustomed to needing to run away, Hina
invoked the help of the gods and it was Maui who came to her aid. He
chopped her unwelcome suitor into three parts and, wrapping the head in
plant fibres, he told Hina not to let go of it until she had reached her home.

However, after all the excitement, Hina wanted to take a dip in the sea
with her friends, so she placed the package on the sand. There it began to
grow, and by the time they emerged from the waves, it had become a tall
palm, with a sinuous eel-like trunk, from which were hanging the first
coconuts. The young women swarmed up the tree to see what these fruits
were, and enjoyed the refreshing drink and the tasty flesh. How Hina's
friends laughed when she threw the shell away from her with a shriek. She
had just noticed, after drinking from one end, how the shell resembled her
eel fiancé with its design of an eel's eyes and mouth! Even after death he
had managed to steal a kiss from her.

EEL LOVER WELCOMED

MAUI, POLYNESIA

Hina loved to swim in a particular deep pool close to the shore. It was also frequented by eels, but they always made room for her and she was not disturbed by them. One day, however, an eel that was larger than the rest approached, and began to caress her. She did not discourage it and the eel became bolder and bolder, knowing that she welcomed its attentions. Certain of this, it transformed itself into a young man and, whether in eel or human form, he became a favourite lover.

This liaison did not remain undetected as they were observed by Maui, who was Hina's brother-in-law. At that time, Maui was involved in a dispute with Hina's husband, and was delighted to be able to cause more trouble by telling him that his wife was being unfaithful with an eel lover. Hina then warned her lover that they had been discovered and that retribution was on the way.

Due to his 'mana', his personal power, combined with his watery nature, her lover was able to tell her that a great downpour accompanied by a tidal surge was on the way. The flood would reach her house, where she was to wait for him on her threshold. He would come to her there, but when he laid his head in her lap she must cut it off and take it to a higher place on the island to escape the flood. All happened as he had predicted, so Hina knew she should obey him. Although she hated to do so, she decapitated him and took his head to the nearest foothills. As soon as she placed it on the ground it grew into a palm tree with strange fruits.

What a gift the coconut tree was; apart from the most nutritious nuts, the coconut milk sustained Hina and her people when the sweet waters on the island had been contaminated by the sea surge and flooding. Soon the people learned how to make roofs from the leaves, and mats and clothing from the fibres. The trunks were used for canoes and building materials, and every part of the coconut palm became a blessing for the people. When they see the face of the eel at the end of the coconut, they are grateful to Hina's lover.

WHY TERMITES BECAME STARS

AUSTRALIA

Known by European settlers as the 'didgeridoo', a purely onomatopoeic word, the original name for this instrument exists in several Australian aboriginal languages. It has become the national instrument of Australia.

Some say that Yidaki was the name of the great hunter and warrior, some say Yidaki is the name of what he created and so he became that name afterwards. One night, returning home alone, he came across a branch that had fallen in a storm. How straight it was, but there was movement at one end – a host of termites. The man picked it up and it was lighter than he expected, so he looked down it and saw that it was almost hollow. The termites were still swarming at the far end, so he raised it high and blew through the branch as hard as he could. How strong his breath was – the termites were blown into the sky, and there they turned into stars.

Yidaki lit a fire and thrust burning twigs into the hollow branch to burn away any remains of the nest, and it became as smooth inside as outside. His breath had made stars – what else could it make? He blew down it again, and the strangest, most compelling, powerful sound emerged. It was as though thunder had been plucked from the sky and fed to the earth. It was the roar of water falling into chasms, it was a sound to summon the ancestors. Yidaki took the instrument to his people. How they rejoiced, painting their bodies and dancing to its music. Since then it has been sacred, used for healing ceremonies and bridging the way from this world to other worlds.

TO MAKE AN ENDING:
THREE OF THE SAME?

There was once a king who delighted in receiving strange and exotic gifts. One day he found that a parcel had been left for him. In it he found three identical wooden dolls. A note fluttered to the floor. It said: 'How are we different?' Intrigued, the king examined them carefully and could detect no differences at all. He summoned his advisors – neither could they. He asked his courtiers but none of them could either. He summoned his fool, who said, 'I am not foolish enough to try. Ask your storyteller.'

The storyteller was summoned and looked at the dolls minutely. Suddenly she smiled and, just as quickly, plucked a hair from the king's beard.

'That had better be worth it,' threatened the king.

The storyteller was threading the hair through the ear of one of the dolls. It went straight through and emerged at the other side. Quick as a whip, her hand flashed out and pulled out another hair.

'I am warning you …' growled the king.

The second hair had already been inserted through the next doll's ear and had disappeared. The king tried to duck, but was not quick enough. A third hair from his beard lay between the storyteller's thumb and index finger.

'That was your last chance,' hissed the king.

The third hair had already disappeared into the third doll's ear but was emerging through the mouth, and although it had entered the doll as a straight hair, it was coming out as curly as a corkscrew.

'I have solved the riddle Your Majesty: the first doll is a fool. Anything it hears goes into one ear and immediately comes out of the other. The second doll is wise, it retains what it hears. The third doll is a storyteller. The stories it has heard come out of its mouth with a twist and a spin that the storyteller has put upon them.'

BIBLIOGRAPHY

www.africansayings.com/sayings/tortoise-and-hawk

www.austhrutime.com/aboriginal_astronomy_reconstruction_star_knowledge_
   aboriginal_tasmania.htm

Ba, Amadou Hampate, *La Revolte des Bovides*, Hatier, Paris, 2013

Chinese Myths, Juvenile and Children Publishing House, 1986, Shanghai, China

Erdoes, Richard and Ortiz, Alfonso, eds, *American Myths and Legends*, Pantheon, 1984

Deep Time Diligence: An Interview with Tyson Yunkaporta, *Emergence
   Magazine*, https://emergencemagazine.org/interview/deep-time-
   diligence/?utm_source=Emergence+Magazine&utm_campaign=f35c17987f-
   DeepTime%E2%80%9420240225&utm_med

Dosedla, Heinrich, 'The Kind and Unkind Papuan Girls: Tumbuna Tales from the
   Highlands of Papua New Guinea,' *Fabula*, Vol. 53 No. 1–2, 2012.

Couzen, Jeni, *Creation of the World in /Xam Mythology*, Firelizard Press, 2016

Fox, Charles E. and Drew, Frederic H., 'Beliefs and Tales of San Cristoval (Solomon
   Islands)', *The Journal of the Royal Anthropological Institute of Great Britain and Ireland*,
   Vol. 45 (Jan.–Jun., 1915), pp. 131–185, https://doi.org/10.2307/2843390, www.jstor.org/
   stable/2843390

Garrow, Duncan and Wilkin, Neil, 'The World of Stonehenge', The British Museum,
   2022

Getty, Laura and Kwon, Kyounghye, *Compact Anthology of World Literature*,
   www.human.libretexts.org/Bookshelves/Literature_and_Literacy/World_Literature/
   Compact_Anthology_of_World_Literature_(Getty_and_Kwon)/03%3A_
   India/3.02%3A_The_Mahabharata

www.goodreads.com/work/quotes/3802528-sha-naqba-imuru?page=3

Guirand, Felix, *New Larousse Encyclopaedia of Mythology*, Hamlyn, 1968

Hayes, Barbara and Ingpen, Robert, *Folk Tales and Fables of the World*, Random House,
   1987.

Howart, Crispin, 'Mugus – the terrible blind god, the lord of pigs – a unique sculpture
   from Papua New Guinea', *Oceanic Art Society* Vol. 29 No. 2, 2017, www.oceanicart-
   society.org.au/mugus-the-terrible-blind-god-the-lord-of-pigs-a-unique-sculpture-
   from-papua-new-guinea/

Jacksties, Sharon, *Animal Folk Tales of Britain and Ireland*, The History Press, 2021

Jacksties, Sharon, *The International Handbook of Therapeutic Stories and Storytelling*,
   Routledge, Kegan & Paul, 2022

Jain, Narendra P., *Folk Tales of Mexico*, Oriental University Press, 1986

Kigshill, Sonia and Westwood, Jennifer, *The Fabled Coast*, Random House, 2012

Littleton, Scott C., *The Illustrated Anthology of World Myth and Storytelling*, Duncan Baird, 2002

Lupton, Hugh, *The Dreaming of Place*, Propolis Books, 2020

Matthews, John, *Secret Camelot*, Blandford, 1997

McCosh Clark, Kate, *Maori Tales and Legends*, David Nutt, 1896

'Mother or Wife? An African Dilemma Tale and the Psychological Dynamics of Sociocultural Change', *Social Psychology*, Vol. 43 No. 4, Hogrefe Publishing, 2012, www.researchgate.net/publication/263922218_Mother_or_Wife_An_African_Dilemma_Tale_and_the_Psychological_Dynamics_of_Sociocultural_Change

Mudrooroo, Nyoongah, *Aboriginal Mythology*, Thorsons/Harper Collins, 1994

www.nzetc.victoria.ac.nz/tm/scholarly/tei-TuvAcco-t1-body1-d48.html

Niane, Djibril Tamsir, 'SUNDIATA an epic of old Mali', www.scarsdaleschools.k12.ny.us/cms/lib5/NY01001205/Centricity/Domain/202/Sundiata.pdf

Poignant, Roslyn, *Oceanic Mythology*, Hamlyn, 1967

Ramsay Smith, William, *Aborigine Myths and Legends*, Senate, 1996

Reed, Alexander W., *Aboriginal Myths, Legends and Fables*, A.H. & A.W. Reed Ltd, 1982

Reed, Alexander W., *Aboriginal Stories*, Reed New Holland, 2002

'Tasmanian Aboriginal oral traditions among the oldest recorded narratives', University of Melbourne, 2023, www.unimelb.edu.au/newsroom/news/2023/august/tasmanian-aboriginal-oral-traditions-among-the-oldest-recorded-narratives

Tayib, Abdulla El and West, Michael Philip M.A., Phil, D., *Stories from the Sands of Africa*, Longman Group Ltd, 1962

Veenker, Ronald A., 'Gilgamesh and the Magic Plant', *The Biblical Archaeologist* Vol. 44, No. 4, 1981, https://doi.org/10.2307/3209664, www.jstor.org/stable/3209664

'Why did the gods spare Gilgamesh?', https://mythology.stackexchange.com/questions/1269/why-did-the-gods-spare-gilgamesh

Zielinski, Sarah, 'Ten Ancient Stories and the Geological Events That May Have Inspired Them', *Smithsonian Magazine*, www.smithsonianmag.com/science-nature/ten-ancient-stories-and-geological-events-may-have-inspired-them-180950347